DELTA'S EMPLOYEES'
PROJECT
767 A REALITY!

From Christy Kelly
6'1'00

The Spirit of DELTA

DELTA

DELTA

An Airline And Its Aircraft

The Illustrated History of A
Major U.S. Airline And The People
Who Made It

OTHER BOOKS BY R.E.G. DAVIES

A History of the World's Airlines
Airlines of the United States Since 1914
Airlines of Latin America Since 1919
Continental Airlines — the First Fifty Years
Rebels and Reformers of the Airways
Pan Am: An Airline and Its Aircraft
Lufthansa: An Airline and Its Aircraft

DELTA
An Airline And Its Aircraft

The Illustrated History of A Major U.S. Airline And The People Who Made It

By R.E.G. Davies

Illustrated by Mike Machat

Paladwr Press

DEDICATION

Like Old King Cole, I called on my fiddlers three when
in need of inspiration and encouragement. The
combined experience and knowledge of Steve Caisse,
Paulette O'Donnell, and Paul Talbott ensured the
accuracy of the text, the tables of data, the maps, and
the illustrations in this book. Their contribution has
been essential to its compilation, and with their
invaluable help, the author, with his artist and editor,
have been inspired to play a merry tune.

Published by Paladwr Press, P.O. Box 521238, Miami, FL 33152.

Manufactured in Hong Kong.

Designed by R.E.G. Davies

Artwork by Mike Machat

Edited and Produced by John Wegg

Typesetting by Fisher & Day

Prepress and Press Management by The Drawing Board

Printed by C & C Offset Printing Co., Ltd.

ISBN Ø-9626483-Ø-2

Library of Congress Catalog Card Number 90-91572

First Edition

CONTENTS

No Silver Spoon

During the evolution of air transport in the United States, and especially in the embryo years when success or failure depended upon favorable glances from the authorities and agencies in Washington, D.C., a privileged few airlines emerged that were so much bigger, so much richer, and so much the better endowed by government subsidy, that the other airlines could only survive at all by picking up the crumbs — specifically the occasional route award or rare Post Office contract that the Big Four did not want.

The privileged were United Air Lines, American Airlines, TWA, and Eastern Air Lines, as well as the Chosen Instrument for all overseas routes, Pan Am. Among the underprivileged were all the components of the present-day Delta. Whatever Delta is today, it did itself.

When C.E. Woolman started the first Delta Air Service in 1929, he was forced to abandon the modest route from Fort Worth to Atlanta simply because it did not fit into the Postmaster General's grand plan. Only a political scandal on the scale of Watergate permitted Delta to get back into business, and even then it was awfully slow going. Western Air Express was deprived of its birthright in the disreputable Shotgun Marriage, out of which emerged TWA but which almost killed Western; and its subsequent history was a series of rescue operations from a series of crises. Northeast had the cards stacked against it from the start, with no routes to speak of, and with a short-sighted management, at least until long after World War II, whose horizons did not extend south of New York. Even Pacific Northern, one of the smaller boughs of the Delta family tree, was the victim of a route realignment policy that clearly favored its competitors.

Delta's steady progress, therefore, has been almost entirely of its own making. To paraphrase the axiom about prominent people: that some are born great, some become great, and some have greatness thrust upon them; Delta made itself great by careful planning and intuitive wisdom. The merger with Chicago & Southern in 1953 was a textbook exercise in how to amalgamate two good airlines into a potentially great one. The acquisition of Northeast in 1972 not only consolidated Delta's position and growing stature, but it solved a long-term problem for the CAB. And the addition of Western in 1986 was a masterstroke that put Delta Air Lines into the Big Leagues.

This last corporate move came after airline deregulation, and after Western itself had rejected many suitors for its hand. But deregulation itself, which opened up previously locked windows of opportunity, did not go to Delta's head, as it did in some cases, leading to many a cynical takeover and many a bankruptcy. With a track record of wise decision-making, Delta is now firmly in the driver's seat.

Time was when neither Delta, Western, Northeast, nor Chicago & Southern could afford to buy a Douglas DC-3 from the manufacturer. Thus the early part of this book features the smaller Lockheed Electra or the Stinson tri-motors and even smaller aircraft that were sized to the modest traffic volumes of the early routes of the 1930s. The situation is different today. Since the DC-8 and the DC-9, Delta has no longer followed the pack. It has led it. With its critical role in the development of McDonnell Douglas's MD-11, one of the great airliners that will welcome the next century, it will maintain its place as one of the world's great airlines.

Delta may not have been born with a silver spoon in its mouth but, in making its own way, it has become its own silversmith.

Acknowledgments

Outstanding among those who contributed to this book are two stalwarts of Delta Air Lines. Paul Talbott is one of those rare types who can not only take airplanes apart and but can also tell you the ancestry of every airplane in the fleet. In delving into the innermost recesses of Delta's extensive archives he has saved me countless weeks of painstaking work. Also, he has been of considerable help to Mike Machat to decide which of many individual aircraft or particular color schemes should be used.

Working closely with Paul, Steve Caisse has assiduously sought and selected most of the photographs that appear in this book. We have tried to include some pictures that may not be familiar to some readers; but have not excluded good pictures solely because they are well-known. Steve also checked all my maps to ensure that everything was correctly in place.

Presiding over this industrious activity and acting as a faithful communications channel was Paulette O'Donnell, who coordinated the efforts, did a little progress-chasing from time to time, and above all, kept the author going when at times he was feeling a little jaded and wondering if it was all worthwhile.

Closer to home, Bob van der Linden has once again served as my technical conscience, ensuring that I do not commit heinous errors such as confusing a Lockheed Model 10-A with a 10-B or a GE CF6-80C2D1F from your common-or-garden CF6.

Other contributions have been no less valuable. The Western Air Lines archives were presided over by Linda Dozier and their safe keeping in Atlanta today is largely thanks to her sense of history in handing them over to Paulette O'Donnell. The works of valiant researchers, historians, and writers such as Rick Allen, Peter Bowers, Bill Larkins, John Stroud, Harry Gann, Peter Brooks, Don Thomas, Roger Bentley, Norm Houle, and a host of others; Harriette Parker, the "founder" of the Delta archives, and Jackie Pate who took over the reins for more than a decade; Terri Hanson, Bruce Henry and Charles Burcher at Delta's photography department; Ken Klatt, legal department; and Gordon Barrington, public affairs: all these are gratefully acknowledged.

Finally, I would like to thank Bill Berry, who gave this book his blessing and ensured its production; and all the employees, past and present, of the parent company and its antecedents, without whom Delta Air Lines may not have become the great airline that it is and thereby qualify for inclusion for this series of books.

—R.E.G.D.

Further Reading

The purpose of this series of books is to encourage interest in the fascinating history of the world's airlines. While every effort has been made to make this one on Delta as useful a reference source as it is an attractive portrayal of a great story, some readers may wish to consult the following:

Delta — The History of an Airline, by David Lewis and W.P. Newton; *The Delta Family History* by George W. Cearley; *Adventures of a Yellowbird,* by Robert W. Mudge; *Air Transport at War,* by Reginald M. Cleveland; *The Only Way To Fly* by Robert Serling; *High Journey* by Carleton Putnam; and *Airlines of the United States Since 1914,* by R.E.G. Davies.

Machat's Law

In my previous airline book partnerships with Ron Davies, I have drawn attention to the bewildering complications inherent in the accurate illustration of airliner markings, and I have labeled this phenomenon Machat's Law, which states: "The only consistency in airline color schemes is their inconsistency." The corollary states: "In a given number of similar aircraft types from the same airline, there will be a like number of color scheme variations." One of my favorite examples of this occurrence is a first-generation jetliner that appeared in no less that nine major color scheme variations in its first 18 months of service with a major airline!

The problem is more than academic, for it leads to the suspicion that mistakes have been made, often because eye-witnesses will swear that they have photographs that don't agree with the illustrations depicted herein, and that subsequently prove the artwork to be incorrect.

I can only assert that each illustration in this book was carefully chosen to represent a specific aircraft at a specific moment in its history with either Delta, or one of the airlines that joined the Delta family. In many cases, titles, logos, and subtle details of aircraft markings have been enlarged to enhance the artwork, and to deal with technical printing limitations.

Many of the profile drawings are accompanied by "Artist's Notes" to clarify various aspects of color schemes or structural details, and where appropriate, I have drawn attention to aircraft design features that may be unusual, and which may escape notice at first glance.

—*Mike Machat*

Author

To write a succinct but at the same time comprehensive history of Delta Air Lines, following the same formula as in the previous books in the series (on Pan American and Lufthansa) has been quite a challenge: to present the many achievements of disparate elements in a form that preserved the correct chronological balance and continuity. Four separate histories would have been too simplistic, too disjointed. The end of the stories of Chicago & Southern, Northeast, and Western, would have implied a note of finality. But the presence of so many Chicagoans, New Englanders, and Westerners in the Delta team today bear witness to the insistency of the family spirit that is part of the company policy. Carleton Putnam, Paul Collins, and Harris Hanshue have never been condemned to historical anonymity.

Equally, to have told the story of all the four elements, and including other ancestors such as Art Woodley's Pacific Northern, Al Frank's National Parks Airways, or Dick Leferink's Wyoming Air Service in chronological order would have been hopelessly confusing.

I have attempted, therefore, to weave the pieces together, carefully identifying eras of evolution, and tracing the development of the main airline groups between watershed events that can readily be recognized by the reader as logical break points in the individual stories, to be picked up later after pausing, as it were, to observe what was going on elsewhere in a "meanwhile, back at the ranch..." approach.

Once again, I have started by writing a prelude — for airlines do not just happen. There is invariably some special motivation that leads to their existence. Back in the 1920s, C.E. Woolman's flying experience was the key to the creation of aerial crop-dusting, and was the inspiration that led to the formation of the Delta Air Service. Such qualities of experience, vision, and inspiration are still to be found, 60 years later, in the Delta of today. History is still unraveling, just as it did in days gone by.

The same format is followed as in previous books. Mike Machat's precision drawings are the eye-catching attractions of the right-hand pages, while my maps, if not containing as much visual impact, are aimed to be at least as informative on the left. The right-hand pages are usually about aircraft, while those on the left are usually about segments of airline history related to the aircraft. The cause-and-effect relationship works in both directions.

I have attempted to concentrate all the available data on a given theme into one place. Appendices listing aircraft fleets, for example, are inserted as far as possible adjacent to the text, photographs, and drawings of the subject aircraft. Where relevant, comparison tabulations or charts are inserted to answer unspoken questions as to the difference between aircraft variants, such as a Douglas DC-7 or a DC-7B. The main objective of this layout scheme has been to save the reader the annoyance of constantly having to refer to the back of the book, or worse, at the end of a chapter, to seek elucidation of detail. Cross-references to other pages have been made only to avoid repetition, for example, when one aircraft type is the prime subject more than once, because it served more than one of the Delta ancestor airlines.

I hope that *Delta: An Airline and Its Aircraft* will have succeeded in its main objective: to offer a reliable and accurate history of a great airline that is at the same time a good reference source, a pleasure to read, and a delight to the eye.

—*R.E.G. Davies*

Artist

Depicting the 46 featured aircraft presented special challenges, and many design decisions had to be made with regard to specific color schemes used, the historical significance of certain aircraft, and technical production considerations as well. Adding to this was the specter of Machat's Law (see previous page), creating a plethora of possible color scheme and design variations on everything from the Western Indian head to Delta's famous widget. Thankfully, the comprehensive Delta historical archives, together with the resources of Paladwr Press, saved the day.

The scale comparisons of each aircraft were made with Delta's upcoming flagship of the 1990s, the McDonnell Douglas MD-11, rather than the Boeing 747, used in previous books in this series. Delta operated only five 747s for a limited period of time.

To me, *The Spirit of Delta* is not just the name of the Boeing 767 that graces the cover of this book, but rather a state of mind. Delta's motto "We Love To Fly And It Shows" is almost an understatement, and I trust this book captures the ebbulient spirit.

On a personal note, my first experience aboard Delta was in 1968 when, as a young serviceman, I was returning from overseas on special leave to attend my Father's funeral. In that difficult time, the courteous and understanding people of Delta went out of their way to get me home swiftly and safely, making a challenging experience that much more comfortable. I have never forgotten that trip, and today it is with considerable pride and enthusiasm that I undertake this exciting endeavor to illustrate the many significant and historic aircraft of Delta Air Lines.

—*Mike Machat*

Editor

This story of Delta Air Lines and of its affiliates and ancestors (the third in the series on the World's Great Airlines), brings together many diverse talents: the artistry and precision of one of the best commercial aviation artists in the U. S., the skilled cartography from Ron's own pen and his inspiring writing style, and aircraft listings that for the aficionados are the last word on the subject, thanks to Delta's own faithful (and unofficial) historians.

For although the illustrations are often the most obvious features of the complementary double-page spreads, they are only part of a composite whole. The text sometimes has to lie in the shadow of a Machat "special" or as a peripheral comment on a map or a set of excellent pictures. But all these component parts are interdependent. A good picture or map is worth a thousand words but the text is the mortar that holds the bricks together. Conversely, without the supporting material, the text would have had to be ten times as long and only one tenth as interesting.

For that has been the main objective: to produce an attractive book that is a joy to peruse at leisure, with each double-page spread a self-contained essay in its own right; at the same time to compile a totally reliable source of reference.

Every fact and figure in the book has been rigorously scrutinized. Wherever possible, exact dates are given, in the text, the tables, and the maps. These are the essential signposts and milestones of history. The specifications included in the aircraft tables and information band with each profile drawing feature Delta's weights and passenger seating capacities at delivery; performance figures are representative. Photographs, except where otherwise credited, are from Delta's extensive archives.

The fleet lists have been closely checked against corporate records and, in many cases, are published here for the first time. Abbreviations have been kept to a minimum and most will be familiar. The manufacturer's serial number —that all-important aircraft identification number that remains with an aircraft for its whole life — is abbreviated to"MSN" rather that the industry's commonly-used "s/n", and avoids the ambiguous term "c/n" (constructor's number).

Production has been made that much easier by the support of the talented efforts of Brian Day and Kimberley Fisher, Scott Piazza, and the Delta triumvirate to whom this book is dedicated.

When I wrote my first full-length book, Mike Machat and Ron Davies were valued consultants and contributors. To be with the same team of close friends again, is to work with acknowledged specialists. Fashioning with them the history of one of today's trend-setting airlines, with roots in such diversified traditions, has been a privilege indeed.

—*John Wegg*

Prelude in Peru

Dr. B.R. (Bert) Coad and C.E. Woolman

Dr. B.R. Coad was appointed by the U.S. Department of Agriculture in the early 1920s to establish a field laboratory at Tallulah, Louisiana. An experienced entomologist, he launched a war against the boll weevil, the tiny insect that annually destroyed whole swathes of the precious cotton crop in the southern states. In this effort, he was assisted by an Agricultural Extension Agent, **C.E. Woolman**. Together they experimented with two dry powder insecticides, lead arsenate and calcium arsenate, and to speed up the process of applying the powder, deadly to boll weevils, they realized the value of aerial crop-dusting. And so a new industry was born.

Seasonal Dusting

The Huff-Daland Dusters, Inc., crop-dusting company had quickly established itself in 1924, first at Macon, Georgia, and then in Monroe, Louisiana. It was moderately successful, laying the foundations of what has become a world-wide industry. The only interruptions in its story of success was the annual falloff in business after the crop was picked; and it sought to put idle airplanes to use by transferring them to the southern hemisphere where the seasons are reversed from those in the United States.

Huff-Daland selected first Mexico, then Peru, for its seasonal migration. Late in 1926 it moved five aircraft, disassembled and crated, by ship to Lima, where the idea was promoted and soon accepted by the local cotton growers. Having established a base, the company sought additional work and on 28 May 1928 received permission to establish passenger, mail, and freight services within Peru and to foreign destinations from an appreciative Peruvian government. In this enterprise, the initiative had been taken by **Harold R. Harris**, Huff-Daland's operations manager, and C. E. Woolman, its chief entomologist, who also happened to be a natural-born salesman.

A Peruvian Airline

At this time, powerful financial and industrial, even political forces were jockeying for position in Latin America. In air transport, the Haydon Stone banking group formed the **Peruvian Airways Corporation** in New York on 4 September 1928 with a **Fairchild FC-2**, possibly with a view of fending off German incursions from Colombia and Ecuador. An agreement was made between Huff-Daland and Haydon Stone, with the result that when regular air service started from Lima to Talara on 13 September 1928, it was made under the terms of the Huff-Daland operating certificate from the Peruvian Government.

This organization, headed by the ambitious and visionary **Juan Trippe**, was obliged to make a pact with **W.R. Grace & Company**, the dominant trading organization along the west coast of South America, and the outcome was the formation of **Pan American-Grace Airways (PANAGRA)**, on 25 January 1929, on which date Peruvian Airways was absorbed. The inspiration for this branch of a future worldwide system may be traced back to Huff-Daland and to C.E. Woolman, whose innovation in bringing crop dusting to Peru also sowed the seeds of air transport in that country.

C.E. Woolman (left, holding hat), with the President of Peru (right, hands folded) in 1928, on the occasion pictured below.

Dr. B.R. (Bert) Coad (far left), a noted entomologist, directed the field laboratory at Tallulah, La., in the early 1930s to develop insecticides to combat the scourge of the boll weevil.

Collett Everman (C.E.) Woolman was Bert Coad's assistant at Tallulah.

The Fairchild FC-2

One of the pioneer passenger aircraft produced in North America, this sturdy little four-seater began the first air service in Peru, on 13 September 1928. It was operated by the **Huff Daland Dusters Air Navigation Company**, just two days before another pioneer from the U.S.A., Elmer Faucett, began a parallel air service along the Peruvian coast with Stinson Detroiters. Peruvian Airways had extended its Lima—Talara route to reach the northern and southern frontiers of Peru just a day before PANAGRA was incorporated. This aircraft passed to that airline and eventually found a home at the National Air and Space Museum in Washington.

This Fairchild FC-2 was pictured at Lima in 1928 at the inauguration of the Peruvian Airways service. This aircraft passed to PANAGRA for whom it also inaugurated the first service. It now resides in the National Air & Space Museum, Washington, D.C.

Huff-Daland Duster (Petrel 31)

106 mph (max)

Liberty 12 (400hp) ■ 5,250 lb. max. gross take-off weight ■ Length 38 feet ■ Span 50 feet ■ Height 14 feet

One of the Huff-Dalands in Peru. Harold Harris, Operations Manager of Huff-Daland Dusters is on the right.

A Huff-Daland Duster in Peru with the La Llama Volador logo.

Founded by Thomas H. Huff and Elliott Daland in 1921, the Huff, Daland & Co., Ltd., changed its name to **Huff-Daland Airplanes, Inc.**, in 1925 and moved from Ogdensburg, New York, to an extensive plant at Bristol, Pennsylvania. Known as a builder of light bombers, such as the Pegasus, it also produced a three-seat commercial aircraft, the **Petrel**, among other small types.

The Model 5 version of the Petrel was used to conduct experiments in crop-dusting (see opposite page and overleaf) and successfully proved its qualities of low flying speed, maneuverability, good field of vision, and low maintenance costs. The Petrel 5 was lengthened by a

whole ten feet, fitted with a 400hp Liberty engine to replace the 200hp Wright Whirlwind radial, and the gross weight doubled — to produce a quite different airplane, the Petrel 31, or more familiarly, the **Huff-Daland Duster**, able to carry up to 1,500lb of calcium arsenate.

On 8 March 1927, Huff-Daland Airplanes became the Keystone Aircraft Corporation, and went on to build heavy aircraft, including the 10-seat tri-motor, the Pathfinder. The Petrel 31 became the Keystone "Puffer," a droll reference, presumably, to its manner of disposing of its payload.

Delta Air Service

Monroe Doctrine

Having been the scourge of the Peruvian variety of the boll weevil, and also having acquired a taste for air transport — a taste that invariably becomes an addiction — **C.E. Woolman** returned to the United States in 1928. There he found the Huff-Daland Dusters in a state of disarray, because the parent company, Huff-Daland Airplanes, now Keystone Aircraft, was in financial straits, and wished to pull out of the dusting subsidiary in Monroe, where the original company name had been retained.

Seeking support from local businessmen at Monroe, he found that the crop-dusting efforts had generated a great deal of sympathetic interest in the contribution that Huff-Daland had already made to the community. Woolman was able to glean enough capital to start his own aviation enterprise, the **Delta Air Service**. The company's president was D. Y. Smith, a Louisiana planter; "C.E." was the vice-president and general manager, effectively running the operation; other directors were C.H. McHenry, Travis Oliver, M.S. Biedenharn; and Johnny Howe was the chief pilot.

The support given by the Monroe community has never been forgotten. Every year, the descendant of the tiny Delta Air Service, which has grown steadily to become one of the five largest airlines in the world, and whose name is recognized and respected from London to Singapore, holds its annual general meeting at Monroe. The Louisiana city has become as much of a pilgrimage destination as Mecca is to the Moslem world.

Delta Air Service

On 12 November 1928 C.E. Woolman, with the backing of the Monroe investors to the amount of $40,000, of which $20,000 was in cash, purchased the crop-dusting operation from Keystone, and three days later acquired the equipment. Delta Air Service, Inc., received its charter in Monroe on 3 December. The name was suggested by a secretary, **Catherine Fitzgerald** — later to become affectionately known as " Miss Fitz," — to relate to the Delta region, to acknowledge not only a customer community, but also an investment community at the lower reaches of the Mississippi River.

The Saga Begins

Right from the start, Woolman realized that the Huff-Daland Duster was good for spraying crops but not much good for carrying passengers. The same shortcoming applied also to other small aircraft which supplemented the Huff-Dalands. The problem was partially solved when, early in 1929, he purchased the assets of the **Fox Flying Service**, whose resources included two six-seat (including the pilot) **Travel Air Model S-6000-Bs**. On 17 June 1929, at 8 a.m., the first passenger service departed from Dallas' Love Field, and hurtled to Jackson, Mississippi, at 90mph, stopping at Shreveport and Monroe. Johnny Howe, chief pilot, was at the controls.

The local press described the **Travel Airs** as "the giant monoplane of Delta Air Service," or "large cabin planes," or, better yet, "the last word in airplane construction." One newspaper described the Delta inaugural as a "New Episode in Aviation," in a banner headline. One early less-publicized episode was to take place when the pilot, Elmer Rose, received permission from Woolman to take his wife on a flight. Billie Rose may have been the first beneficiary of the staff travel privileges that are one of the perquisites of airline employment today.

Selman Field, Monroe, La., in 1929. Note the crates to the left of the hangar. These contained aircraft delivered from the adjacent rail line.

The original Delta Air Service "crew" of pilots and mechanics in 1929. C.E. Woolman, "father" of what became the Delta "family" is second from left. John Howe, who piloted Delta's first scheduled flight, is to his right.

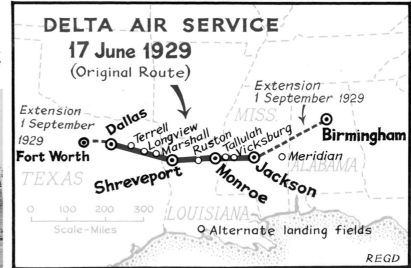

DELTA AIR SERVICE
17 June 1929
(Original Route)

Extension
1 September 1929

Extension
1 September 1929

Dallas
Terrell
Longview
Marshall
Ruston
Tallulah
Vicksburg
Birmingham

Fort Worth
MISS.
Meridian
TEXAS
Shreveport
Monroe
Jackson
ALABAMA

0 100 200 300
Scale-Miles

LOUISIANA

Alternate landing fields

REGD

War on the Boll Weevil

This selection of photographs of operations by the versatile crop-dusting aircraft tell their own story. The advantages of the use of the airplane are obvious. To spray by hand would need armies of laborers, with the attendant risk of crop damage, not to mention damage to the sprayers themselves. One of the illustrations shows a similar operation, "fogging" a lakeside on a mosquito-control project.

A lineup of Huff-Daland Dusters (with one Travel Air 2000 in center stage) at Monroe, La.

C.E. Woolman.

A Stearman makes a typical low pass.

DELTA'S CROP-DUSTERS

Huff-Daland		Stearman C3B	
MSN	**Regn.**	**MSN**	**Regn.**
30	NR487	106	NR3863
34	NR275K	144	NR6253
43	NR3359	166	NR7550
49	NR2963	207	NR6496
53	NR2952	227	NR8813
54	NR2950	228	NR8814
56	NR395N		
57	NR2955	*106 was a C3B Special, 207*	
59	NR2951	*was a C3BM; 106, 144, 207*	
62	NR2953	*and 227 were purchased*	
	NC2961	*from the Texas Dusting Co.*	
70	NR17606		
71	NR17607	**Travel Air 4000**	
73	NR17608	154	NR64E
		501	NR5395
NR274K was a Model HN;		502	NR5396
54-59 were Petrel models.			

DELTA AIR CORPORATION
MONROE, LA.

Huff-Daland Dusters in action against the boll weevil. One of these aircraft types is in the collection of the National Air and Space Museum, and is on loan to the Delta Air Lines Museum in Atlanta.

Brief Encounter

Dreams of Expansion

C.E. Woolman was never the type to cherish illusions of grandeur. But he did hold sensible views on what needed to be done to survive as a small airline with a limited catchment area from which to draw passenger traffic. For the Delta Air Service had no mail contract, and the chances of getting one were diminishing, as the Postmaster General, **Walter Folger Brown**, made it clear that he was going to construct a U.S. airline system with routes that, in his words, "went from somewhere to somewhere." And apparently he did not consider that a route from Dallas to Jackson, via Shreveport and Monroe, fitted that category unless it was connected with major cities such as Atlanta and elsewhere. The Route 28 mail contract from Chicago to Atlanta had already been awarded in 1928 to Interstate Airways, purchased by American Airways in 1930, and the Dallas — Jackson segment was essential for Brown's plan to create the transcontinental line that subsequently became American Airlines.

Undeterred, Woolman pressed ahead cautiously. On 1 September 1929, the route was extended at both ends, to Fort Worth and to Birmingham, the important steel city in northern Alabama. From here, only a short step remained to link up on 18 June 1930 with Atlanta, the biggest and fastest-growing city of the southeastern United States, and even more important, a key point on Eastern Air Transport's (EAT) trunk route from New York to Miami. A link with Eastern would have put Delta Air Service on the airline map. Early in

1930, an idea was discussed with Eastern which, like Delta, had acquired its name when its parent company, Pitcairn Aviation, decided to separate its manufacturing and airline divisions early in 1929. Eastern and Woolman agreed upon a coordinated plan whereby EAT would submit a bid for a mail route from Atlanta to New Orleans, which would then be flown under sub-contract by Delta.

Unfortunately for Woolman and the Delta Air Service, the Postmaster General, holding the authority to award mail contracts, without which no airline in the early 1930s could hope to stay in business, had other ideas.

David and Goliath

To some extent, the Postmaster General, Walter Folger Brown, was a man of great vision. He was not impressed with the way in which the railroads had not yet succeeded in fashioning a cohesive coast-to-coast route. Canada had two, but the United States had none. With transcontinental mail service as his prime objective, Brown was determined his air mail route map would not follow the labyrinthine course set by the railroads.

He therefore resolved that, instead of the almost entirely localized companies that resulted from the first Air Mail Act (the "Kelly") Act of 1925, each with its own parochial sphere of interest, he would establish a structure for a coordinated nationwide air mail service, come what may. To do this he persuaded Congress to pass, on 29 April 1930, the Third Amendment to the Kelly Act to legalize the fundamental changes that he wished to make. The **McNary-Watres Act,**

as it was known after its sponsors, changed the basis of air mail payments from weight carried to space offered; laid down strict qualifications for aspirant bidders for the lucrative contracts; and permitted extension clauses to existing routes, covered by the Commercial Air Mail (CAM) contracts.

Under this new legislation, C.E. Woolman and Delta Air Service didn't have a prayer. Any illusions that might have been held on the analogy of the David and Goliath confrontation did not apply. In this case Walter Folger Brown — the very name sounded ominous — was on the side of Goliath.

Three Strikes and You're Out

The new system of payments by space offered favored the big airlines that had the larger equipment, such as Ford Tri-Motors or Fokker F-10s. The qualifications included proof of two years operating experience, including night flying. And the little airline from Monroe had none of these.

Further, the Postmaster General awarded contracts to large, well-capitalized corporations that could pour heavy investment into buying aircraft, establishing ground support, and setting up commercial organizations on a large scale. Favoring three large conglomerates, United Aircraft Corporation, General Motors, and the Aviation Corporation (AVCO).

On 16 September 1930, Walter Brown awarded the coveted southern transcontinental air mail contract to **American Airways**, AVCO's operating airline. Part of this route was from Dallas to Atlanta, precisely along Delta's only route. Later on, by a machiavellian manipulation of the terms of the route extension clauses of the McNary-Watres Act, the issue became moot, as American obtained a short-cut from Nashville to Dallas, via Memphis. American was relieved of the indignity of claiming "coast-to-coast, Great Lakes to the Gulf" only to have its critics allege that it was "coast-to-coast via the Great Lakes and the Gulf."

Delta Air Lines' original headquarters at Monroe, La.

Travel Air S-6000-B.

Travel Air S-6000-B

5 seats ■ 110 mph

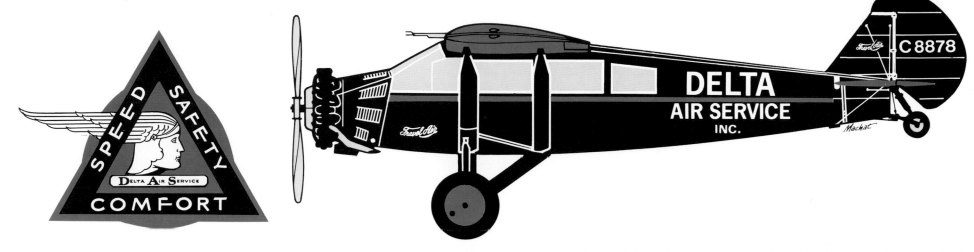

Wright J6 Whirlwind (300hp) ■ 4,230 lb. max. gross take-off weight ■ Range 500 miles ■ Length 31 feet ■ Span 49 feet ■ Height 9 feet

Thanks to the collusion of the Postmaster General, American shaped up its transcontinental route network. Exactly two weeks after losing the Dallas — Atlanta route, Delta Air Service suspended operations and sold all its equipment to Southern Air Fast Express (SAFEway), another American victim, on 29 October. Keeping his powder dry, C.E. Woolman prudently reorganized and incorporated his company as the Delta Air Corporation and, after repurchasing some aircraft from SAFEway, returned to crop-dusting.

An Array of Talent

The **Travel Air Manufacturing Company, Inc.**, was incorporated at Wichita, Kansas, on 4 February 1925. Two of its promoters were **Walter H. Beech**, a demonstration pilot, and **Lloyd C. Stearman**, a designer, both of whom had left the Wichita Aircraft Company to pursue their wish to build single-seat sports biplanes, using welded steel tubing for the main fuselage frame rather than wood, the material favored by "Matty" Laird of Wichita Aircraft. Beech and Stearman were soon joined by **Clyde V. Cessna**, a promising aviator and planebuilder from Rago, Kansas. The first Travel Air flew on 13 March 1925.

Stearman left in October 1926, and Cessna in January 1927, both to start their own companies. Beech stayed on until the company passed under the control of the **Curtiss-Wright Corporation**, which moved the production entirely to St. Louis in August 1929. Walter Beech went back to Wichita and, like Cessna and Stearman, started his own company.

Travel Air was one of the victims of the Great Depression, as companies folded at the end of the Roaring Twenties. It had built hundreds of airplanes, of many different types, with several sub-variants of each type. Possibly the best of them all was the **Model S-6000-B**, a six-place monoplane with neat, clean lines. **Delta Air Service** had three of them, two from Fox Flying Service, and one directly from Wichita. One of them opened Delta's first scheduled service, on 17 June 1929.

CHARACTERISTICS OF SELECTED TRAVEL AIRS

Type	Model	Dimensions (ft)			Pass. seats	Engines		MGTOW (lb)	Speed (mph)	Date of First Service*
		Length	Span	Height		Type	hp			
Biplane	2000 (Model B)	24	35	9	2	Curtiss OX5	90	2,180	100	Mar. 28
Biplane	4000 (Model BW)	24	35	9	2	Wright J5	220	2,400	130	Mar. 28
Mono-plane	S-6000-B	31	49	9	5	Wright J6	300	4,230	130	Mar. 29

*Aircraft listed are representative of the most widely used models. * Date of Approved Type Certificate (ATC).*

DELTA AIR SERVICE FLEET 1929-30

MSN	Regn.	Remarks
Travel Air 2000		
369	NC4316	Built 12 Mar. 28, delivered 14 Mar. 29; retired 1 Sep. 37
Travel Air S-6000-B		
988	C8878	Opened first Delta service, 17 Jun. 29
1072	C9905	Acquired in purchase of Fox Flying Service
1081	C9930	Delivered from Travel Air

The S-6000-Bs were sold to Southern Air Fast Express (SAFE) on 29 October 1930.

Stinson SM-1 Detroiter		
M-216	NC3350	From Fox Flying Services; sold to SAFE

Prelude in California

The Kelly Act

The first major piece of legislation enacted towards the ideal of an organized and systematic U.S. airline industry was the **Contract Air Mail Act**, passed on 2 February 1925. Popularly known as the Kelly Act, after its main advocate, Representative Clyde Kelly of Pennsylvania, its main objective was to curb the efforts made by the U.S. Post Office to carry the mail by air. Curiously its main supporters were the railroads, which viewed airlines as possible partners in offering a mail service.

The provisions of the Act called for the now nationwide network operated by the Post Office to be transferred to private contractors. Each of these would be the successful bidders for individual routes, the longest of which was from San Francisco to Chicago.

Subsequently, after much preparatory work by the Joint Committee of Civil Aviation, set up by Secretary of Commerce Herbert Hoover, and supportive recommendations by the Morrow Board, the Air Commerce Act was signed into law on 20 May 1926, to place air transport in the United States on a firm footing.

Western Enterprise

Air Mail Contract No. 4 (CAM 4) was awarded to **Western Air Express**, of Los Angeles. The company had been promoted by Harris M. "Pop" Hanshue, a former racing car driver and car dealer, and backed by Harry Chandler, of the *Los Angeles Times,* and James A. Talbot, of Richfield Oil. When the company was founded, on 13 July 1925, no doubt the motivation was to challenge the assumption that San Francisco

This rare picture, taken in the winter of 1925-26 (courtesy, the DeGarmo Family Collection) shows a survey team — with transport of two previous generations — locating a good site for an airstrip in the scrub desert of Western Air Express' route between Los Angeles and Las Vegas.

was the natural western terminus of a transcontinental air route. How close Hanshue came to achieving his ambition, and how it was cynically plucked from his grasp, is narrated on pages 18 and 22.

Western Air Express (WAE) began mail service on 17 April 1926, from Vail Field, Los Angeles, to Salt Lake City, via Las Vegas. The service connected with the main Post Office mail route — not contracted until 1927 — and Western had aspirations of winning that prize too, but Boeing Air Transport won the coveted San Francisco — Chicago mail contract.

Western started passenger service on 23 May 1926. During the remainder of that year, 209 stalwarts paid $90.00 each for the privilege of sitting in an unheated and only partially protected cockpit, squeezing in beside the mailsacks. Occasional stops were made in the Mojave Desert or the Nevada scrub, where, however, there were no comfort stations. The one-way trip took 6-1/2 hours. Incredibly, WAE completed all 518 of the flights scheduled for 1926, a tribute to the aircraft, the pilots, and the standards of maintenance.

This original route (see map on page 20) was the foundation around which Western's network grew, but it was to outlast all the others.

Claims to "Firstliness"

There have been many arguments as to which U.S. airline can fairly claim to being the first. Much depends on the definition and a clear distinction must always be made between the terms first and oldest. Of the contract mail carriers, Varney Air Lines made a flight on 6 April 1926 but postponed regular service until two months later. Henry Ford's airline had already been offering private express service on its own behalf since April 1925 and was therefore ready to carry the mail as soon as the Kelly Act took effect. Robertson began mail flights from St. Louis to Chicago two days before Western's inaugural. These, and many others, can lay some kind of claim for truly veteran status.

Western could with justification place much emphasis on the quality and reliability of its service, and the key role it played in accelerating the mail service in the far west. The route has been operated continuously ever since it started, and both Salt Lake City and Los Angeles are key hubs in Delta's network today. As a matter of interest, Western Air Express did inherit, by its acquisition of Pacific Marine Airways in 1928 (see page 18) one of the oldest routes in the United States that has been operated more or less continuously since 4 July 1919.

Harris M. (Pop) Hanshue, President of Western Air Express, hands over the mail to Fred Kelly, one of the famous quartet, known as the Four Horsemen. Note that each pilot was assigned his own airplane.

The scene at Vail Field, Los Angeles, as three Douglas M-2 mailplanes are readied for the historic inaugural service on 17 April 1926 to Las Vegas and Salt Lake City (see map page 20.)

Douglas M-2

2 seats ■ 118 mph

WESTERN
AIR
EXPRESS
INC.

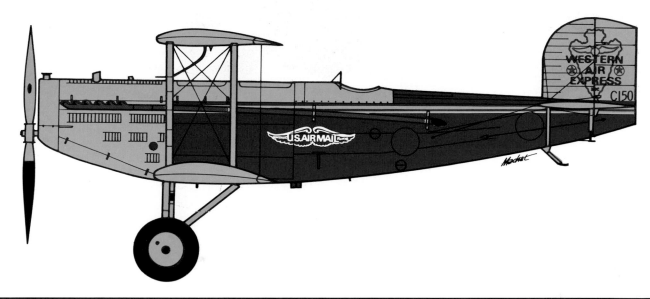

Liberty (400 hp) ■ 4,755 lb. max. gross take-off weight ■ Range 650 miles

This sturdy mailplane was selected by the U.S. Post Office as well as by Western Air Express as the best aircraft of its day able to meet the challenging specifications for construction, performance, and flying characteristics. Its mail compartment, situated in front of the pilot's cockpit, and sealed from the engine by a fireproof wall, was lined with reinforced duralumin. The compartment was six feet long, with a capacity of 58 cubic feet, and could carry up to

LENGTH 29 feet
SPAN 40 feet
HEIGHT 9 feet

1,000lb of mail. Two removable seats could be installed to carry passengers or reserve pilots on assignment.

An improved version, designated the M-3, was selected by National Air Transport, and a further improvement, that added five feet to the wing span, resulted in the M-4, which saw extensive service with National. One of the Western M-4s (C1475) is now restored, having been carefully rebuilt by a volunteer group of Western and Douglas employees in Los Angeles, and flown across the U.S.A. to the National Air and Space Museum in Washington in May 1977. The fact that it could make a second "first flight" on 2 June 1976, 46 years after it crashed in 1930, is a remarkable tribute to the ruggedness of the original design and to the longevity of the Liberty engine that powered it.

WESTERN AIR EXPRESS — THE FIRST FLEET

Fleet No.	Type	MSN	Regn.	Purchase Date	Remarks
Douglas Mailplanes					
1	M-1	244	C150	8 Mar. 26	Converted to M-2; sold to Charles F. Dycer, 7 Apr. 32
2	M-2	245	C151	22 Mar. 26	Sold to Lincoln Air Svce., 29 Sep. 31
3	M-2	246		22 Mar. 26	Crashed, Salt Lake City area, 8 Dec. 26
4	M-2	247	C1489	29 Mar. 26	Sold to T.T. Brown, 20 Aug. 31
5	M-2	248	C1490	29 Mar. 26	Sold to Lincoln Air Svce., 29 Sep. 31
6	M-2	252	C1491	15 Apr. 26	Sold to L.A. Weedle, 5 Oct. 31
7	M-4	357	C1512	10 Sep. 26	Sold to Elmer A. Riley, 1 Oct. 31
8	M-4	338	C1475	16 Jun. 27	
9	M-2		C1476	16 Jun. 27	Crashed, Denver, 10 Dec. 27
The first six aircraft were purchased from Douglas; the other three from the Post Office Department					
De Havilland DH-4B (all from Post Office Department)					
A	A-99		C1488	30 Nov. 26	Sold to Paramount Famous Lasky Corp., 14 Nov. 27
B	A-98		C1487	7 Nov. 26	
C		100	C640	30 Nov. 26	

The Model Airway

The Guggenheim Fund

The success of Western's Los Angeles — Salt Lake City mail service led to an interesting development. The **Daniel Guggenheim Fund for the Promotion of Aeronautics**, formed on 18 January 1926, selected Western to conduct a full-scale passenger service in California as an experiment in promoting air transport. For this "Model Airway" and having sought in vain among U.S. aircraft manufacturers for a suitable aircraft, the Fund supported the choice of the **Fokker F-10**, a 12-seat landplane that introduced new standards of comfort when it opened service on the Los Angeles — San Francisco route on 26 May 1928.

For the first time, meals were served on board, at least, box lunches were provided from the *Pig 'n' Whistle* cafeteria in Los Angeles, and Miles Davis had the honor of being the first steward. The Model Airway offered limousine service to the airports, and provided log-books for the passengers to record the thrill of riding the airways in comparative comfort.

Cabin meal service on board the Fokker F-10.

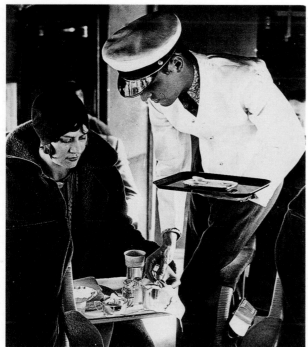

Radio and Weather Reporting

With Dr. Carl-Gustav Arvid Rossby, a well-known meteorologist, as consultant, Western Air Express installed 37 en route weather stations between the two great Californian metropolitan areas. This permitted five different choices of route, an unprecedented luxury for the pilots in 1928.

WESTERN'S FOKKER TRIMOTORS

(In order of delivery, Fleet Numbers 100-125)

MSN	Regn.	Delivery Date	Remarks
Fokker F-7A			
602	C3908	2 Mar. 28	From Atlantic Aircraft; sold to Continental Air Express, 11 May 29
Fokker F-10			
1000	NC4458	24 Apr. 28	Retired from service, 30 Apr. 31
1001	NC5170	9 May 28	Written off, Alhambra, 26 Jan. 31
1002	NC5358	11 May 28	Crashed, Oakland, 26 Dec. 29
1005	NC8048	14 Nov. 28	} Sold to TWA, 24 Mar. 31
1006	NC8047	10 Dec. 28	
All from Atlantic Aircraft Corp. (Fokker).			
Fokker F-10A			
1009	NC9716	24 Dec. 28	From Atlantic Aircraft Corp.; sold to SAFE, 9 Oct. 30
1011	NC279E	2 Feb. 29	From Fokker; crashed, Lake Arrowhead, 23 Feb. 30
1013	NC393E	Mar. 29	From Fokker; destroyed in storm, Wichita, 2 Jun. 29
1007	NC392E	3 Mar. 29	} From Fokker; sold to TWA, 24 Mar. 31
1017	NC455E	27 Mar. 29	
1019	NC456E	8 Apr. 29	
1020	NC489E	21 Apr. 29	From Fokker; sold to SAFE, 9 Oct. 30
1021	NC591E	6 May 29	From Fokker; crashed, Alhambra, 22 Dec. 30
1042	NC582K	7 Aug. 29	Fokker; sold to Chas. H. Babb, 12 Feb. 35
1043	NC583K	12 Aug. 29	} From Fokker; sold to TWA, 24 Mar. 31
1063	NC999E	31 Oct. 29	
1028	NC39N	1 May 30	Ex-Standard Airlines; crashed Lynndyl, Utah, 11 Dec. 32
1054	NC580K		} From Standard Airlines; sold to SAFE, 9 Oct. 30
1055	NC581K	8 May 30	
1038	NC9169		
1058	NC528M	10 Jun 30	Ex-Standard Airlines; sold to TWA 24 Mar. 31
1045	NC584K	20 Jul. 31	From Pacific Air Transport } Sold to Chas. H. Babb 2 Dec. 35
1044	NC215M	7 Aug. 31	
1057	NC586K	22 Nov. 32	Ex-Standard Airlines
1015	NC394E	6 Jan. 33	From Richfield Oil Co.

Herbert Hoover, Jr., Western's radio specialist, pictured here with (left) Jimmy James, and (right) Fred Kelly.

Herbert Hoover Jr., Western's own radio specialist, together with Thorp Hiscock, a communications engineer with Boeing Air Transport, developed a system of two-way radios, replacing the airborne radio-telegraph (Morse Code). Geoffrey Kreusi, a Swiss, and Gerhardt Fischer, a German, both hired by Western to work with Hoover, developed the first radio-compass. This was subsequently sold to Bendix and was improved to become the automatic direction finder (ADF) that became standard equipment for all airliners until the advent of the inertial navigation system.

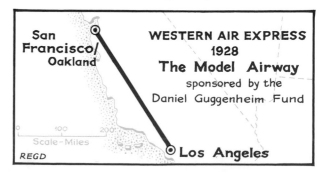

San Francisco/ Oakland

WESTERN AIR EXPRESS
1928
The Model Airway
sponsored by the
Daniel Guggenheim Fund

Scale—Miles
0   100   200

REGD

⊙ Los Angeles

Fokker F-10

12 SEATS ■ 110 mph

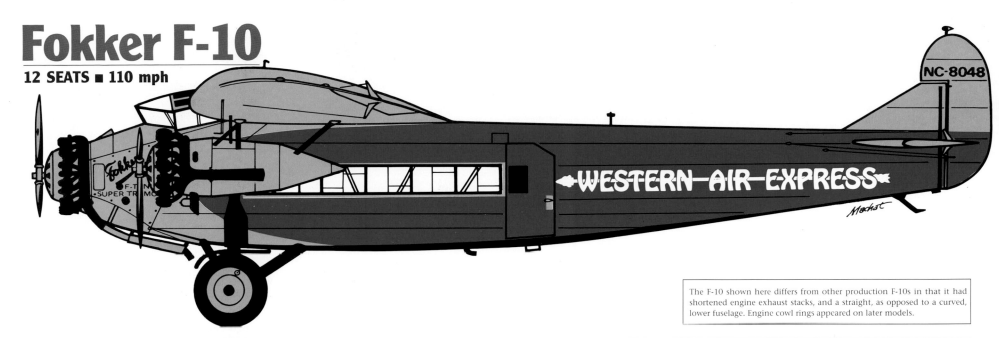

NC-8048

Fokker F-T... SUPER TR...

WESTERN AIR EXPRESS

Machat

The F-10 shown here differs from other production F-10s in that it had shortened engine exhaust stacks, and a straight, as opposed to a curved, lower fuselage. Engine cowl rings appeared on later models.

Pratt & Whitney Wasp (400 hp) x 3 ■ 12,500 lb. max. gross take-off weight ■ Range 700 miles

Western Air Express spent the entire $180,000 from the Guggenheim Fund to purchase three Fokker F-10 tri-motors. With three Pratt & Whitney Wasp engines, they were among the finest aircraft of their time — this was before the Ford Tri-Motor swept all before it — and in 1928, the shock of the TWA crash which hit the newspaper headlines because of its distinguished passenger (see below) was still three years away. Its impressive performance, which enabled it to maintain altitude with two engines out, and actually to be able to climb to 7,000 feet with only one out, was more than satisfactory in an era when engine failure with a single-engined aircraft was all too frequent, and all too often catastrophic.

As the table of aircraft on the opposite page shows, Western had quite a few F-10s and F-10As (the A version had a slightly longer wing and could carry two more passengers than the ten in the F-10). They flew with Western Air Express until 1935.

The Fokker F-10 was innovative in that it boasted wheel brakes, a lavatory, a lighted instrument panel, and "full cabin-length windows" that could be opened in flight to allow the fresh air in. A total of 124 were built, of which 59 were Fokker-10As.

One of the F-10s and F-10As that passed to **TWA** with the WAE/TAT merger was NC999E, the aircraft that crashed at Bazaar, Kansas, on 31 March 1931, and which gained special notoriety because the Notre Dame football coach, Knute Rockne, was killed. Of more importance to the annals of airliner development history, the Fokker F-10, as a direct result, was the first aircraft type to be grounded, albeit briefly, by the Director of Aeronautics in the Department of Commerce, a landmark decision which epitomized a new attitude towards safety standards by the regulatory authorities, and a grave suspicion of wooden aircraft construction thereafter.

LENGTH 50 feet
SPAN 79 feet
HEIGHT 102 feet

Fokker F-10 at Alhambra Airport in 1930.

17

Pacific Marine and Colorado Airways

The Airway to Catalina

One of the earliest passenger air routes in the United States is the over-water connection between Los Angeles Harbor and Catalina Island, where the little resort community of Avalon invites jaded Angelinos to get away from the Big City.

First to spot the opportunity was none other than Syd Chaplin, elder brother of the famous Charlie, who started the **Chaplin Air Line** on 4 July 1919, using a Curtiss MF flying boat. It operated three round-trips a day, with a staff of three, until mid-September, by which time it was known as Catalina Airlines. Subsequently, one of the pilots continued to make trips on demand, until the end of 1920, when **Pacific Marine Airways** took over the route.

Pacific Marine was incorporated in Los Angeles on 7 August 1924 by Foster Curry, the same vacation promoter who had helped to make Yosemite National Park an attractive tourist destination. His fleet consisted of two Curtiss HS-2Ls and the service was maintained until **Western Air Express** took over the company on 29 June 1928.

As shown in the accompanying table, Western utilized a number of different aircraft types to replace the old Curtiss boats. When its contract to serve the island ended in May 1931, a new company, the **Wilmington-Catalina Airline** was organized by Philip K. Wrigley, of the chewing gum empire, starting service on 6 June 1931, with Douglas Dolphin amphibians.

Colorado Airways

On 31 May 1926, Anthony F. Joseph started new service as **Colorado Airways**, to connect Cheyenne, on the transcontinental air mail route, with Denver, Colorado Springs, and Pueblo. Using at first Standard biplanes, later replaced by Ryan M-1s, the latter were replaced by Stearmans when **Western Air Express** acquired the CAM 12 mail contract.

Colorado Airways operated Ryan M-1s in 1926.

THE COLORADO AIRWAYS RYAN M-1 FLEET

MSN	Regn.	Delivery Date	Remarks
	NC4281 NC4282		} Sold to Western College of Aeronautics, 18 Dec. 28

Fleet Numbers 22/24; one other was No. 20, sold to Wilson Aero Service, 23 Jul. 28; all were taken over by WAE December 1927.

THE WAE STEARMAN C3B FLEET

MSN	Regn.	Delivery Date	Remarks
105	NC3709		Crashed, Denver, 7 May 29
106	NC3863	15 Dec. 28	Crashed, Denver, 10 Aug. 30
108	NC4011	17 May 29	
193	NC6495	15 Dec. 28	
235	NC8820	17 May 29	Crashed, Denver, 6 Jan. 30
4011	NC774H	22 Mar. 30	
229	NC8815		

Fleet Numbers 200-206; NC3863 was C3B Special, NC4011 a C3MB, and NC774H a 4DM.

One of three Curtiss HS-2Ls used by Pacific Marine Airways.

Keystone-Loening Air Yacht amphibian of W.A.E.

Western's one and only Sikorsky S-38.

AIRCRAFT ON THE ROUTE TO AVALON

MSN	Regn.	Remarks
Curtiss HS-2L		
A-1373	C652	} Operated by Pacific
A-1981	C2420	Marine, 1922-30,
111	C5419	Fleet Numbers 225-227
Loening C2H		
220	NC9773	} Ordered by Pacific Marine, operated by
230	NC135H	WAE after purchase; Fleet Numbers 301-302
Sikorsky S-38A		
14-5	NC8021	*Flying Fish*, Fleet Number 300; operated by WAE Sep. 28; written off, Avalon, 5 Jun. 29
Boeing 204		
1076	NC874E	Introduced May 1929, Fleet Number 228; sold to Gorst Air Tpt., 7 Jan. 31

Standard and West Coast

Standard Air Lines

On 3 February 1926, the Aero Corporation of California, an aircraft dealership and flying school in Los Angeles, formed a subsidiary, **Standard Air Lines**. The officers included Lieut. Jack Frye, president; Lieut. Paul Richter, Jr., treasurer; and Walter Hamilton, 2nd vice-president.

Standard began scheduled service on 28 November 1927 with a daily flight between Los Angeles and Tucson, via Phoenix. (This fleet is included in the tabulation on page 16). Standard also had a single **Fokker F-7**, of a lesser breed apparently, for there was a contemporary reference to "Fokker single-engined comfort facilities (being) limited to men, a brief stop being made for women at Desert Center, California, where a solitary filling station boasted two crude outhouses." Standard was incorporated as a Nevada Corporation on 1 May 1928.

The First Air-Rail Transcontinental Route

During 1929, several railroads linked up with airlines to offer joint air-rail services, aimed to reduce the transcontinental time for passengers as well as mail. The most publicized of these, the **Transcontinental Air Transport (TAT)** service, operating jointly with the Pennsylvania Railroad, started on 7 July. But preceding this was that of the Universal Aviation Corporation and the New York Central, on 14 June. Both TAT and Universal depended on the Santa Fe for their western rail links.

Even before these was the claim of **Standard Air Lines**, which, on 4 February 1929, announced the inauguration of "America's First Trans-continental Air-Rail Travel Route," by extending its route eastward to El Paso, via Douglas, and linking up with the Texas and Pacific Railroad. This may have been stretching the definition of the word transcontinental, but air-rail it certainly was, and the claim was given more le-

The Bach Air Yacht trimotors had different combinations of engines. This one, a Model 3CT-5 Cascadian in service with West Coast Air Transport, had a Pratt & Whitney Hornet in the nose and two Siemens-Halske radials under the wings. (Photograph courtesy Sam Parker)

gitimacy on 4 August when a complex link-up was made with **Southwest Air Fast Express (SAFE)** and the New York Central.

These fine aspirations came to an end when, with the collusion of the Postmaster General, **American Airways** was able to purchase the Standard Air Lines route (not the airline) in October 1930, having already negotiated the control of SAFE. Thus another of Hanshue's plans was summarily removed from the Postmaster General's grand plan; for the opportunist **Western Air Express** leader had purchased Standard on 1 May 1930, possibly trying to play one last card for Californian interests in the nationwide game of air-mail poker. Standard Air Lines was eventually dissolved on 27 July 1934.

West Coast Air Transport

On 5 March 1928, West Coast Air Transport Corporation started passenger and express service, on a daily schedule, between San Francisco and the northwest cities of Seattle and Portland, with intermediate stops. The company was owned by Union Air Lines of Sacramento, and operated a fleet of eight tri-motored Bach Air Yachts. It was incorporated in Delaware on 27 June 1929.

Late in 1929, **Western Air Express** acquired the

company, which had been quite successful, carrying almost 5,000 passengers in 1928. But with the crisis of the 1930 Shotgun Marriage (see page 22) Hanshue had to retrench, terminating service in December of that year, and selling the company to **Pacific Air Transport,** part of the Boeing-United conglomerate, on 16 March 1931, for $250,000.

BACH AIR YACHTS OF WEST COAST AIR TRANSPORT

MSN	Regn.	Remarks
1	NC3997	Model 3CT-2 Crusader; written off, Seattle, 8 Jun. 28, but re-registered NC7065 10 Jul. 29
2	NC4184	Model 3CT-5 Cascadian; taken over by WAE and sold to Dick Rankin, re-registered NC7092.

WCAT acquired up to six other unidentified Air Yachts from Bach in 1928.

*West Coast Air Transport also had a **Breese** (msn 6/C3017) purchased on 16 Oct. 29 and taken over by WAE.*

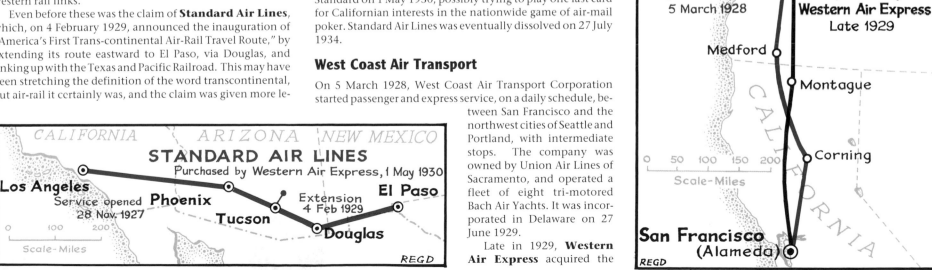

STANDARD AIR LINES
Purchased by Western Air Express, 1 May 1930

CALIFORNIA · ARIZONA · NEW MEXICO

Los Angeles
Service opened 28 Nov. 1927
Phoenix
Tucson
Douglas
Extension 4 Feb 1929
El Paso

0 · 100 · 200
Scale-Miles

REGD

WEST COAST AIR TRANSPORT
Opened service 5 March 1928

Portland
OREGON
Acquired by Western Air Express Late 1929
Medford
Montague
Corning
San Francisco (Alameda)

CALIFORNIA

0 · 50 · 100 · 150 · 200
Scale-Miles

REGD

Western Air Express Expands

While **Western Air Express** was concentrating on its Californian Model Airway, it was obliged to review its longer-term and wider-ranging aspirations to establish a network of nationwide scope. It turned its eyes away from the central route, via Salt Lake City, inwards to opportunities for expansion to the east via the southwestern states of the U.S.

The progress is illustrated in the map below. The first step was to open a daily passenger service, without the benefit of a mail contract, on a direct route to Albuquerque, straight across Arizona, on 15 May 1929. Within a month, on 1 June, this was extended to Kansas City, and feelers were put out towards renting office space in Chicago. The following year, on 1 April 1930, Western acquired the **Aero Corporation of California** and its subsidiary, **Standard Air Lines**. This gave Western a second route to the east, to the Texas cities, and a month later, the rich oil centers of Oklahoma were added to the network.

Supplementing these new arteries, Western acquired airlines on the West Coast and in the Rocky Mountain area, as indicated on the map on this page.

By the middle of 1930, Harris Hanshue had systematically fashioned the largest commercial air network in the United States, but only two routes, Los Angeles — Salt Lake City, and Pueblo — Cheyenne, were operated with the support of mail contracts. The financial losses became intolerable, and the Postmaster General, Walter F. Brown, was obdurate in his refusal to grant the coveted CAM 34 New York — Los Angeles mail contract. The story of how Hanshue was deprived of the reward for pioneering service to the public is outlined on page 22.

Left: Western's famous quartet of hardened airmail pilots was known as The Four Horsemen. Fred W. Kelly, C.N. (Jimmy) James, Alva R. DeGarmo, Maury Graham, and (extreme right) Major C.C. Moseley, V.P. operations of WAE.
Right: The luxurious interior of the Fokker F-32.

WESTERN'S EARLY BOEING FLEET

MSN	Regn.	Delivery Date	Remarks
Boeing 95			
1063	C419E	30 Mar. 29	Crashed, St. George, Utah, 24 Feb. 30
1064	C420E	10 Apr. 29	Crashed, Cedar City, Utah, 21 Jan. 30
1065	C421E	30 Mar. 29	Sold to Mildred F. Obbink, 3 Jul. 34
1066	C422E	15 Apr. 29	Sold to Elenore Riley, 25 Jul. 34
Fleet Numbers 50-53			
Boeing 40B-4			
1149	C742K	5 Mar. 30	Crashed, 9 Feb. 32
1169	C843M	6 Mar. 30	Sold Jul. 34
Fleet Numbers 54-55; All aircraft purchased new from Boeing			

*WAE also acquired a **Lockheed Model 3 Air Express** (5/NC4897, Fleet Number 250) but this was damaged when landing at Las Vegas on its inaugural flight, 6 June 1928, and returned to the manufacturer.*

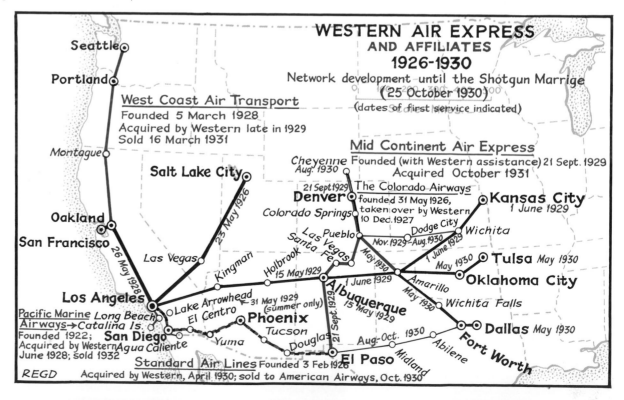

WESTERN AIR EXPRESS AND AFFILIATES 1926-1930
Network development until the Shotgun Marriage (25 October 1930)
(dates of first service indicated)

West Coast Air Transport
Founded 5 March 1928
Acquired by Western late in 1929
Sold 16 March 1931

Mid Continent Air Express
Founded (with Western assistance) 21 Sept. 1929
Acquired October 1931

The Colorado Airways
founded 31 May 1926, taken over by Western 10 Dec. 1927

Pacific Marine Airways → Catalina Is.
Founded 1922; Acquired by Western June 1928; sold 1932

Standard Air Lines Founded 3 Feb 1926
Acquired by Western, April 1930; sold to American Airways, Oct. 1930

REGD

Seattle
Portland
Montague
Salt Lake City 23 May 1926
Oakland
San Francisco 26 May 1928
Las Vegas
Kingman
Los Angeles
Lake Arrowhead 31 May 1929 (summer only)
El Centro
Long Beach
San Diego
Agua Caliente
Yuma
Phoenix
Tucson
Douglas
Aug.-Oct. 1930
El Paso
Midland
Abilene
Fort Worth
Dallas May 1930
Wichita Falls
Oklahoma City
Tulsa May 1930
Amarillo May 1930
Albuquerque 15 May 1929
Holbrook 15 May 1929
Santa Fe
Las Vegas
Pueblo Nov. 1929-Aug. 1930
Dodge City
Wichita 1 June 1929
Kansas City 1 June 1929
Denver
Colorado Springs
Cheyenne Aug. 1930
May 1930
1 June 1929
21 Sept 1929

Fokker F-32

32 SEATS ■ 123 mph

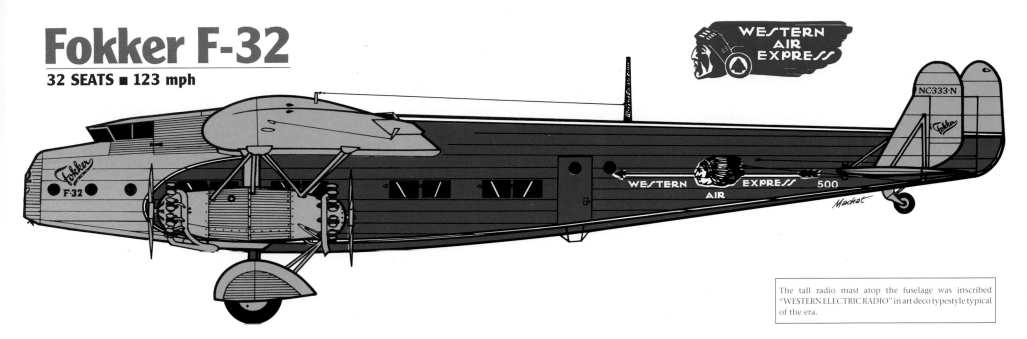

The tall radio mast atop the fuselage was inscribed "WESTERN ELECTRIC RADIO" in art deco typestyle typical of the era.

Pratt & Whitney Hornet (575 hp) x4 ■ 24,250 lb. max. gross take-off weight ■ Range 740 miles

A Giant before its Time

This enormous aircraft was a marvel of its time and, like all big things, attracted comment solely because of its size. It was, in fact, the heaviest aircraft to enter commercial service in the United States until the Douglas DC-3, which it exceeded in both length and wing span.

Western introduced the F-32 on 17 April 1930, between Los Angeles (Alhambra) and San Francisco (Oakland) but, as the table below shows, it was not very successful. Still, it had its brief hour of glory and received much praise for its plush appointments, with eight compartments, each seating four passengers on reclining seats which were well upholstered — a welcome change from the wicker chairs that had hitherto been provided. The decor was artistic, the woods and fabrics were the best. There were call buttons, lavatories, folding tables, galleys, reading lights: in fact all the modern amenities that were to become standard equipment in the mid-1930s when the modern airliners made their appearance.

The instrument panels were better than anything seen before; the fuel tanks were kept well away from the passengers, in the wings; and each engine had its own fire-extinguishing system. This ponderous four-engined aircraft may have been ungainly but no-one could have called it an ugly duckling, at least judging by the furnishings, illustrated opposite. Furthermore, it gave Western the honor of operating the first four-engined commercial airplane in the United States.

LENGTH 70 feet
SPAN 99 feet
HEIGHT 17 feet

WESTERN'S FOKKER F-32 FLEET

MSN	Regn.	Remarks
1201	NC124M	Prototype; WAE markings but not placed in service
1202	NC130M	Crashed before delivery
1203	NC333N	Operated 1 Apr. 30 to 1 Oct. 30, Fleet Numbers 500-
1204	NC334N	501; sold to TWA 24 Mar. 31

The giant Fokker F-32 (32 seats) is shown here in front of the hexagonal hangar especially built for it at Alhambra Airport, near Los Angeles.

The Shotgun Marriage

The Master Plan

The Postmaster General of the Coolidge Administration, Walter Folger Brown (see page 12), had a clear vision of what he felt would constitute a sensible air network: three transcontinental lines, coast-to-coast (with a northern route west of Chicago); linked with several north-south lines at the coasts, along the Mississippi, and down the Rocky Mountains, plus a few supplementary cross-feeds where traffic volumes appeared to justify them. Unfortunately, only one route, Boeing Air Transport's San Francisco-Chicago artery, had transcontinental potential— it quickly became **United Air Lines**. A second, based flimsily on the Universal Aviation Corporation system, eventually grew into **American Airways** by the applicationof extension and consolidation opportunities that had much to do with what the Postmaster General wanted, but little to do with logic, nor, many would suggest later, to do with legality. The third route presented a problem. Two airlines, **TAT** and **Western Air Express**, both wanted it. Each had a good case.

TAT had pioneered a passenger air route from the Southern Plains to the Midwest, but much of its enterprise succeeded in its impact on the public attitude towards flying, more than in traffic volumes generated, or in revenues earned, to cover the heavy investment made according to an elaborate and very expensive plan and route laid down by Charles Lindbergh, technical adviser to the airline. TAT lost close to $3,000,000 within two years of operation.

Western Air Express had strenuously stretched its network eastwards from California in several directions (see page 20) and by the summer of 1930 had reached Dallas, Tulsa, and, more significantly, Kansas City, key staging point for TAT. Harris Hanshue's route, in fact, closely paralleled the one laid down by Lindbergh, and an extension was planned to Chicago. Dangling the carrot of a very lucrative New York — Los Angeles space-available mail contract before the two rivals, Walter Brown informed both airlines that he would not award it to either one. They must merge so as to eliminate unnecessary and self-destructive competition. And so the third transcontinental route award was made in what became known as the Shotgun Marriage, with Postmaster General Brown notarizing the marriage certificate, duly solemnized on16 July 1930. The merged airline became **Transcontinental and Western Air (TWA)** on 24 July, 1930. Harris Hanshue was president of the new corporation.

Walter Folger Brown (left), Postmaster General during the Hoover administration, whose master plan for a nationwide airline network relegated Western Express to a minor role. A TAT Ford Tri-Motor at Port Columbus, Ohio (right).

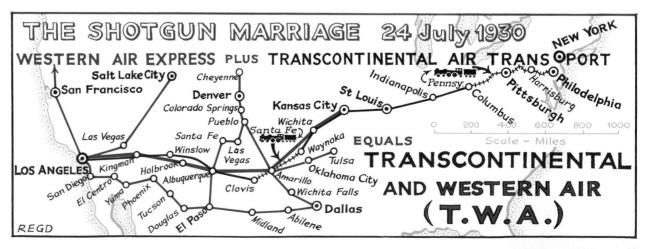

Western Recovery

Down But Not Out

After serving as president of TWA for eight months, Harris Hanshue was forced out of that position by TAT's former management and returned to his previous position at WAE. He embarked on a painful policy of retrenchment.

By the end of 1930, Western Air Express was only a shadow of its former self. In October, the ex-Standard Air Lines Los Angeles — El Paso route was sold to American Airways. This was a bitter pill to swallow, as Hanshue not only lost a route that could have formed the nucleus of a southern transcontinental route; he was obliged to help the powerful **Aviation Corporation of America (AVCO)** to fulfill its coast-to-coast ambitions and consolidate the position of what was to become American Airlines.

In December 1930, service to Seattle was suspended and on 16 March 1931, West Coast Air Transport Corporation, which nominally held the route, was sold to Pacific Air Transport, part of the United Air Lines group, another favored giant of the Postmaster General.

Mid-Continent Air Express

Mid-Continent Air Express was incorporated in Delaware on 19 June 1929, and on 21 September 1929, began operations on a route from Denver to El Paso, via intermediate points (see map). Financial support came from Western Air Express and aircraft were supplied by the General Aviation Corporation. By the end of the year, a second route was opened from Denver to Kansas City, and an extension was made to Dallas in August 1930. These routes, operated by six-seat Fokker Super-Universals, were part of WAE's expansionist moves towards the east; but were frustrated by the TWA Shotgun Marriage coup which forced Harris Hanshue to his knees.

Nevertheless, with General Aviation taking a greater role in Western Air Express's affairs (see page 24) Mid-Continent was fully absorbed into the parent company on 27 September 1931, its fleet strengthened by the addition of Boeing 40B-4s and Boeing 95s, and was officially dissolved as a separate corporation on 16 December of that year.

Western's Lockheed Air Express was damaged upon landing on its inaugural flight and returned to Lockheed.

Western operated this Stearman 4DM in 1930.

One of Western's Boeing Model 95 mailplanes.

The prototype Fokker F-14, although painted in Western Air Express colors, was never operated by WAE.

WESTERN'S SINGLE-ENGINED FOKKERS

MSN	Regn.	Delivery Date	Remarks
Fokker Super-Universal			
812	NC8011		Destroyed by fire, Watrous, N.M., 3 Dec. 33
826	NC9724		Sold to Chas. H. Babb, 7 Mar. 34
830	NC9789		Crashed, Las Vegas, N.M., 31 Dec. 33
861	NC99K	16 Apr. 32	Sold to Chas. H. Babb, 25 Jun. 34
862	NC121M		
863	NC122M		Crashed, Colorado Springs, 2 Dec. 33
864	NC123M		Sold to Chas. H. Babb, 5 Feb. 34
865	NC126M		Sold to Chas. H. Babb, 25 Jun. 34

*Fleet Numbers 211-218; all ex-**Mid-Continent Air Express** which was first promoted by, then absorbed by WAE in October 1931. The first three and last listed were, in turn, ex-**Standard Air Lines**. Mid-Continent also used Universal 438/NC128M; and Standard had Universal 426/NC3317 plus the following aircraft (registered to Aero Corp. of California): Fokker F-7A 617/NC7888 (crashed, Beaumont, Calif., 29 Mar. 29), and Universals 416/NC696 (sold to Pacific Air Trspt., 9 Nov. 27), and 423/NC3193.*

Fokker F-14			
1404	NC129M	16 Dec. 29	Sold to TWA 24 Mar. 31; the prototype (1401/NC150H) was painted in WAE colors but not operated
1409	NC328N	28 Jan. 30	
1411	NC331N	24 Mar. 30	

Fleet Numbers 400-402. One other aircraft (1408/NC327N) reported but no other details available.

Mid-Continent Express also had two **Boeing 40B-4s**, as follows:			
1149	NC742K	5 Mar. 30	Acquired from Boeing Air Transport
1169	NC843M	6 Mar. 30	

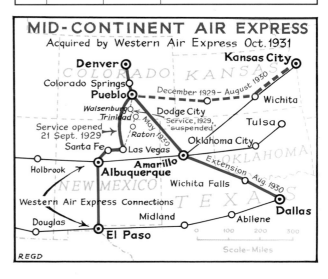

MID-CONTINENT AIR EXPRESS
Acquired by Western Air Express Oct.1931

General Motors Control

The General Aviation Corporation

To offset severe financial losses incurred during 1929 and 1930, and with the loss of the one route that would have enabled it to reverse the negative trend, **Western Air Express** was forced into a corner and obliged to surrender its western independence and ownership. On 3 March 1931, in a significant corporate transaction, the **General Aviation Corporation** acquired a 30 per cent shareholding in Hanshue's company. The significance lay in the fact that General Aviation was a subsidiary of the mighty **General Motors Corporation**, which also controlled TWA and Eastern Air Transport, and which now tried to establish itself in the airline arena, as it had challenged Henry Ford on the roads of the United States.

On 1 August 1931, the Postmaster General extended the former Colorado Airways mail route (CAM 12) by creating separate north-south links with Albuquerque and Amarillo, and Western Air Express moved in to acquire Mid-Continent Air Express so as to consolidate General Motors' position in the Rocky Mountain region. Cleaning up the western end of the operation, the Catalina Island route was sold to the Wrigley gum interests (Wrigley himself owned Catalina Island) in 1932.

North American Aviation

Early in 1933, Western Air Express became a subsidiary of **North American Aviation**, when complete control of this holding company was taken over by the **General Aviation (Manufacturing) Corporation**, which by now owned the majority of the stock.

By the beginning of 1934, the three largest shareholders in Western Air Express were the General Aviation Corporation, the National Aviation Corporation, and — curiously — the Aviation Corporation of America (AVCO), i.e. American Airways. But the real direction was in the hands of General Motors. Under its control, WAE changed its name to **General Air Lines** on 28 February 1934, and once again became an independent corporation, General Air Lines Inc. (Western Air Division), on 17 April of that year. Harris Hanshue, who had fought so valiantly for western airline interests, was forced to leave, and he died in 1935, undoubtedly embittered by the injustice handed out to a pioneer airline that had done so much for U.S. aviation as a whole.

General Air Lines Interlude

After the cancellation of the air mail contracts on 9 February 1934, when President Roosevelt stepped in to eliminate the appalling abuse of the contractual system of route awards and mail payments, Western Air Express started afresh under the new name, **General Air Lines**. It was awarded the San Diego — Los Angeles — Salt Lake City route, and was effectively right back where it started in 1926.

General began service on 8 May 1934, with aircraft technically leased from Western. But the life of the renamed airline was short. The Black-McKellar bill, passed by Congress on 12 June of that year, made far-reaching changes to airline regulations. One of these was to disqualify any manufacturer or other aviation enterprise from holding an interest in an airline. The new law was effective on 31 December 1934 and on that date General Motors pulled out and yet another era began for Western Air Express.

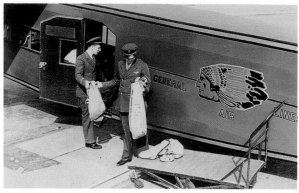

Loading the mail on a General Air Lines Fokker F-10.

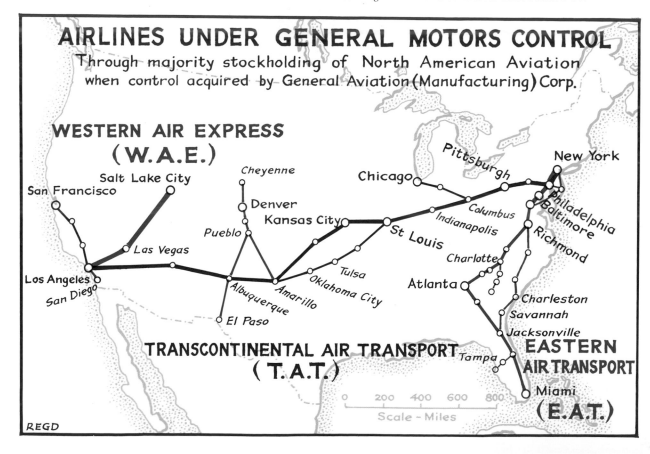

Improved Passenger Comfort

The Modern Airliner

Coincidentally with the sweeping change of ownership of Western Air Express came an equally far-reaching change in the design and construction of the aircraft that served it. Until 1933, all aircraft, including those used for air transport, had been built mainly of wood. The fuselages were typically of metal frameworks, rather like railroad coaches, and were covered with fabric or plywood; while the wings were also of fabric-covered wood construction. In fact the Fokker wings were entirely of wood. The notable exception was the Ford Tri-Motor, widely deployed in the U.S.A., but not with Western.

In 1933, Boeing put together a number of aeronautical innovations from Europe, notably the use of stressed skin, a semi-monocoque fuselage, retractable landing gear and cowled radial engines; and unveiled the twin-engined **Boeing 247** (having first built a few Monomails as a kind of prototype). A later innovation, variable-pitch propellers, gave the improved **Boeing 247D** an even more distinct edge — about 65 per cent more speed — over the 100mph Fokker and Ford predecessors. The famous Ford Tri-Motor, although metal-clad with corrugated aluminum, was slow and ungainly. The 247 was clean and, by comparison, elegant.

In 1934, the **Douglas DC-2** usurped the 247 for design and performance leadership, with a larger, cleaner, and altogether more comfortable airplane. One of the Boeing 247's short-comings was the intrusion of the two wing spars into the lower part of the fuselage, requiring a certain agility to step into the forward seats. Its width and headroom were also somewhat cramped. The DC-2, on the other hand, was a revelation. Its 14 seats were well spaced and a tall man could stand comfortably in the aisle. With box-spar wing construction, there were no annoying main spars to step over. It was a handsome design and, for the first time, the word *airliner* could be used to describe an airplane whose primary purpose was to carry passengers, who, moreover, did not have to share the cabin with mail sacks, were provided with refreshments on board, and were served by cabin staff.

Western Air Express, in its new guise as **General Air Lines**, was among the earlier operators of these watershed types, introducing DC-2s on 15 October 1934, although these were replaced almost immediately by Boeing 247Ds in December the same year.

Maude Campbell became WAE's first female passenger in June 1926. (Harris Hanshue doing the honors).

WAE operated one 10-passenger Clark GA-43 (NC13903/MSN 2204) for a brief period during 1934.

Western Air Lines operated two Lockheed 18 Lodestars acquired from Inland Air Lines (see page 37) as a result of a merger in 1944.

25

Delta Air Lines Recovers

The Black-McKellar Act

When the McNary-Watres Act of 1930 (see page 12) effectively disfranchised Delta Air Service as a bona fide airline, this could have been the nadir of C.E. Woolman's fortunes. But having been pushed off center-stage, as it were, he waited in the wings, learned by that hard taskmaster, Experience. When the opportunity came to get back on stage, he did so with aplomb and began the slow but steady upward curve of the new **Delta Air Corporation**. Even if somewhat limited in its immediate horizons, it now became a member of the U.S. airline fraternity, with equal rights even to those of the "Big Four" aristocrats with their inherited wealth of aircraft, routes, and favors from Washington.

In a far-reaching piece of legislation, the Air Mail Act of 1934, known as the **Black-McKellar Act** after its sponsors, removed most of the inequities, and certainly the perceived illegalities of McNary-Watres. Although the activities of the Big Four (American, United, Eastern, and TWA) were not fragmented, as this would have caused near-chaos, their routes and mail contracts had to be renewed under a new round of bidding. The involvement of non-airline corporations, especially manufacturing interests, was prohibited; and the smaller airlines were not deliberately disfranchised by connivance, craft, or conspiracy.

A New Delta

C.E. Woolman seized his chance and formally re-entered the airline business when the Delta Air Corporation made the lowest bid for the new Route 24 air mail contract and on 8 June 1934 received the coveted award. The only aircraft it had at the time were crop-dusters and Woolman hastily purchased, on 23 June, six **Stinson SM-6000B (Stinson T)** tri-motors from American Airlines, the reconstructed American Airways, itself now moving into larger Curtiss and Douglas equipment. After surveying the route with a Curtiss Robin, the rejuvenated company, now calling itself **Delta Air Lines**, opened air mail service on a great day — in more ways than one — the Fourth of July 1934.

Early Ups and Downs

On 4 July the first flight connected only Dallas and Monroe, via Tyler and Shreveport. A second aircraft departed Monroe for Atlanta on 4 July, but got no further than Birmingham due to weather. The Birmingham — Atlanta portion was completed the following day; Atlanta — Charleston service began 7 July.

THE DELTA AIR LINES STINSONS

MSN	Regn.	Remarks
Stinson SM-6000B (Model T)		
5035	NC10814	Sold to Atlantic & Gulf Coast Airline, Mar. 37
5042	NC10843	
5045	NC10846	
5026	NC11176	Sold to Roger Inman, Coffeyville, Ky. 4 Jun. 36
5027	NC11177	Sold to Strachan Skyways, Savannah, 5 Dec. 36
5024	NC11174	

All purchased from American Airways, 23 Jun. 34; Fleet Numbers 1-6.

MSN	Regn.	Remarks
Stinson A		
9102	NC14598	Sold to M.A. Gelabert, Panama, 31 Mar. 38
9103	NC14599	Crashed, Gilmer, Tex., 14 Aug. 35
9111	NC15134	Crashed, Atlanta, 27 Aug. 36

All purchased from Stinson, 22 Jun. 35; 29 Jun. 35; and 8 Jan. 36; Fleet Numbers 7-9.

*During World War II, Delta also operated a **Stinson SR-5** (NC420).*

While the Georgian capital was outstandingly the most important point on the route, Delta retained its ties with the city of its birth, Monroe, Louisiana. Strengthening these ties, in 1935, a Monroe banker, **Clarence E. Faulk**, became president of Delta, after buying a controlling interest and demonstrating the faith of a financier in C.E. Woolman's enterprise. Faulk was to become Chairman of the Board in 1945, and remained in that capacity until his death on 31 August 1951.

The year 1935 was quite eventful, as Delta Air Lines (the corporate name was still Delta Air Corporation) got into its stride. It leased some fast aircraft from Bowen Air Lines, especially for the mail service (see table this page) and purchased two new **Stinson Model As** from the manufacturer, all ready for the summer schedules. Demonstrating a promotional ingenuity that would be the envy of the Public Relations Department today, Delta came up with the **Trans-Southern Route**, a phrase born of semantic genius.

EARLY DELTA MAIL (AND EXPRESS) AIRPLANES

MSN	Regn.	Remarks
Lockheed 5C Vega		
124	NC107W	Leased from Bowen Air Lines, 1935 for mail
127	NC161W	carriage only
Lockheed 8A Sirius		
167	NC167W	Leased from Bowen Air Lines, 1935 for mail only; crashed, Birmingham 24 Dec. 35

*Delta also operated a **Stearman C3B** (247/NC8837) as an instrument trainer from 20 Aug. 34 to 31 Mar. 37; a **Curtiss Robin 4C-2** (704/NC510N) was rented in 1934 for training and survey flights; a **Curtiss CW-1 Junior** (1134/NC10956) was also used as a trainer; and early in 1940, **Delta Air Corp.** purchased a **Fairchild FC-2** (51/NR3984) from C. S. Robinson.*

Laying to rest one of the shortcomings in its operation that had disqualified it from receiving air mail awards, Delta Air Lines opened its first night service on 15 July 1935. But as if to remind it that the way ahead was fraught with obstacles and strewn with hazards, it sustained its first fatal accident on 14 August of that year, when a Stinson A operating Flight 4 between Dallas and Shreveport crashed at Gilmer, Texas, killing four occupants. But Delta entered its third full year of service firmly resolved to wipe out the memory through a standard of excellence that permitted no repetition of this sad experience, short of an Act of God.

THE TRANS-SOUTHERN ROUTE

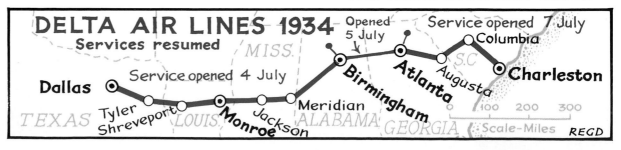

DELTA AIR LINES 1934
Services resumed
Opened 5 July
Service opened 7 July
Service opened 4 July
Dallas · Tyler · Shreveport · Monroe · Jackson · Meridian · Birmingham · Atlanta · Augusta · Columbia · Charleston
TEXAS · LOUIS. · MISS. · ALABAMA · GEORGIA · S.C.
0 100 200 300 Scale-Miles
REGD

Delta's Early Aircraft

The Delta Stinsons

The purchase of six **Stinson SM-6000Bs (Model T)** from American Airways in 1934 (see opposite page) must have seemed like a case of poetic justice to Delta officials for it was to American's forerunner, AVCO, that Delta had sold its passenger fleet four years earlier after it had lost the quest for an air mail route between Texas and Georgia.

Delta records indicate that the decision to acquire Stinson Ts was made because American was willing to sell the aircraft at a bargain basement price of $5,400 each (they had cost $22,500 each when new) after grounding them when Delta received CAM 24. The Stinson Ts carried Delta's first revenue passengers over CAM 24 on 5 August 1934, following the mandatory 30-day probationary period when only mail could be carried. The trip between Atlanta and Dallas took almost eight hours with the Stinson Ts, and the tariff was $49.14 one-way or $88.45 round-trip. The eastbound service departed Dallas at 11:45am and arrived at Atlanta at 7:30pm; the westbound flight left Atlanta at 7:30am and reached Dallas at 4:00pm.

The **Stinson A** tri-motors were purchased for $34,000 each (the first new aircraft Delta had acquired since the Travel Airs in 1929), specifically for overnight services across the Trans-Southern Route. Described by Delta as "Deluxe Tri-Motors," the Stinson As offered passengers a substantial improvement in comfort over the Stinson Ts, with sound-proofed cabins and reclining seats upholstered with leather-edged whipcord. The new tri-motors entered service on 2 July 1935 and introduced a second cockpit crew member. Although the precursor of today's first officer, the new addition was referred to by Delta as a "handyman" and performed a number of duties on the ground as well as assisting the pilot while in-flight.

With the Stinson As, Delta started a tradition of bestowing names on its most prestigious services and the flights between Dallas and Atlanta were, appropriately enough, referred to as *The Georgian* and *The Texan*. The fast tri-motors (see page 49) reduced travel time on the route to 5hr 55min, with four stops.

Faster With Lockheed

Perhaps conscious of the need to carry air mail as expeditiously as was technically possible, Delta leased two **Lockheed Model 5C Vegas** early in 1935 from Bowen Air Lines. Delta also operated a **Lockheed Model 8A Sirius** for a short time, again on lease from Bowen. This was the same type that Charles Lindbergh selected for his remarkable survey flights to the Orient and to Europe in 1933.

Clarence E. Faulk, newspaper publisher and banker of Monroe, La., who acquired a controlling interest in Delta Air Lines in 1934.

Delta used the Stinson SM-6000B tri-motor (known also as the Stinson Model T) when it re-entered scheduled service on 4 July, 1934. (Griffin Studios, Monroe, LA)

Preserving the Pioneers

By a combination of circumstances, several of Delta's early aircraft can be inspected today. At the Atlanta headquarters, a **Huff-Daland Duster** (see page 9) is lovingly preserved in the company's museum, where it is on loan from the National Air and Space Museum (NASM) of the Smithsonian Institution. A Western Air Express **Douglas M-4** (painted as a M-2) and Huff-Daland's original **Fairchild FC-2** (in PANAGRA markings) resides in the Hall of Air Transport of NASM in Washington.

And a Curtiss-Wright 6B Sedan (see page 13) has recently been restored with immaculate care and pride by a group of Delta enthusiasts at Atlanta and painted with Delta markings to represent one of its **Travel Air S-6000-Bs**.

Stinson Model A, introduced by Delta in 1935 to supplement the Model T (SM-6000B).

Streamlining the Image

Named services such as the *Georgian* and the *Texan* — started on 2 July 1935 — were not enough to erase the impression that **Delta Air Lines** was a little behind the times, operating as it did Stinson tri-motors. C.E. Woolman recognized that a modern fleet would be a competitive asset in the growing airline industry. This policy, issued in 1935, became an integral part of Delta corporate policy, and prevails today.

Coming up strongly on the outside track was a third manufacturer from the west coast, Lockheed, at Burbank, California, which, with help from the Reconstruction Finance Corporation, undertook to produce an airliner that preserved the reputation for streamlined speed gained with the Vegas and Orions. The result was the **Lockheed Model 10 Electra**.

Delta Air Lines introduced the first of its five **Model 10-Bs** at the end of 1935 and these became the flagships of the line during the latter 1930s. All the Stinsons were gone by the end of 1937, as were the Vega and Sirius mailplanes. The Electras were fast, had the most modern instrumentation of the day, and — unlike the normal custom today — its co-pilot served box lunches. They were Delta's first all-metal aircraft.

The Lockheed 10 Electra interior set new standards of comfort for a hitherto somewhat austere Delta Air Lines.

DELTA'S LOCKHEED ELECTRAS
In order of delivery

MSN	Regn.	Delivery Date	Remarks
Model 10-B			
1049	NC14990	21 Dec. 35	Retired 1 Jun. 42; to USAAF (as UC-36C 42-57219)
1050	NC14991	28 Dec. 35	Retired 1 Jun. 42; to USAAF (as UC-36C 42-57220)
1051	NC14992	2 Feb. 36	Retired 2 Mar. 41; sold to Waterman Air Lines
1077	NC16053	15 Jan. 37	Retired Jun. 42; to USAAF (as UC-36C 42-57221)
1038	NC14960	37	Ex- Eastern Air Lines; retired Jun. 42; to USAAF (as UC-36C 42-57217)

Fleet Numbers 20-24; first four aircraft purchased new from Lockheed.

MSN	Regn.	Delivery Date	Remarks
Model 10-A			
1028	NC14939	Dec. 39	Leased from Braniff Airways until 20 Mar. 40, Fleet Number 403
Model 12 (Electra Junior)			
1266	NC14999	23 Jan. 45	Operated until 11 Jul. 46 for training and route surveys; ex-USAAF C-40A 38-582; sold to Transair

A Lockheed 10 Electra (right), pictured in 1939 with Delta's entire Atlanta Maintenance and Operations Department.

Lockheed 10 Electra

10 SEATS ■ 190 mph

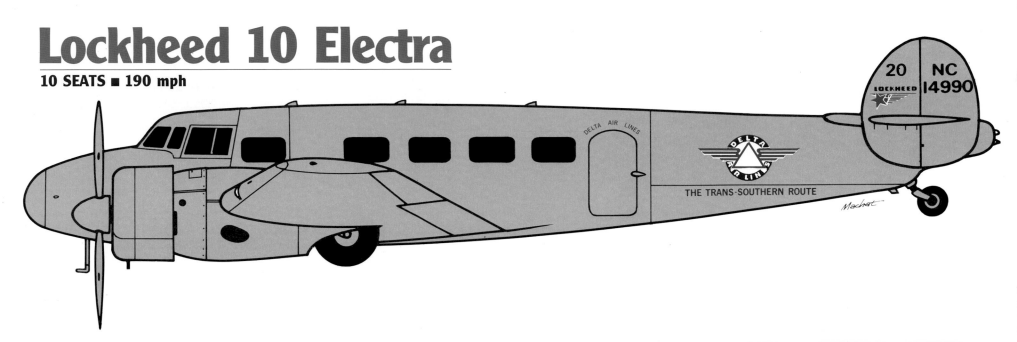

Pratt & Whitney Wasp (450 hp) x 2 ■ 10,300 lb max. gross take-off weight ■ Range 350 miles

The Lockheed Twin

Against the well-known story of the **Boeing 247** v. **Douglas DC-2/DC-3** competition (see page 31), the presence of a third participant in the technical breakout from the era of the Ford Tri-Motor is often forgotten. Yet Lockheed was in the same race for commercial recognition and success, and the twin-engined Model 10 and its smaller cousin, the Model 12, were in many ways just as influential as the 247 and the DC-2. For the traffic level on most airline routes in the mid-1930s was still insufficient to justify even the 14-seat capacity of the DC-2. The **Lockheed Electra** was a little faster than its rivals, and this was a promotional asset.

The Electra went into service with **Northwest Airlines** on 11 August 1934, less than three months after the DC-2 had made its debut with TWA, and almost two years before American introduced the DC-3. It was especially popular with those airlines that were not big enough to be classified as the Big Four (United, American, TWA, and Eastern), all of which bought the larger Douglas twins.

As narrated on the opposite page, Delta was among the satisfied customers, as were, interestingly, all but one of the major airlines that in due course became part of the Delta family. Indeed, the Electra could be seen everywhere in the United States, and especially in those regions where air travel was, as yet, available only to a few.

LENGTH 39 feet
SPAN 55 feet
HEIGHT 10 feet

THE LOCKHEED TWINS

Type	Dimensions			Pass. Seats	Max. Payload (lb.)	Engines			Max. Gross Tow (lb.)	Cruise Speed (mph)	Normal Range (st.miles)	First Service		No. Built
	Length	Span	Height			No.	Type	hp (ea)				Date	Airline	
10 Electra	38'7"	55'0"	10'1"	10	1,825	2	P&W Wasp	450	10,300	190	800	11 Aug. 34	Northwest	149
12 Electra Junior	36'4"	49'6"	9'9"	6	1,375	2	P&W Wasp Jr.	400	8,650	213	800	1937	Santa Maria	130
14 Super Electra	44'4"	65'6"	11'5"	14	4,060	2	P&W Hornet	875	17,500	215	900	Sep. 37	Northwest	231
18 Lodestar	49'10"	65'6"	11'10"	18	7,000	2	P&W Twin Wasp	1,200	20,000	229	1,000	Mar. 40	Mid-Continent	625 *

* Inc. military

The First Delta Douglases

The Twos and the Threes

Fast and modern though the Lockheed Electras were, **Delta Air Lines** needed larger airplanes as it shared in the rapid expansion of air traffic that occurred throughout the United States during the 1930s, especially after the Douglas airliners had swept the field, first with the **DC-2**, which although competing against racing aircraft almost won a race from England to Australia in October 1934, and whose successor, the **DC-3**, was to become one of the most famous aircraft of the world's airways. The Australia race established beyond all doubt the superiority of the Douglas product. Unlike the specially-built de Havilland Comet racer that won the exciting contest, and the Boeing 247 that came in third, KLM's DC-2 carried four passengers and a load of mail, and stopped at all the commercial airline stations en route.

Early in 1940, Delta purchased four 14-passenger Douglas DC-2s from American Airlines. The first one entered service on 15 March, with an extra crew member, Delta's first flight attendant (see page 55). The DC-2s were soon replaced by five DC-3s, delivered at the end of 1940, and the first of which entered service on Christmas Eve. At last, Delta was operating the same type of equipment as its mightier neighbors, even though, as yet, it was not in direct competition with the likes of American or Eastern on the same routes.

A Major New Route

In a further step towards progressive legislation to keep pace with the burgeoning growth of commercial aviation in the United States, the **Civil Aeronautics Act of 1938**, sometimes known as the Lea-McCarran Act after its sponsors, was passed on 23 June. It created the **Civil Aeronautics Au-**thority (CAA) which, with its offshoot, the **Civil Aeronautics Board (CAB)**, were to bring not only a semblance of order to an industry that had been without direction but also offered the prospect of future growth in an administrative environment that was both fair but also (in the language of the British legal system) seen to be fair. The CAB awarded "Grandfather" Certificates of Public Convenience and Necessity to all those airlines with a record of at least six months continuous scheduled service. Delta Air Corporation received the first one.

An early beneficiary of the new deal for the commercial airlines was Delta Air Lines. Early in 1941, the CAB awarded it an important new route from Atlanta to Cincinnati in the northerly direction, and one to Savannah to the south. By this time, Delta had transferred its headquarters from Monroe to Atlanta, where, with this route award, traces of a possible future air traffic hub could be discerned, with Eastern Air Lines already firmly established.

Delta opened service to Cincinnati on 15 April 1941 and to Savannah on 1 May. In a further route award, Delta also reached New Orleans, with an extension from Shreveport, starting on 15 October 1943, so as to offer through flights from Dallas and Fort Worth to the great city of the Mississippi Delta. These routes changed the Delta map from a single route into the beginnings of a network; but the onset of World War II in December 1941 postponed any further ambitions until the cessation of hostilities.

DELTA'S DOUGLAS DC-2 FLEET

MSN	Regn.	Delivery Date	Remarks
1038	NC14275	4 Feb. 40	All purchased from
1401	NC14921	19 Feb. 40	American Airlines and sold
1403	NC14923	6 Mar. 40	to British Purchasing Commission,
1410	NC14924	20 Mar. 40	Jan.-Feb. 41

Fleet Numbers 30-33; all Model DC-2-120.

Delta's first Douglas DC-3, City of Atlanta, *went into service on 24 December 1940.*

A Delta Douglas DC-2, photographed at Shreveport, during its brief service in 1940-41.

DELTA AIR LINES 1934-1943

Service opened 4-7 July 1934

Route Extension 15 April 1941

Route Extension 1 May 1941

Route Extension 15 Oct. 1943

(1 November 1943) Alexandria

Baton Rouge (1 November 1943)

Fort Worth — Dallas — Tyler — Shreveport — Monroe — Jackson — Meridian — Birmingham — Atlanta — Augusta — Columbia — Charleston — Savannah

Cincinnati — Lexington — Knoxville

New Orleans

OHIO · KENTUCKY · TENNESSEE · TEXAS · LOUISIANA · MISS. · ALABAMA · GEORGIA · S.C.

Scale-Miles 0 100 200 300

REGD

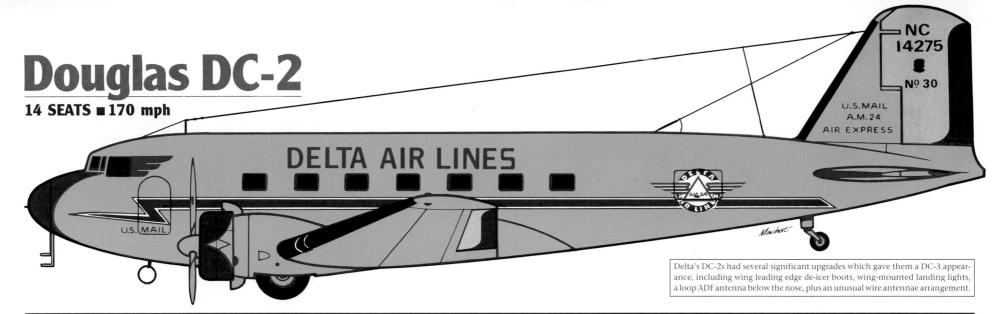

Douglas DC-2

14 SEATS ■ 170 mph

NC 14275
№ 30
U.S. MAIL
A.M. 24
AIR EXPRESS

DELTA AIR LINES

U.S. MAIL

Machat

Delta's DC-2s had several significant upgrades which gave them a DC-3 appearance, including wing leading edge de-icer boots, wing-mounted landing lights, a loop ADF antenna below the nose, plus an unusual wire antennae arrangement.

Wright Cyclone (710 hp) x 2 ■ 18,560 lb. max. gross take-off weight ■ Range 1,000 miles ■ Length 62 feet ■ Span 85 feet ■ Height 16 feet

Charity Began At Home

In 1933, the **Boeing Airplane Company** came very close to winning the jackpot in the competition to build an airliner that incorporated all the technical and design improvements that had accumulated during the early 1930s. On 8 February 1933, the **Boeing 247** made its first flight. Transcontinental flying time was halved and the airlines beat a pathway to Boeing's door to buy the 247.

They were disappointed. At that time, before the Air Mail Scandals led to new regulations, aircraft manufacturers could own airlines. Boeing Airplane owned Boeing Air Transport, by now a division of United Air Lines. Subsidized by a generous system of mail payments, the airlines were able, at that time, to purchase new aircraft. Boeing, with a fundamental understanding of the free enterprise system, believed it should keep its new product in the family, at least for a year or two, and announced to the other airlines that the Model 247 was not available.

Classic Confrontation

One airline in particular, TWA, was so upset that it sent a letter to five other manufacturers with a specification that would demand an aircraft design to beat the 247 in every respect: size, speed, range, and field performance. The **Douglas Aircraft Company** from Santa Monica, California, promptly responded to the challenge, and produced a prototype aircraft, the DC-1. The DC-1's maiden flight on 1 July 1933, only five months after the 247's debut, met the stringent tests imposed by TWA. On 19 February 1934, the eve of the cancellation of the air mail contracts, which would change the entire complexion of the commercial airline industry, the DC-1 made a dramatic flight from Los Angeles to Newark setting a new transcontinental speed record.

Only one DC-1 was built. Douglas quickly realized that, with slight modifications, the 12-seat layout could be increased to 14, and the **DC-2** was born. It went into service with TWA only one week after its first flight on 11 May 1934, thanks to the DC-1's role as a prototype. **General Air Lines** operated four DC-2s for a brief period late in 1934. In 1940, **Delta Air Lines** was to follow suit, with four DC-2s purchased from American Airlines. These aircraft served Delta less than a year before being replaced by new DC-3s. **Northeast Airlines** operated five former TWA DC-2s during the spring and summer of 1942.

DELTA'S DOUGLAS DC-3 FLEET

MSN	Regn.	Delivery Date	Remarks
3277	NC28340	29 Nov. 40	*City of Atlanta*; sold to Mohawk, Apr. 53
3278	NC28341	23 Dec. 40	Sold to H. Hill, 27 Apr. 58
3279	NC28342	24 Dec. 40	Sold to Florida Airmotive Sales, 31 May 62
3280	NC28343	4 Jan. 41	To USAAF (as C-49) and operated by Delta Mil. Trpt. Div. from 25 Jul. 42. Sold to P.C.A., Feb. 43
3281	NC28344	28 Dec. 40	Sold to Florida Airmotive Sales, 28 Feb. 63

Fleet Numbers 40-44; purchased from Douglas.

MSN	Regn.	Delivery Date	Remarks
2267	NC28343	13 Aug. 44	*City of Miami*; sold to Fla. Airmotive Sales, 2 Feb. 63
2224	NC28345	14 Apr. 44	Crashed, Waskom, Tex., 17 May 53
6259	NC28346	27 Jun. 44	Sold to Executive Air Trpt., Oct. 59
6322	NC33347	19 Oct. 44	Sold to H. Hill, 24 May 58
6337	NC15748	45	Sold to North Central via H. Hill, Apr. 57
4145	NC15849	1 Feb. 45	Sold to Florida Airmotive Sales, 28 Feb. 63
4993	NC20750	45	Leased from Reconst. Fin. Corp; written off, Meridian, Miss. 10 Nov. 46
4984	NC20751	24 Aug. 45	Sold to Jack Adams Acft. Sales, 31 Mar. 63
4174	NC20753	26 Sep. 45	Ex- C-68; sold to Lakeport Lsg. Co., Jan. 48
11677	NC88854	7 Nov. 45	Ex- C-53; sold to H. Hill, 27 Mar. 58
6336	NC10655	22 Jan. 46	Sold to Bush Avn. Enterprises, 30 Jun. 62
4845	NC25656	10 May 46	Ex- C-53; sold to G. Perry, 31 Aug. 62
9066	NC49657	5 Jan. 46	Ex- C-47; destroyed in mid-air collision, Columbus, Ga., 22 Apr. 47
4943	NC39393	12 Feb. 47	Ex- C-53; sold to Jack Adams Acft. Sales, 31 Mar. 63
4962	NC1200M	19 Oct. 47	Ex-USN R4D-4; sold to Fla. Airmotive Sales, 28 Feb. 63

Fleet Numbers 43 (2nd), 45-52, 54-58, and 60; ex-USAAF C-49s except as indicated.

Cargo Aircraft			
4715	NC86553	6 Nov. 45	Ex- C-47; sold to Jack Adams Acft. Sales, Apr. 63
13759	NC51359	1 May 47	Ex- C-47; crashed, Atlanta, 15 Jun. 54
9037	N57539	17 Jan. 49	Ex- C-47; purchased from L.B. Smith, sold to Aircraft Ferry Services, Sep. 59

Fleet Numbers 53, 59, and 61.

Western Starts Again

Down But Not Out — Once Again

Reacting to the conditions imposed by the Black-McKellar Act, **William A. Coulter**, who had financed Pennsylvania-Central Airlines (PCA), tried to buy General Motors' shares in both Western Air Express and Eastern Air Transport. He was successful in the former case, on 29 December 1934, but as a condition of sale, General Aviation, General Motors' aviation subsidiary, forced a liquidation dividend, almost wiping out Western's assets. The airline was forced to sell its flagships, the Douglas DC-2s, to Eastern in December 1934.

Alliance with United

Coulter appointed **Alvin P. Adams** as President. He pulled Western out of the TWA association and set up an independent **Western Air Express Corporation**, dissolving both General Air Lines and Western Air Express, Inc. He also established a close operating and commercial air link with United Air Lines, integrating routes and schedules, and leasing **Boeing 247** aircraft to supplement the severely depleted fleet.

Western's only route was the San Diego — Los Angeles — Las Vegas — Salt Lake City airway across the Mohave Desert and the western scrubland of Nevada and Utah. But it provided a vital link to United's transcontinental air route, a mutually convenient arrangement that at least enabled Western to survive precariously during the mid-1930s.

Western used such aircraft as the Boeing 40B-4 as it recovered from the crisis of the Shotgun Marriage.

Douglas DC-2, during the brief period in 1934 when Western Air Express became General Air Lines.

This Douglas DST (the original DC-3) in combined United/WAE colors was a step toward an interchange program that would be launched in 1940 (see page 37).

THE WESTERN AIR EXPRESS BOEING 247D FLEET

MSN	Regn.	Delivery Date	Remarks (L) = leased
1686	NC13305	12 Apr. 35	(L)
1687	NC13306	23 Dec. 34	Purchased from United when Western was renamed General Air Lines; to SCADTA (Colombia) 15 Dec. 37
1690	NC13309	23 Dec. 34	(L)
1691	NC13310		(L)
1693	NC13312	(1935-36)	(L)
1694	NC13313	(1935-36)	(L)
1695	NC13314	12 Apr. 35	(L) Crashed, Burbank, 1 Sep. 35
1696	NC13315	13 Jun. 35	Crashed, Newhall, Calif., 12 Jan. 37
1697	NC13316	29 Apr. 38	(Also leased in 1937)
1699	NC13318	(1935-36)	(L)
1700	NC13319		(L)
1702	NC13321	(1935-36)	(L)
1707	NC13326	(1935-36)	(L)
1708	NC13327	6 Dec. 35	Purchased from United; to SCADTA 7 Dec. 37
1710	NC13329	(1935-36)	(L)
1712	NC13330	(1935-36)	(L) To Wilmington-Catalina Airlines, 30 Jul. 38
1715	NC13333	1 Jul. 35	(L)
1717	NC13335	(1935-36)	(L)
1718	NC13336	30 Apr. 38	Purchased from United
1719	NC13337	1 Aug. 37	Acquired through purchase of National Parks Airways
1721	NC13339	(1935-36)	(L) Destroyed in hangar fire, S.L.C., 12 Jan. 41
1723	NC13341	31 Jan. 41	(Also leased in 1936); purchased fr. Penn.-Central Airlines (PCA)
1724	NC13342	(1935-36)	(L) To PCA Dec. 39
1734	NC13352	(1935-36)	(L) To PCA 29 Jan. 37
1735	NC13353	(1935-36)	(L) To PCA 26 Jan. 37
1736	NC13354	1 Aug. 37	Acquired through purchase of National Parks Airways
1741	NC13359	(1935-36)	(L) To PCA 31 Mar. 37, crashed
1948	NC13362	(1935-36)	(L)
1949	NC13363		(L)
1950	NC13364	(1935-36)	(L)
1953	NC13369	(1935-36)	(L) To Union Electric Light, St. Louis, 11 Jan. 37
1954	NC13367	(1935-36)	(L)
1957	NC13370	6 Sep. 35	From Boeing Aircraft; crashed nr. Alpine, Utah, 15 Dec. 36
1958	NC13365	(1935-36)	(L) United Flight Research

All aircraft except NC13370 were owned by United Air Lines and most of them leased (L) to WAE Unless otherwise indicated, aircraft requisitioned by the USAAF, June-July, 1942 as C-73s. Fleet numbers last three digits of registration.

Boeing 247D

10 SEATS ■ 180 mph

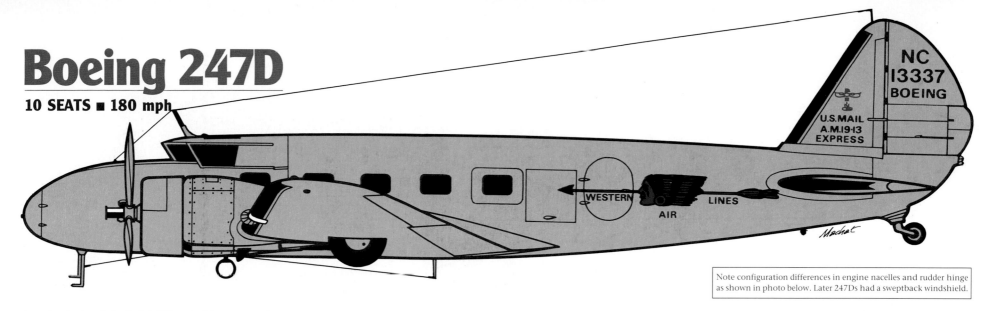

Note configuration differences in engine nacelles and rudder hinge as shown in photo below. Later 247Ds had a sweptback windshield.

Pratt & Whitney Wasp (550hp) x 2 ■ 13,650 lb. max. gross take-off weight ■ Range 750 miles

THE WESTERN AIR LINES DC-3 FLEET

MSN	Regn.	Delivery Date	Remarks
1900	NC16060	5 May 38	From United Air Lines; crashed, Fairfield, Utah, 15 Dec. 42
2265	NC19964	Aug. 40	*City of Las Vegas*, purchased from Douglas; sold to United 7 Jun. 42
3283	NC28379	21 Mar. 41	Purchased from Douglas; sold to United, 7 Jun. 42
Fleet Numbers 60, 964, and 379.			
4811	NC33670	Aug. 41	Purchased from Douglas; sold to Bonanza Air Lines, Dec. 48
4812	NC33671	31 Aug. 41	Purchased from Douglas; sold to Gopher Aviation, Feb. 59
4126	NC33647	1 Jun. 42	From United; sold to Hil-Drown Venture
4123	NC33644	2 Jun. 42	5 Apr. 58
Fleet Numbers (in order) 107, 105, 108, and 102.			
3286	NC33621	10 Feb. 44	Ex- C-48; crashed, Hollywood, 24 Apr. 46
1959	NC18101	10 Jun. 44	Ex- C-48; sold Hil-Drown Venture, 5 Apr. 58
4813	NC19387	10 Jun. 44	Ex- C-52; sold to Airesearch Aviation, Jul. 56
4941	NC15563	20 Nov. 44	Ex- C-53; sold to Central Airlines, 31 Mar. 59
11729	NC49554	17 Jan. 45	Ex- C-53; sold to L.A. Clarke, 27 Jul. 56
4900	NC18600	23 Jan. 45	Ex- C-53; sold to Piedmont, 7 Feb. 56
11662	NC18645	21 Mar. 45	Ex- C-53; crashed, Mt. White, Calif., 14 Nov. 46
11642	NC45395	4 Oct. 45	Ex- C-53; crashed, Mt. Laguna, Calif., 4 Oct. 45
4912	NC45363	27 Sep. 45	Ex- C-53; sold to Page Airways, Mar. 55
4400	NC56589	16 Oct. 45	Ex- C-47; sold to Wes Durston, Oct. 48
6017	NC56592	16 Oct. 45	Ex- C-47; sold to Douglas Aircraft Dec. 48
Fleet Numbers (in order) 106, 101, 104, 109-112, 114-117.			
4887	NC15569	7 Oct. 43	Acquired with Inland Air Lines acquisition; crashed, Los Angeles, Calif. 29 Jun. 53
26676	N49319	Dec. 53	Ex- C-47; from Pacific Northern Airlines; sold to Red Dodge, Aug. 67

All but the last listed ex-military aircraft were from the USAAF, most of them via the Reconstruction Finance Corporation.

*WAE also used two **Lockheed 12-A Electra Juniors** (1243/NC18955 and 1244/NC18956) between Dec. 37 and Apr. 38; a **Waco EQC-6** (4544/NC17469) from 27 Feb. 37 until 31 Jul. 38 when it was written off by wind damage; and a **Waco EGC-8** (5058/NC19382) from Jul. 38 until 14 Oct. 42.*

LENGTH 52 feet
SPAN 74 feet
HEIGHT 13 feet

Western Air Express Boeing 247D, pictured in 1935.

National Parks Airways

Al Frank's Airline

On 27 October 1927 the U.S. Post Office invited bids for Air Mail Route No. 26, from Salt Lake City to Great Falls; and somewhat to the surprise of other established air carriers, the contract was awarded on 30 December to **Alfred Frank**, a Salt Lake City mining engineer. The rate was $2.47-1/2 per pound of mail carried. Together with some associates he incorporated, on 2 March 1928, **National Parks Airways**, with a capital of $200,000, soon increased to $1,500,000. On 6 April, Al Frank assigned the contract to National Parks, and with local support, built a hangar at Salt Lake City, and purchased three **Fokker Super-Universals**.

Mail and passenger service on the contracted route opened on 1 August 1928, with one flight each way per day. Early in 1930, more aircraft were acquired (see opposite page). On 1 February 1930, National Parks began carrying express packages for the Railway Express Agency.

During 1933, modest extensions were made, northward to Havre, and a branch line from Butte to Livingston and Billings. The latter was on an east-west orientation and Al Frank no doubt cherished ambitions to spread his network throughout the length and breadth of the state of Montana. A similar east-west extension from Butte to Missoula would seem to have been logical. But the Postmaster General awarded a series of generous extensions to Minneapolis-based **Northwest Airways**. Al Frank was furious and made representations to the Black Committee, then collecting evidence for infringements of government-subsidized transport operations. He had a case. Subsequent analysis revealed that Frank's National Parks Airways had had 509 contracted route miles, with no extensions; Northwest had only 407 original miles, but was granted 1,621 miles of "extensions."

Scandal!

Such manipulation was perceived by the Black Committee to be a bizarre interpretation of the law by Postmaster General Walter Folger Brown. This led to the cancellation of all the 34 air mail contracts on 9 February 1934. Summarizing what soon became known as the Air Mail Scandal, the new Postmaster General, James Farley, observed "that the contractors were all guilty of fraud and collusion, with the possible exception of the National Parks Airways Inc." Al Frank received a new contract on 7 May and resumed service on 15 May 1934.

One of the provisions of the Black-McKellar Act demanded that the old companies should be divorced from the former contractors. Possibly to pay lip service, at least, to the

Al Frank, founder of National Parks Airways.

A Stearman C3MB used to carry the mail on CAM 26 during the late 1920s.

terms of the Act, the airline described itself as the "**Salt Lake City-Great Falls Airline**, formerly National Parks Airways, operated by Alfred Frank."

National Parks in Name and Service

On 1 November, the first modern airliner, a **Boeing 247**, entered service, and on 1 December 1934 the mail contract was formally sublet from Al Frank to **National Parks Airways**. Fulfilling the expectations of its name, service to a national park was introduced on 1 August 1935. After clearing a swathe through 60-foot high pine trees, an airstrip was opened at West Yellowstone, whence connections were made to Old Faithful by the Yellowstone Transportation Company. For this special service, operated only in the summer, National Parks leased a **Boeing 80A** tri-motor.

Al Frank ran into financial difficulties, stemming from a precarious population base that could not generate enough passenger or mail traffic. He was ultimately forced to sell out, and on 1 August 1937 the Salt Lake City — Great Falls route became an extension of **Western Air Lines'** trunk route from San Diego and Los Angeles to Salt Lake City.

When the end came, National Parks had proudly announced the acquisition of two **Lockheed 12-A Electra Juniors** but these were in Western's colors when they entered service in December 1937. Al Frank's airline was later liquidated after nine years of pioneering service. In spite of the difficult operating conditions, often in severe weather, and invariably over formidable terrain, National Parks had only one fatal accident, at Pocatello, in 1928.

NATIONAL PARKS AIRWAYS 1928-1936

Fokker Super-Universal

8 SEATS ■ 118 mph

A Fokker Super-Universal of National Parks Airways.

Pratt & Whitney Wasp (420hp) ■ 5,150 lb. max. gross take-off weight ■ Range 675 miles ■ Length 37 feet ■ Span 51 feet ■ Height 9 feet

A Formidable Line-up

In December 1927, the Dutch **Fokker** company, riding on the crest of a wave of success in Europe, and having supplied Pan American with its first aircraft, established a branch affiliate in the United States at Teterboro (Hasbrouck Heights), New Jersey, and built a new factory in Glendale, West Virginia. The interlocking relationship with other established corporations was significant. The president was Harris Hanshue, of Western Air Express; Eddie Rickenbacker was vice president; and Tony Fokker was the chief engineer.

The Universals

Much publicity was given to the giant Fokker F-32 four-engine transport, and the Fokker F-10 trimotor, a development of the famous Fokker F-VIIb that had been such a great success in Europe and had been assembled for Pan Am in the U.S. As these were the larger aircraft of the Fokker family, they tended to attract most of the publicity, especially during a period when multi- engine types were identified with safety. Consequently the single-engine Fokker **Universal** and the **Super-Universal** have tended to be overlooked.

Yet they were well-named. They were to be found all over the United States and played an important role as the story of air transport unfolded in the late 1920s. The Universal and the Super-Universal both had the typical steel-tube fuselage frame and the thick wooden wing characteristic of all Fokkers for a decade or more. The Universal was powered by a 220hp Wright Whirlwind engine and could carry four passengers at a little more than 100mph. The Super-Universal was a little larger, had a 425hp Pratt & Whitney Wasp, and could carry six passengers at about 120mph. In the late 1920s, this alone would have been Super enough. But the Super's distinguishing feature was trend- setting. The extra speed forced the intrepid pilot to require a closed cockpit, and the days of helmet, goggles, and scarf were over.

THE NATIONAL PARKS AIRWAYS FLEET

Aircraft Type	MSN	Regn.	Remarks
Fokker Super-Universal	804	NC6769	Acquired July 1928
	807	NC6880	
	808	NC7048	
	809	NC7242	Crashed, Pocatello, 4 Sep. 28
	866	NC326N	Crashed, Pauline, Id., 28 Nov. 33
	867	NC330N	
Fleet Numbers 1-4, 9 and 10; last two listed acquired in 1930.			
Stearman C3B	103	NC1598	Model C3MB
	172	NC6486	Model C3MB
	178	NC6487	Acquired 13 Oct. 28; sold to Johnson Flying Svce., 27 Jul. 34
	232	NC8818	Acquired 6 May 28, Fleet Number 7; sold to Nick O. Mamer, 7 Sep. 34
NC6487 Fleet Number 6.			
Boeing 40B-4	1167	NC841M	Acquired 1930
	1437	NC10356	Delivered 4 Nov. 31
Fleet Numbers 8 and 11.			
Boeing 247D	1719	NC13337	From United Air Lines, 28 Dec. 35
	1731	NC13349	Leased from United Air Lines, 1935
	1736	NC13354	From United Air Lines, 31 Dec. 35.
Boeing 80A-1	1084	NC226M	Leased from United, 1936
Ford 5-AT-C Special	5-AT-70	NC411H	From Braniff Airways, Jun. 37; sold to Babb, 1938.
Used exclusively for scenic flights over Yellowstone Park; special version of aircraft, with engines lowered 6 inches.			
Lockheed 12-A	1243	NC18955	Delivered, Dec. 37, returned to Lockheed, Apr./May 38
	1244	NC18956	
All aircraft, unless otherwise noted, passed to WAE.			

Inland Air Lines

Wyoming Air Service

Originally headquartered at Casper, **Wyoming Air Service** was founded as a fixed-base operator on 9 May 1930 by Dick Leferink. The initial capital was $50,000. In September of that year, he approached Earl Vance, heading up **Border Airlines** at Great Falls, Montana, with a proposal to establish an air route from Great Falls to Denver, with the two companies linking up at Sheridan, in northern Wyoming. At first, the two airlines operated separately, Border starting from Great Falls to Billings, in February 1931, and Wyoming Air Service from Casper to Denver, with a **Stinson SM-8A**. Both companies extended to Sheridan in the summer as the **Wyoming-Montana Air Lines**.

In September 1931, Border suspended operations, but Wyoming Air Service extended its route as far as Billings. In February 1934, Wyoming Air Service received a mail contract for the Pueblo — Cheyenne route, starting service on 3 May 1934 with three **Stinson Reliants**. On 4 June, a similar contract was received for the Cheyenne — Billings route, two more Reliants were purchased, and service started on 20 June. A **Boeing 247D** was leased from United Air Lines in 1935. The company then became the second, and only operator, other than United, of the **Boeing 221A Monomail**.

Sale of Assets

Lucrative air mail contracts at this time were essential for financial viability; and airlines such as Wyoming had only a small population base. In October 1936 United Air Lines applied to the Post Office for diversion of its transcontinental route from Cheyenne to Denver, but this was successfully opposed by Wyoming, Varney, and TWA. However, Leferink had to sell the Denver — Pueblo segment to Varney Air Transport (later Continental), for $35,000; and the Denver — Cheyenne segment to United, for $209,000.

Inland Air Lines

In compensation for this loss, Wyoming Air Service extended its mail route northward to Great Falls on 1 August 1937, and passenger service on 15 August. Then a new route was added to Huron, South Dakota, via Rapid City and Pierre, with mail on 14 April 1938 and passengers on 25 April. Leferink purchased three Boeing 247s from Pennsylvania-Central Airlines and had them upgraded to 247Ds.

Marking its expansion beyond the immediate vicinity of Wyoming, the name of the pioneering airline of the region

was changed on 1 July 1938 to the more appropriate **Inland Air Lines**. Merger discussions were held during 1941 with Mid-Continent Airlines but these were suspended at the outbreak of World War II.

In April 1942, Inland contracted with the USAAF to operate a cargo route within its catchment area, and extended its meandering network back into Denver again. It also operated to the Pacific Northwest, purchased a **Lockheed 18 Lodestar** from Continental, acquired two **Beech C17B Staggerwings**, and trained a group of pilots for Air Transport Command.

But the sands were running out. On 1 June 1944, 83.57 percent of the stock was sold to Western Air Lines and Inland was absorbed into its route system on 9 April 1952, following approval of the Wyoming State Legislature.

Inland operated the rare Boeing 221A Monomail.

THE FLEET OF WYOMING AIR SERVICE/INLAND AIR LINES

MSN	Regn.	Delivery Date	Remarks
Stinson SM-8A			
M-4104	NC901W	Jun. 30	Flt. No. 1; withdrawn Aug. 34
	NC10801	Apr. 31	Flt. No. 10; sold Feb. 35
	NC240W	20 Oct. 32	
M-4227	NC987W		From Wallace England
Stinson Model S			
8008	NC10824	Aug. 32	Flt. No. 24; sold May 37
8024	NC10830	Jun. 32	Flt. No. 30; sold Jun. 35
Stinson SR-5A			
9251-A	NC13872	} 25 May 34	Sold to Northwest, Feb. 36
9252-A	NC13873		
9253-A	NC13874		
9268-A	NC14168	} 14 Jun. 34	Sold May 1936
9269-A	NC14169		
9270-A	NC14170		
Fleet Numbers 2-4, 8-9, and 70.			
Stearman 4D			
4025	NC796H	Jun. 34	Sold May 1935
Boeing 221A Monomail			
1153	NC725W	} 24 May 35	Crashed 100mi north of Cheyenne, 29 May 35
1154	NC10225		Crashed, Pueblo, Fall 35
Both were ex-United Air Lines.			
Lockheed 9D Orion			
206	NC13748	6 Aug. 35	From Northwest
207	NC13749	6 Aug. 35	From Northwest Airlines; crashed, Buffalo, Wy. 24 Oct. 36
201	NC230Y	7 May 36	From Blue Bird Air Serv., Chicago
Fleet Numbers 48, 49, and 230. Latter two sold to Harold S. Johnson, Oak Park, Ill., 1940-41.			
Boeing 247D			
1688	NC13307	1 May 35	Leased from United, purch. 1 May 36
1951	NC13360	1 May 36	} From United
1949	NC13363	24 Feb. 37	
1689	NC13308	} 24 Aug. 37	} Purchased from PCA
1692	NC13311		
1726	NC13344		
1691	NC13310	3 May 38	From United
1707	NC13326	42	From U.S. Govt. (ex- C-73); to TWA 28 Jul. 42
Fleet Numbers were last three of registration. The first aircraft, NC13307, was named City of Denver. The four ex-United aircraft passed to the USAAF (as C-73s) in mid-1942; the three ex-PCA aircraft went to the Canadian Government.			
Lockheed 18-08-01			
2025	NC25634	2 Jun. 42	} Transferred to Western, 7 Oct. 43;
2074	NC25638	4 Jun. 42	} Fleet Numbers 52 and 51
Beech C17B Staggerwing			
86	NC15843	7 Oct. 43	} From J.W. Marshall, Dallas; sold
110	NC15838		} to Vaughn Krug, 1945/46
Douglas DC-3			
4887	NC15569	1 Jan. 45	From USAAF (ex- C-53); to Western at merger 1952; crashed, Los Angeles, 29 Jun. 53

Wyoming Air Service became Inland Air Lines on 1 July 1938, at which time the fleet consisted of the last two Orions and the first seven 247Ds.

Western's Eastward Struggle

The First Route Extension

During the mid-1930s, **Western Air Express** cautiously re-established its traditional route from California to Salt Lake City, and was able to celebrate a ten-year safety record on 17 April 1936. On 1 August 1937 it acquired **National Parks Airways**, and thus extended its influence northward, at the same time obtaining access to the popular Yellowstone National Park (see map), and introducing its first **Douglas DC-3s**.

Flirtation with United Air Lines

William Coulter had always worked closely with United Air Lines, which had been cooperative in aircraft leasing arrangements during the recovery period following the Air Mail Scandal of 1934. This association proved so attractive that, on 26 June 1939, a group of stockholders persuaded him to sell Western to United. After debate at the Civil Aeronautics Board, the merger proposal was turned down on 19 June. The Board felt that United's hold in the west would be increased to monopoly proportions, a view shared by Western's President Alvin Adams, who lost his job in the process. An interchange agreement with United still permitted convenient transcontinental connections at Salt Lake City.

Confidence in a New Name

In 1941, WAE extended its line across the Canadian border to Lethbridge, Alberta, to become an international airline; and on 17 April 1941 the company was officially renamed **Western Air Lines**. Joint offices with United were abandoned, new uniforms were adopted. The fleet consisted of seven Douglas DC-3s and five Boeing 247Ds, but most of these were requisitioned, on 15 May 1942, by the U.S. Government, in support of the war effort (see page 48).

Western certainly had to use its imagination to achieve Harris Hanshue's ambition of a route to the east. It finally gained such access with a route to Huron, North Dakota, on 1 June 1944, when it acquired 83 per cent of the stock of **Inland Air Lines** (see opposite page), considerably expanding its geographical sphere of influence.

Inland operated the Boeing 247D during the latter 1930s.

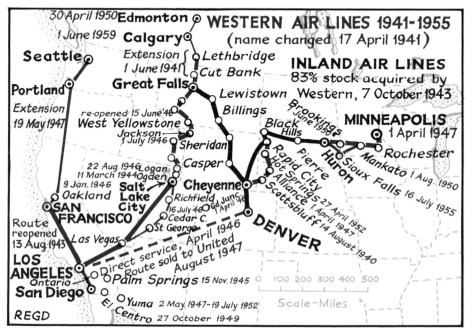

Boston-Maine/Central Vermont

The First Experiment

Commercial aviation made its first cautious step north of Boston because of the initiative of Laurence Whittemore, a senior official of the Boston and Maine Railroad. He had become interested in the possibility of starting an airline during the aviation boom of the late 1920s and persuaded his management that to participate in this new form of transport was preferable to trying to compete with it. On 20 July 1931, accordingly, **Boston-Maine Airways, Inc.**, was organized by the Boston and Maine and the Maine Central Railroads, the latter's participation becoming necessary because the proposed route to northern Maine and beyond encroached on its territory. Service started on 1 August and the entire operation was carried out under contract by **Pan American Airways**, whose experience was judged to be the essential guarantee of success, and infinitely preferable to Boston-Maine's trying to start its own airline without the necessary experience.

As shown on the map, the route was flown by Fokker F-10A landplanes as far as Bangor, and Pan Am flew its Sikorsky S-41B flying boats on to Halifax, as no suitable airfields were available. The route was short-lived. It started on 1 August 1931, and was discontinued on 30 September, only two months later. One of the S-41Bs crashed in Massachusetts Bay on 27 August, a grim reminder that conditions along the New England coastline were not ideal for airlines in the experimental stage.

A Real Airline for the Northeast

Whittemore never lost his enthusiasm for starting an airline, and two years later another opportunity arose. Once again he sought help from an airline but this time not from a going concern but from one that was still in the embryo stage.

A group of airline men from **Ludington Airlines**, of Philadelphia, had been deprived of their successful commuter business between New York and Washington, by the manipulations of the Postmaster General. Two of the disenchanted Ludington executives were Paul Collins, an ex-air mail pilot, and Eugene Vidal, an aviator and West Point graduate. They had met a businessman, Sam Solomon, in New York, and subsequently recruited **Amelia Earhart**, the famous aviatrix of the day, to form a team that could run an airline. With a capital of only $10,000, sufficient to purchase two Stinson SM-6000B tri-motors, Collins founded **National Airways, Inc.**, and contracted with Boston-Maine to fly the route. Service began on 11 August 1933. On 27 October of the same year, Collins made a similar agreement

with the **Central Vermont Airways**, which had been founded by the Central Vermont Railroad (owned by the Canadian National Railways) in a similar manner to the people in Maine. With Collins providing the operational know-how, Vidal the high-level contacts, Solomon the sound management, and Earhart the image, National Airways coordinated the two railroad-sponsored airlines as one, with the two railroad names hyphenated, and issuing joint timetables and fares.

Route development during 1934 was entirely on the western half of the V-shaped route map, with an extension to Burlington, from Montpelier, on 7 February and an important extension to Montreal (turning National into an international carrier on 20 March). As a continuing reminder,

however, of the stringent operating conditions during the winters in northern New England, the Montreal route had to be terminated in November of that year.

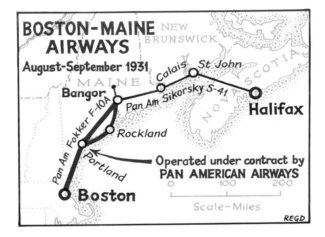

Passengers disembarking from a Fokker F-10 on the Boston-Maine/Pan American joint service.

BOSTON-MAINE/CENTRAL VERMONT AIRWAYS
THE FIRST FLEETS

MSN	Regn.	Remarks
Fokker F-10A		
1041	NC147H	Started service, Boston-Bangor, 31 Jul. 31. Aircraft operated under contract by Pan American until 30 Sep. 31
Sikorsky S-41B		
1100	NC41V	Started service 31 Jul. 31, Bangor-Halifax, under contract to Pan American in conjunction with the Fokker F-10A. Aircraft crashed in Massachusetts Bay on 27 Aug. 31, but salvaged later
1105	NC784Y	Started service 31 Jul. 31
Stinson SM-6000B (Model T)		
5006	NC975W	Began service 11 Aug. 33; sold 20 Jun. 41 to E. G. Germain
5007	NC976W	Crashed Burlington 8 Apr. 36
5011	NC429Y	Derelict Boston 1940-41
All acquired from Eastern, *formerly* Ludington.		

Downeast to the Cape and Beyond

Mayflower Airlines

Early in 1936, **Mayflower Airlines** was founded in Boston. It purchased two Stinson U tri-motors from American Airlines on 4 April and opened a route from Boston to Nantucket (see map).

This route would hardly be worthy of a small commuter airline today, but in the Thirties, there was no classification system to segregate the giants from the pygmies. Mayflower was undeterred. It advertised its aircraft as "Tri-Motor Clippers" — blissfully unaware (or belligerently defiant) of the fact that Juan Trippe and Pan American had registered the Clipper designation as a brand name.

Such an aggressive posture was ill-advised and it was a grand illusion as the honeymoon lasted only a year (see aircraft table). Mayflower Airlines appears to have remained dormant — World War II was imminent — and was acquired by **Northeast Airlines** — in an uncharacteristic burst of acquisitive expansion — in 1944.

In one respect, Mayflower deserves recognition: it identified some short-haul air routes — very short-haul — that, with the right equipment, could be operated effectively in competition with surface transport, because of either circuitous or over-water itineraries needed by the latter. John van Arsdale started the Cape Cod Flying Service in February 1946 and this developed to become the Provincetown-Boston Airline, one of the first postwar companies that were the prototypes of what were later to become the ubiquitous commuter airlines.

Airline Feeder System

On 4 October 1937 the precisely named **Airline Feeder System** started service with **Stinson Model A** tri-motors, on a route from Springfield to Newark, New Jersey (serving New York), via Hartford, New Haven, and Bridgeport. This connected with a new route from Boston to Springfield started by Mayflower Airlines on the same day (see elsewhere on this page) so that, theoretically, this little combination of diminutive airlines could actually offer a form of competition with the established railroad system.

Indeed, in a display of inspired marketing, the AFS offered "for the first time in airline history a Commutation Ticket ... which entitles any passenger to fly at rail fares." The regular fare from Springfield to Newark was $10.05 but the commutation fare, at $4.80, was less than half that figure. The claim was incorrect as to its firstliness, as Stout Air Services had offered the same privilege between Detroit and Cleveland back in 1929; but this does not detract from the praiseworthy initiative shown by the Airline Feeder Service.

Sadly, the innovation did not result in an operational or financial success for the company, which discontinued its service in October 1939. **Northeast Airlines** took over the route authority on 12 June 1944, two months before it acquired Mayflower Airlines; and presumably, with CAB approval, this combination effectively formed the basis of the Boston — New York route authority.

A rare photo of a Mayflower Airlines Stinson Model U. The American color scheme has been retained and the points served by the Oak Bluffs Clipper *are listed under the cockpit. (Photo courtesy Sam Parker)*

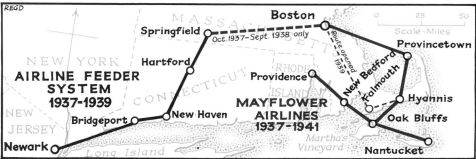

MAYFLOWER'S STINSON U FLEET

MSN	Regn.	Remarks
9008	NC12120	License expired 15 Jul. 41
9009	NC12121	Destroyed by fire in ground accident at Nantucket, 3 Sep. 38
Aircraft purchased from American Airlines.		

An Airline for New England

National Airways Bows Out

As the U.S. airline industry recovered from the crisis of the Air Mail Scandals of 1934, the little company in the northeast had to struggle more than most. One of the sequels to the investigation by the Black Committee was that interlocking relationships between different transport modes was prohibited, as was the ownership of airlines by aircraft manufacturers. This was especially critical in the case of **Boston-Maine/Central Vermont**, and the existence of the operating arrangement with Paul Collins's **National Airways** was convenient as a temporary expedient. In fact, when the air mail contracts were re-awarded in April 1934, the same routes went to National.

As time went on, however, the need for a drastic improvement became acute. Collins, as a veteran air mail pilot, with a sub-conscious urge to ensure that "The mail must go through," whatever the conditions, had its drawbacks. There was no ground radio north of Boston, no lighted airfields, much less lighted airways; and the instructions to the pilots, as a slogan for survival, was "fly low and slow."

Winter conditions were appalling. Deep snow was a barrier to operations, and frozen snow was worse, as the Stinsons' wheels simply spun on the icy surface. They were probably the only aircraft in commercial airline service to be fitted with truck chains on the wheel tires. In the spring the landing fields became marshlands, and in the summer some of the local communities felt that the flat fields could be put to a better purpose. On one occasion, a complete circus obligingly moved over to make room for the Stinsons to land.

This state of affairs could not go on, if Boston-Maine/Central Vermont was to hold up its head among its peers. In November 1936 it purchased two new **Lockheed 10-A Electras**. National Airways did not have the money to buy them and so the operating agreement was terminated on 1 March 1937, control passing to the railroad interests. The Electras took over the "trunk" routes from Boston to Bangor

and from Boston to Burlington, while the Stinsons continued to brave the elements north of Bangor, on a new route to Caribou, in northern Maine, started on 5 August 1937.

Northeast Airlines

On 19 November 1940, the airline itself took steps to remove the railroad connotation in its image. The name was changed to a wholly appropriate **Northeast Airlines**, and every effort was made to create a traditionalist theme, complete with a smiling Pilgrim as its insignia and air hostesses with white "pilgrim" collars.

Northeast Airlines began to flex its muscles, modest though they were in comparison to the mighty sinews of the trunk lines. It bought its first 21-seat **Douglas DC-3s** and introduced them in service on 1 July 1941, by which time the faithful Stinsons, that had been through so much toil and tribulation during the formative years of the Boston-Maine, were pensioned off.

Stinson SM-6000B of Boston-Maine/Central Vermont Airways with chains on the wheels for improved ground control.

One of Boston-Maine's Lockheed 10-A Electras at Boston.

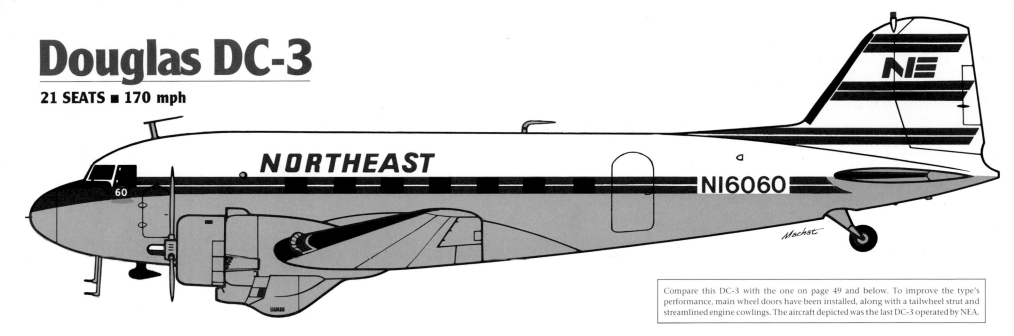

Douglas DC-3
21 SEATS ■ 170 mph

NORTHEAST

NI6060

Compare this DC-3 with the one on page 49 and below. To improve the type's performance, main wheel doors have been installed, along with a tailwheel strut and streamlined engine cowlings. The aircraft depicted was the last DC-3 operated by NEA.

Pratt & Whitney R-1830 (1,200hp) x 2 ■ 25,200 lb. max. gross take-off weight ■ Range 500 miles ■ Length 65 feet ■ Span 95 feet ■ Height 16 feet

The Old Indestructible

The Douglas DC-3 made its first flight on 17 December 1935 (the anniversary of the Wright brothers' famous feat at Kitty Hawk) and went into service with American Airlines on 25 June 1936. Many books have been written about this famous airplane, which to some enthusiasts has become, with some justification, almost an object of worship. Its dominance of the airline scene became such that, of the 322 aircraft in U.S. airline service in 1941, 260, or 80 per cent, were DC-3s; and the percentage of seats offered was much higher.

A total of 430 Douglas DC-3s were delivered to the airlines before the outbreak of World War II halted civilian production. During the war, the "Gooney Bird" was built in Japan and the Soviet Union, as well as in the U.S. and more than 13,000 were estimated to have been built altogether, in all versions, military and civil; and some hundreds of them are still flying today, a few even in scheduled service.

One of Northeast's three pre-war DC-3s photographed at Boston during its few brief months of service before being traded for DC-2s.

THE FIRST MODERN AIRCRAFT OF BOSTON-MAINE/CENTRAL VERMONT AIRWAYS
(NORTHEAST AIRLINES from 19 November 1940)

MSN	Regn.	Delivery Date	Remarks
Lockheed 10-A Electra			
1069	NC16055	6 Oct. 36	} Ex-National Airways
1070	NC16056	13 Oct. 36	
1037	NC14959	28 Jul. 37	From Eastern Air Lines
1021	NC14915	Feb. 38	From Northwest Airlines; sold to National Airlines, 1939
1026	NC14337	41	} From Braniff Airways
1030	NC14941	41	

*Fleet Numbers were last two of registration. All aircraft except NC14915/16056 requisitioned by the Civil Aeronautics Authority (CAA) in 1942, but operated by Northeast; NC16056 to USAAF as UC-36A, 11 Jun. 42. A **Lockheed 12-A Electra Junior** (NC17397/1269 Sky Baby) was also operated briefly.*

MSN	Regn.	Delivery Date	Remarks
Douglas DC-2-112			
1243	NC13717	} 16 Apr. 42	All aircraft from TWA and requisitioned as C-32As by U.S. Army (via Treasury Dept.) 19-22 Jul. 42
1294	NC13784		
1246	NC13720		
1293	NC13783		
1297	NC13787	} 22 Apr. 42	

Northeast Shakes Off the Past

The First U.S. Domestic Overseas Airline

When **Northeast Airlines** introduced **Douglas DC-3s** in July 1941 (see page 40) it must have thought that at last it had reached true senior status, with equipment that could be classified as modern. It could not have known that, within a few months, its sudden elevation in operational capability from the old Stinsons and Lockheed Electras would be put to a rigorous test. For it became the first U.S. domestic airline to offer overseas services on a regular schedule.

On 11 January 1942, Northeast made a survey flight with a **Douglas C-39** (one of the military versions of the DC-2) on behalf of the United States Army Air Force. The route was from Presque Isle, in northern Maine, to Gander, Newfoundland, via Moncton, Goose Bay, and Stephenville, and the purpose was to determine the practicality of starting a scheduled service. Gander had suddenly become a vital staging point on the aerial highway across the Atlantic Ocean, and under the Lend-Lease program launched by President Roosevelt even before the United States was plunged into World War II, a new airfield with concrete runways had rapidly been constructed.

This was the first sortie into this area since Charles Lindbergh's *Jelling* expedition of 1933, made on behalf of Pan American Airways. Lieutenant Crocker Snow, who directed the operation, decided that the C-39 should be replaced by the **C-53** (a military version of the DC-3), which had more powerful engines. Northeast Airlines began carrying passengers and freight on 13 February 1942, a contract having been approved on 31 January. Operations during the month of February on a route to Newfoundland could not have been easy; but with its experience in pioneering its services in Maine and Vermont, Northeast was ideally suited to the task, and in its element.

Back at base, the airline had to come to terms with some commercial realities. In April 1942 it had been obliged to trade in its brand-new DC-3s in exchange for some of TWA's DC-2s; but Northeast got five aircraft in place of three. But no sooner had these been received than they were requisitioned, as **C-32As,** by the U.S. Army Air Force; and they were promptly put into service under contract to Northeast in support of the war effort, pioneering routes to Europe via Labrador, Greenland, and Iceland.

Into the Wild Blue Yonder

On 24 April, Northeast Airlines extended its Gander service northward via Goose Bay, Labrador, to Narssarssuak, Greenland, (given a military code-name Bluie West 1) and this was soon extended to Søndre Stromfjord (Bluie West 8) further north along the eastern coast of Greenland. The veteran Northeast chief pilot, **Captain Milton H. Anderson**, did most of the pioneer route-proving in this inhospitable region. His description of Bluie West 1 (quoted by Reginald Cleveland in *Air Transport at War*) is illustrative of the conditions: "The shore line was reached in a heavy snowstorm which reduced visibility to less than a mile, and with winds later computed to be over 60mph on the surface. Extreme difficulty was encountered in locating the fjord which led to the airport, and it was found only by climbing through the overcast in unfamiliar mountain terrain, orienting on a radio range with countless multiple courses, simultaneously experiencing a 180-degree shift, and finally spiraling down 8,000 feet through a hole in the overcast over the airport."

Across the Atlantic

Greenland was merely the staging point towards Europe. Within a month of opening service to Bluie West 1 and 8, Northeast extended the route to Iceland, via Angmagssalik (Bluie East 2); and on 3 July a further extension brought a Northeast-operated C-53 to Stornoway, on the island of Lewis, in the Outer Hebrides of Scotland, from which key airfield it was but a short segment to Prestwick, near Glasgow, the main wartime terminus for trans-Atlantic landplane services of all kinds. During 1942, Northeast also operated some local services within Iceland, carrying troops needed to garrison the island against the possibility of a German occupation.

The Canadian Arctic

Not long after establishing itself as a pioneer of the northern Atlantic rim, Northeast Airlines blazed another frozen and icebound trail in northern Canada. Under the massive supply effort that was rapidly getting under way from the factories and product sources of North America to beleaguered Britain, a shorter route was quickly planned from the western and middle regions of the U.S.A. and Canada, to reach the Greenland stations without having to fly to the east coast of the American continent. Northeast's first flight to this area was made on 1 November 1942 as far as Frobisher Bay (Crystal 2) (see map); then on 21 November from Crystal 2 to

A Northeast-operated Douglas C-53 in USAAF camouflage. (Photos courtesy NEA/Bob Mudge)

Arctic-suited Northeast crew, with formally attired passengers, ready for a wartime flight.

Pioneering the Frozen North

NORTHEAST'S DOUGLAS DC-3 FLEET

In order of delivery

MSN	Regn.	Delivery Date	Remarks
3286	NC33621	1 May 41	Purchased new from Douglas, but traded to TWA, Apr. 42, in exchange for DC-2s
3287	NC33622	8 May 41	
3288	NC33623	8 May 41	
2253	NC28323	2 Jun. 42	Purchased from American Airlines; sold to Colonial Airlines, early 46
2254	NC28324	2 Jun. 42	
4861	NC30087	18 Jun. 44	From USAAF (C-53); sold to Lake Central Airlines, 3 Feb. 61
4872	NC19942	23 Oct. 44	From USAAF (C-53); sold to Custom Air Sales
3256	NC25612	12 Apr. 45	Ex-USAAF (C-48) through Reconst. Fin. Corp.; crashed, South Weymouth, Mass., 9 Sep. 51
7348	NC45388	20 Sep. 45	From USAAF (C-53) through Reconst. Fin. Corp.; sold to Air Carrier Serv. Corp., Sep. 67
4908	NC45362	27 Nov. 45	Ex-USAAF (C-53) through Reconst. Fin. Corp.; sold to Air Carrier Serv. Corp., Sept. 67
11745	NC17891	45	From USAAF (C-53); crashed, Mt. Success, N.H., 30 Nov. 54
9914	NC65282	17 May 46	From USAAF (C-47) through Reconst. Finance Corp.; sold to Piedmont, Feb. 61
19402	NC65390	28 Jun. 46	Purchased from Exec. Transport Corp. (ex-USAAF C-47); sold to Piedmont, 21 Feb. 48
19648	NC65136	27 Sep. 46	Purchased from Temco (ex-USAAF C-47s); sold to Lake Central Airlines
19025	NC65134	2 Oct. 46	
18984	NC65384	5 Jun. 47	From USAAF (C-47) through Reconst. Finance Corp.; sold to Piedmont, Apr. 48
7337	NC34417	29 Jan. 52	Purchased from TWA (ex-USAAF C-53); crashed, New Bedford, Mass., 15 Sep. 57
11752	N44998	5 Feb. 52	Purchased from TWA (ex-USAAF C-53); sold to Lake Central Airlines, 30 Dec. 60
11648	N19428	27 Feb. 53	Ex-USAAF C-53; sold to Tampa Center Inc., 1967
11738	N44992	2 Mar. 53	Purchased from United (ex-USAAF C-53); sold to Air Carrier Serv. Corp. Sep. 67
1902	N16060	10 Mar. 53	Purchased from United; sold to Air Carrier Serv. Corp. after retirement on 16 Dec. 66, the last DC-3 operated by NEA
2190	N14967	6 Mar. 55	Purchased from PANAGRA; sold to Lake Central Airlines, 30 Dec. 60
2007	N18941	10 Jun. 55	Leased from United Air Lines
2027	NC18953		Leased from TWA; Fleet No. 358

All except NC18953 used last two numbers of registration as Fleet Numbers.

Churchill, via Southampton Island; and finally on 16 March 1943 to a point on Baffin Island (Crystal 3), where the only runway was on the frozen bay, available during the fall, winter, and spring.

On 28 March 1943, the first of four round-trips were made even further north, to Arctic Bay, at the extreme northern end of Baffin Island, and to Fort Ross on Somerset Island. The mission was to replenish supplies and to remove personnel for medical treatment from these vital weather station outposts. In 13 days, 2,300lb of supplies were taken across some of the most inhospitable, barren, and frigid land ever to witness the operation of a civil airliner.

Sometimes the progress of commercial aviation is measured by the growth of airliners, from, say, the DC-3 to the Boeing 747; or by the growth of routes flown, from the multiple-stop transcontinental route to the ability to fly from New York to Tokyo nonstop as a matter of routine. No less an indication of aviation's conquest of the elements is to consider that Northeast's pioneering flights to the Arctic regions, then hailed as battles for survival, are now flown as a matter of routine scheduling by the regional airlines of Canada and Greenland.

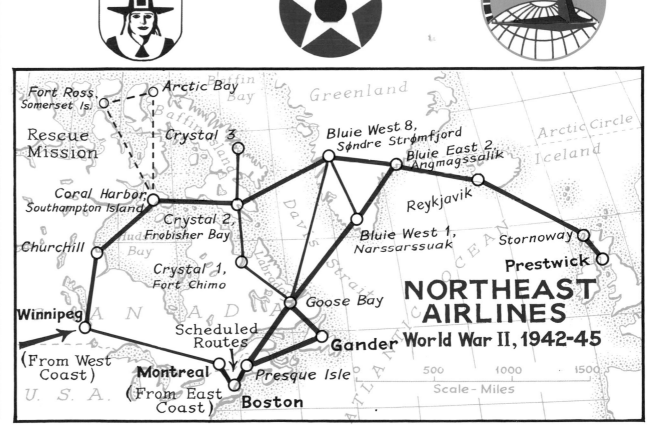

NORTHEAST AIRLINES

NORTHEAST AIRLINES World War II, 1942-45

Pacific Seaboard Airlines

California Milk Run

During the early 1930s, a young law student had learned to fly in a **Bellanca CH-300** that he had purchased, on a whim, in New York, and combined a program of flying lessons with a transcontinental flight to California. There he became interested in starting a small airline, and on 15 June 1933 organized **Pacific Seaboard Airlines.** The student's name was **Carleton Putnam**, and the idea of a coastal route between San Francisco and Los Angeles was suggested to him by Robert E. Gross, of Lockheed.

The route was a delightful way of traveling from the Bay Area to southern California — and it still is — but from the inaugural flight of the Bellanca *Miss San Jose* on 23 June, and in spite of the tempting offer of flying at 3-1/2¢ per mile — "Cheaper than driving your car" — the company lost money heavily and seemed destined to go the way of all airlines that had not done their sums correctly nor had judged the market shrewdly enough.

Fate then took a hand. On 9 February 1934 President Roosevelt canceled all the existing mail contracts, following the revelations of the notorious Air Mail Scandal. After a few weeks, during which the U.S. Army bravely tried to carry the mail, but failed to convince anyone, partly because it had been given an impossible task, the Postmaster General invited new bids for revised air mail contracts. This was on 30 March 1934, and Carleton Putnam, repeating the impetuosity in starting the scenic route along the Californian coast, made a desperate bid for a route in middle America, from the Great Lakes to the Gulf.

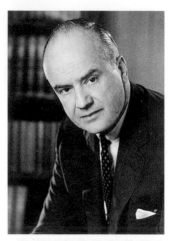

Carleton Putnam, founder of Pacific Seaboard Airlines, forerunner of Chicago & Southern.

The Mississippi Valley Route

When the air mail contracts came up for re-bidding in March 1934, popular aviation opinion assumed that the route from Chicago to New Orleans, via St. Louis and Memphis, would go to the Robertson brothers, who had been pioneers in the area, having employed Charles Lindbergh as a pilot in the 1920s. They had sold out to Universal Aviation Corporation, started again, and sold again; the second time more or less forcibly, to American Airways, as the Postmaster General under the Hoover administration, Walter Folger Brown, played with the aspirant airline entrepreneurs as a chess master moves his pieces. With the air mail contract new deal, this was an opportunity for the Robertsons to win back their birthright.

They bid one of the lowest rates of all the candidate airlines across the country for all the routes; 18-1/2¢ per mile; and must have been astonished to learn that this rock-bottom figure had actually been underbid. Carleton Putnam was the successful gambler, receiving the award on 3 June 1934, and he moved his entire California operation, including the name, Pacific Seaboard Airlines, to Memphis. Passenger and mail services started on 17 July on the route shown on the map, with an augmented fleet of Bellancas.

Pacific Seaboard's first Bellanca Pacemaker.

Stinson SM-6000B, in service with Chicago & Southern, 1934-35.

PACIFIC SEABOARD AIRLINES 1933

SAN FRANCISCO
San Jose
Salinas
Monterey
Paso Robles
San Luis Obispo
Santa Maria
Santa Barbara
LOS ANGELES

Scale - Miles
0 50 100 150 200

REGD

PACIFIC SEABOARD AIRLINES 1934

CHICAGO
Peoria
Springfield
ST LOUIS
Memphis
Greenwood
Jackson
NEW ORLEANS

Name changed to
CHICAGO & SOUTHERN AIRLINES
1 February 1935

REGD

Bellanca CH-300 Pacemaker

5 SEATS ■ 106 mph

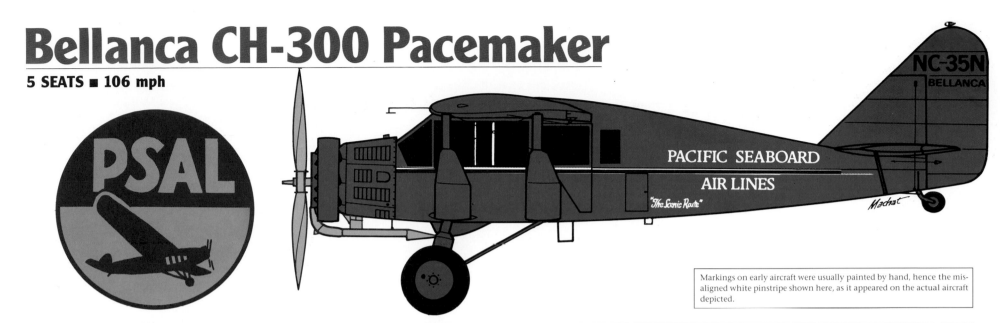

PSAL

NC-35N
BELLANCA

PACIFIC SEABOARD
AIR LINES

"The Scenic Route"

Machat

Markings on early aircraft were usually painted by hand, hence the mis-aligned white pinstripe shown here, as it appeared on the actual aircraft depicted.

Wright J6 Whirlwind (300hp) ■ 4050 lb. max. gross take-off weight ■ Range 350 miles ■ Length 28 feet ■ Span 46 feet ■ Height 9 feet

The Bellanca Story

During the so-called "Golden Age" of aviation, between the two World Wars, the name of Bellanca was seldom far from the headlines. Bellanca's most famous aircraft was undoubtedly the Model MB-2 *Columbia,* flown nonstop from New York to Germany in 1927. Guiseppe Bellanca built many different types of aircraft, most of them characterized by the "lifting strut," an airfoil shape, that offered lift as well as support for the wing.

A PSA Bellanca CH-300 at Grand Central Air Terminal, Los Angeles.

The CH-300 Pacemaker

One of the most successful of Bellanca's designs was the model CH-300 Pacemaker powered by the famous Wright J6 radial engine. A high wing cabin monoplane, the model CH-300 offered a roomy cabin for six, and was able to carry a useful load of just under 1,800lb. More than 35 CH-300s were built.

Interestingly, four of **Pacific Seaboard's** five Pacemakers had mail compartments behind the passenger cabin. Though they were of little use in California, as Putnam did not have a mail contract in 1933, they served him well when he was the successful bidder for the Mississippi Valley route in 1934.

THE PACIFIC SEABOARD AIR LINES FLEET

MSN	Regn.	Remarks
Bellanca CH-300		
170	NC35N	Transferred from Carleton Putnam, 1 Jul. 33; sold to H.F. Klein, 12 Jun. 35
165	NC873M	From Wayne Knight, 1 Jun. 33; sold to Long & Harmon 2 May 35
174	NC167N	From Vermilya-Hoffman Flying Svce., 1 Jul. 33; sold to Cordova Air Svce., 23 Apr. 35
158	NC256M	From Rapid Air Transport, 5 May 34; sold to H.M. Walker 8 May 35
183	NC860N	From Bellanca, 8 May 34; sold to Aeronaves de México, 11 Feb. 35
Bellanca Type D Skyrocket		
634	NC12657	Delivered 19 Jun. 34; sold to C. Putnam, 30 Sep. 36
Curtiss 4C-1A Robin		
702	NC509N	
Pitcairn PA-6		
26	NC585	From Charles Kendall 14 Apr. 34; sold to W.C. Smith, 20 Nov. 35 (instrument trainer)

Chicago & Southern

Essential Name Change

To operate between Lake Michigan and the Mississippi Delta with a name like Pacific Seaboard made no sense at all, at least in the 1930s, when airlines were expected to have some identity with their mission in life. This was long before Eastern Air Lines was to serve Seattle, or Northeast to serve Los Angeles, or Western to fly to Florida. And so Carleton Putnam changed the name of his airline to **Chicago & Southern Air Lines**. It was geographically correct and the very name had an air of gallantry about it. More practically, it was incorporated under Delaware law on 1 February 1935.

Modernizing the Fleet

Single-engined Bellancas were not exactly what the public wanted on the Mississippi Valley route, not least because they were single-engined aircraft, and further because they were beginning to look old-fashioned, compared with the new flagships of the big transcontinental airlines that crossed Chicago & Southern's path — literally — as commercial aviation got under way again in the latter months of 1934. As an interim step, Putnam acquired tri-motored **Stinson SM-6000Bs** in 1935, and then replaced these with a handsome fleet of four **Lockheed 10-B Electras**, in April 1936.

Traffic grew to the extent that, in the spring of 1940, larger aircraft were introduced, 21-seat **Douglas DC-3s** replacing the 10-seat Electras, which were soon retired. Putnam had progressed from five-seat, 100mph, single-engined Bellancas to 21-seat, 160mph, Douglas twins within five years, which was not bad going.

New Routes

With such a fleet, Putnam was fit, willing, and able — to quote the Civil Aeronautics Board's apt phrase — to take on new responsibilities and to expand its sphere of influence. This he did in fine style, winning two route awards that gave the airline access to two more major cities, Detroit and Houston, which effectively opened up two important new market areas: the Great Lakes and Texas. The extension from Memphis to Houston was awarded on 1 March 1941 and inaugurated on 12 June; and the one from Memphis to Detroit awarded in 1944 and started on 1 June 1945. As the map shows, Chicago & Southern had neatly constructed a set of routes that served a large population, including two of the biggest five cities of the U.S.A.; and operationally had linked them all at a central hub at Memphis.

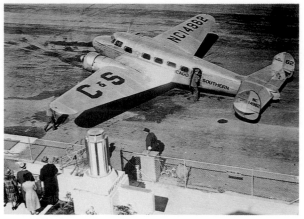

Chicago & Southern's last Lockheed 10-B Electra City of Springfield.

This Chicago & Southern DC-3, photographed here at Jackson, Miss., promoted "The Valley Level Route."

After the end of World War II, the hub principle was further emphasized, and the sphere of influence expanded, when, on 9 September 1948, an additional spoke was added from Memphis to Kansas City, via Springfield, Missouri; and some other intermediate points were added to the existing network. By this time, the aircraft fleet had been further augmented and a dramatic addition made not only to the route structure but to the shape and substance of the airline itself, as described on page 48.

CHICAGO & SOUTHERN'S EARLY FLEET

MSN	Regn.	Delivery Date	Remarks
Stinson SM-6000B (Model T)			
5048	NC10872	21 Dec. 34	Sold to St. Louis Flying Svce., May 36
5050	NC10894	Dec. 34	Crashed, Maywood (Chicago), 28 May 35
5021	NC11153	21 Dec. 34	Sold to St. Louis Flying Svce., Apr. 36
5022	NC11155	21 Dec. 34	Crashed, Yorkville, Il., 11 Feb. 35
5025	NC11175	14 Dec. 34	Sold to St. Louis Flying Svce., May 36
5030	NC10808	28 Feb. 35	
5036	NC10860	25 Mar. 35	Sold, 25 April 1936
5040	NC11167	30 Jun. 35	Sold to St. Louis Flying Svce., May 36

First five aircraft from American Airways; other three from Eastern, Rapid Air Transport, and Central Airlines respectively.

Stinson Junior S			
8059	NC10883		
8062	NC10888	26 Feb. 36	Sold 1940
Stinson Reliant			
9718	NC16148		Model SR-8B } Used for instrument
9767	NC16199		Model SR-8CM } training
Stearman C3R			
5002	NC8822	20 Nov. 35	Mailplane only; sold 30 Nov. 36
Pitcairn PA-6			
26	NC585	14 Apr. 34	From C. Kendall; sold W.C. Smith
	NC7557	6 May 35	Instrument trainer, traded-in 20 Nov. 35 to Long & Harmon

CHICAGO & SOUTHERN AIRLINES 1948

Route opened Sept. 1948
Route to Detroit opened 1 June 1945
Route opened 1 March 1941
Scale–Miles
REGD

Lockheed 10 Electra

10 SEATS ■ 190 mph

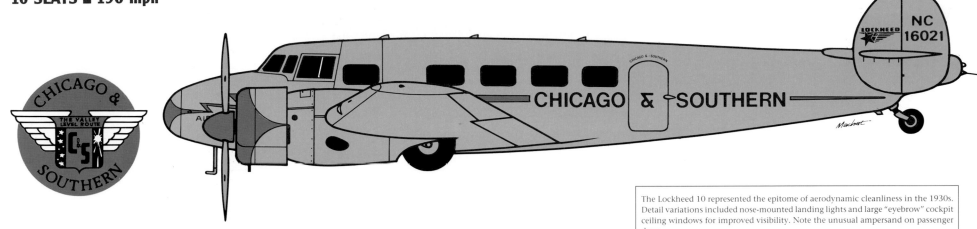

The Lockheed 10 represented the epitome of aerodynamic cleanliness in the 1930s. Detail variations included nose-mounted landing lights and large "eyebrow" cockpit ceiling windows for improved visibility. Note the unusual ampersand on passenger door.

Pratt & Whitney Wasp (450hp) x 2 ■ 10,300 lb. max. gross take-off weight ■ Range 350 miles ■ Length 39 feet ■ Span 55 feet ■ Height 10 feet

CHICAGO & SOUTHERN'S DOUGLAS DC-3 FLEET

MSN	Regn.	Delivery Date	Disposal Date	Remarks	
2218	NC25625	14 Apr. 40	3 Oct. 53		Sold to
2219	NC25626	18 Apr. 40	12 Sep. 53	*City of St. Louis*	Aero
2220	NC25627	24 Apr. 40	31 Dec. 53	*City of Memphis*	Leasing
2233	NC25628	10 Apr. 40	15 Dec. 53		Corp.
2255	NC19977	23 Sep. 40	8 Jun. 42	*City of Chicago*, to USAAF as C-49; crashed, Del Valle, Tex., 10 Mar. 43	
3285	NC28378	3 Apr. 41	18 Jul. 42	To USAAF as C-49; crashed, Memphis, with C & S Mil. Tpt. Div., 6 Nov. 42	
All purchased new from Douglas; first four Fleet Numbers C-25 to C-28.					
4989	NC38938	29 Jun. 44	15 Sep. 53	*City of Detroit*	
6315	NC30083	13 Jun. 44	3 Oct. 53	*City of Little Rock*	
6317	NC31538	8 Feb. 45	15 Dec. 53		Sold to
6328	NC17882	17 Mar. 45	25 Nov. 53	*City of Fort Wayne*	Aero
4998	NC12927	27 Apr. 45	3 Oct. 53	*City of Memphis*	Leasing
6340	NC12958	1 May 45	22 Sep. 53	*City of Chicago*	Corp.
4988	NC44881	11 Aug. 45	3 Oct. 53	*City of Hot Springs*	
6262	NC12926	30 Aug. 45	3 Oct. 53	*City of Evansville*	
Fleet Numbers C-29 to C-36; all from USAAF (ex- C-49s).					
4145	NC15849	19 Aug. 45		Ex-USAAF C-49	
6318	NC19930	45		Leased from Recon. Fin. Corp.	
4585	NC38939	45		Ex-USAAF C-47; sold to D. O'Connor	
4498	NC75411	45		Ex-USAAF C-47; sold to ARAMCO	
13759	NC86599			Ex-USAAF C-47	
13776	NC18618			Ex-USAAF C-47	
Fleet Numbers C-37/C-38; cargo aircraft leased from War Assets Administration after World War II.					
All except the two crashed aircraft and the last five listed passed to Delta with the merger on 3 October 1953.					

CHICAGO & SOUTHERN'S LOCKHEED 10-B ELECTRAS

MSN	Regn.	Delivery Date	Name	Remarks
1040	NC14962	Sep. 37	*City of Springfield*	From Eastern Air Lines; to Royal Canadian Air Force (CF-BQW)
1056	NC16021	31 Mar. 36	*City of New Orleans*	To RAF 12 Jan. 41 as AX766
1057	NC16022	11 Apr. 36	*City of Memphis*	Crashed, St. Louis, 5 Aug. 36
1067	NC16022	10 Sep. 36	*City of Memphis*	Replaced aircraft of same name; retired 1 Jan. 41
1058	NC16023	22 Apr. 36	*City of St. Louis*	Retired 18 Dec. 40
1059	NC16024	28 Apr. 36	*City of Jackson*	To RCAF (CF-BRL)
Purchased new from Lockheed. Fleet Numbers 62, 21-24.				

By 1937, the Chicago & Southern Electras were maintaining three round-trips between Chicago and New Orleans and clearly Putnam's gamble in making an impossibly low bid for the mail contract had paid off. For in addition to the mail payments, passenger traffic was healthy, partly because the citizens of the Windy City were pleased to be able to fly quickly to the warmth, as well as the other attractions, of New Orleans. Rather like Eastern Air Lines, Chicago & Southern did not, as some airlines did, suffer from a severe seasonal problem, because of a dearth of traffic in the winter.

Chicago & Southern Air Lines was typical of the medium-sized airlines that needed the Lockheed Electra during the vital period of consolidation during the latter 1930s, until the first DC-3 arrived in 1940. Because the production of the Lockheed twin was fragmented among many airlines, and the biggest ones did not use them as their first line fleets, its importance as a pre-war airliner is often forgotten. For the record, the commercial (i.e. excluding military versions) production numbers were: **Douglas DC-2**, 130; **Douglas DC-3**, 430; and the **Lockheed twins**, 510. Of these, 149 were Model 10s, 130 Model 12 Electra Juniors, and 231 Model 14 Super Electras.

The Airlines Go To War

Delta Loses a Fleet

The events at Pearl Harbor on 7 December 1941 put the nation into shock and the aircraft and aviation industry in all its facets on a war footing. Of its fleet of ten modern aircraft, five Electras and five DC-3s, **Delta Air Lines** had to surrender all the Lockheeds and one DC-3.

Delta soldiered on with its four remaining DC-3s, on a reduced schedule, carrying passengers on a strict priority basis, according to their importance to the war effort. But Delta's main contribution during World War II was at its home maintenance base, which became one of the many modification centers that coped with the tremendous upsurge of work that became necessary when the U.S. aircraft industry geared up to an incredible pace of output that astounded the world and helped to win the war. As a shrewd manufacturing policy decision, the smooth acceleration of the rate of aircraft coming off the production line was not interrupted or compromised by the constant need for the countless modifications necessary as the designers and project engineers sought innumerable improvements to the basic design of aircraft destined for the theaters of war. Instead, the aircraft, such as Lockheed P-38 Lightnings and Douglas A-20s, were completed according to the original production plan and schedule, and then sent to modification centers such as the one at Atlanta. During World War II, Delta modified more than 1,000 aircraft in this manner, as well as overhauling engines and instruments, and training hundreds of Army pilots and mechanics.

Cometh the Hour, Cometh Northeast

If ever an airline needed a break, it was **Northeast Airlines**; and its chance came when the exigencies of war demanded some very special efforts by some very special people. Partly because of its own conservative policy towards expansion outside the New England hinterland, its network was tiny, even compared with those of Delta and Chicago & Southern. But as some airlines were born great, and some airlines became great, little Northeast had greatness thrust upon it. Strategically placed at one end of the vital supply route to Europe, Paul Collins's airline accepted the unprecedented challenge, and performed magnificently. The exciting story is told on pages 42 and 43.

Chicago & Southern Does Its Bit

Carleton Putnam's airline had established a solid foundation in the Mississippi Valley. At the outbreak of World War II, its

Lockheed Electra fleet had dwindled to two, but it had six Douglas DC-3s. In a situation parallel to that of Delta, **C & S** surrendered most of its fleet to the armed forces. Its two remaining Electras were flown to Canada for the Royal Canadian Air Force, and two of its DC-3s were transferred to the USAAF in the summer of 1942. Like Delta, the airline established a modification center at Memphis, and conducted pilot and mechanic training programs.

Western's Operation Sourdough

Western Air Lines' response to a nationwide call for vital air transport services after Pearl Harbor was one of the most

One of Delta's Douglas DC-3s, obtained in 1944, is shown early postwar at Asheville, NC.

demanding. It joined the hardy Alaskan sourdough pilots and maintenance men in establishing links from the 48 States to the strategically critical Alaskan theater of operations.

Two main routes were operated on a twice-daily schedule. Civilian flight crews wore Air Transport Command (ATC) uniforms, with special wings, insignia, and epaulets. The flying conditions were harsh. During the winter, temperatures plunged to 60 degrees below zero (at that extreme the difference between Fahrenheit and Centigrade/Celsius matters little). Rubber crystallized and shattered like glass; fuel hoses snapped; oil flowed like molasses until heated; grease froze in wheel bearings. Altimeters were unreliable because the intakes were blocked with snow. Radio aids were sparsely deployed and navigational charts were often rough drawings.

Throughout these daunting conditions, Western maintained a perfect safety record and the highest aircraft utilization in Air Transport Command. Western won respect with its war record and emerged from the hostilities into a postwar era where it could take its place among the leading U.S. airlines.

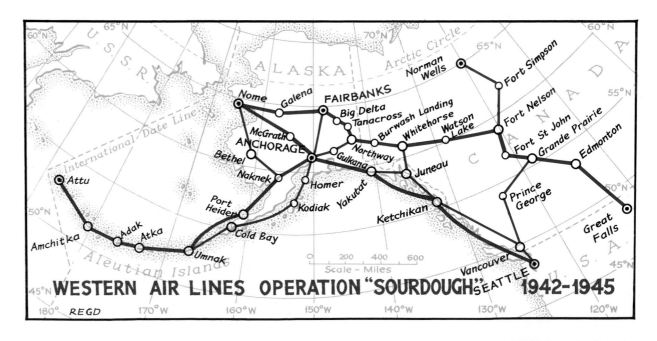

WESTERN AIR LINES OPERATION "SOURDOUGH" 1942-1945

The Age of Transition

This page epitomizes the great technical leap forward that occurred during the mid-1930s. Inventive, intuitive, innovative, intelligent, inspired: all these qualities can be attributed to the brilliant minds that took the United States from the primitive open-cockpit single-engined biplane era to the sharp, almost sleek monoplane tri-motors that graced the commercial skies before the Boeing 247 ushered in a new era. The Stinson Model A, operated by Delta from 1935 to 1938, was typical of these.

The Stinson's framework was of steel, with the skin formed of doped fabric, but it was comfortable enough for the eight passengers that it could carry. It was also quite a good performer — Stinson advertised it as "America's Fastest Tri-Motor." With a cruising speed of around 160mph, it was not far short of the Douglas DC-3's 170mph. But there the resemblance ended. The Stinson A first flew on 27 April 1934 and 31 were built. But the Douglas DC-2's debut was only two weeks later, and its descendant, the 21-seat DC-3, was only eighteen months behind. They were a generation apart. (see also pages 31 and 41 for further notes on the Douglas twins)

The Delta Air Lines DC-3 portrayed here is the *City of Atlanta*, introduced in late 1940, and marking the critical upgrading of the fleet. (Four DC-2s, purchased earlier in the year, had been sold to a beleaguered Britain as a contribution to the war effort.)

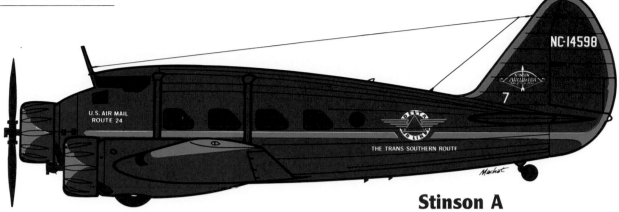

Stinson A

Type	First Flight	Dimensions			Seats	Engines			Max. Gross Wt. (lb)	Cruising Speed (mph)	No. Built
		Length	Span	Height		No.	Type	hp (ea)			
Stinson A	27 Apr. 34	37	60	12	8	3	Lycoming R-680	260	10,200	160	31
DC-2	11 May 34	62	85	16	14	2	Wright Cyclone	710	18,560	180	130 *
DC-3	17 Dec. 35	65	95	16	21	2	Wright Cyclone	1,200	25,200	170	430 *
* Civil DC-2s, DST/DC-3s only.											

The *City of Atlanta* name on the first DC-3 was important as less than four months later, on 1 March 1941, Delta headquarters would be moved from Monroe, Louisiana, to Atlanta.

Douglas DC-3

Across the Caribbean

A Postwar Reward

While **Chicago & Southern Air Lines** had been ambitious and had built up a solid market base in the central region of the United States, it had never aspired to becoming a U.S. flag carrier overseas. But that was before the involvement of the airlines as part of the industrial machine that supported the armed forces during World War II. C & S had done its share (see page 48) and, in company with many other airlines, it participated in a flurry of postwar overseas route expansion as Pan American Airways lost its monopoly position as the Chosen Instrument of U.S. international air transport policy.

On 22 May 1946, the Civil Aeronautics Board awarded to Chicago & Southern an important route: from New Orleans to Havana and Caracas route spanning the Caribbean. Services began to Havana on 1 November 1946 and in the fall of 1947, connections were promoted for an interline service with Peruvian International Airlines to the west coast of South America as far as Lima. The route was extended to Caracas in August 1948.

Further icing on the Caribbean cake was forthcoming with a further route award that gave Chicago & Southern access to the important cities of San Juan, Puerto Rico; Port-au-Prince, Haiti; and Ciudad Trujillo (now Santo Domingo) in the Dominican Republic — a further encroachment into Pan American, and by this time, Eastern Air Lines' markets.

Four-engined Equipment

Douglas DC-4s had already been ordered when the original Caribbean route award was made and the first one went into service domestically on 1 June 1946. When it started the

service to Havana, C & S was able to claim that, of all the airlines benefiting from the all-important Latin American route case, it was the first to demonstrate that it was fit, willing, and able in deeds as well as words.

In October 1950, Chicago and Southern Air Lines introduced the **Lockheed Model 649 "Gold Plate" Constellation**, a vastly improved version of the original "Connie" but of the same dimensions (see page 59). Once again it saw service on the Mississippi Valley trunk domestic line first, and then went into Caribbean service in December of the same year. On 1 April 1953, it was C & S's flagship at the start of an interchange agreement with TWA (which also had Constellations) on a route that provided a through-plane service from Houston to New York, utilizing C & S points from Indianapolis southwards, and with a TWA stop at Pittsburgh. This was just in time for one of the most impor-

C&S's Lockheed 649A, City of San Juan.

tant mergers to take place during the reign of the CAB when, on 1 May 1953, Carleton Putnam joined forces with Delta's C.E. Woolman.

C&S' DC-3 City of Chicago *in green and yellow colors at Fort Wayne, Indiana, in 1952 attended by a 1940 Ford refueling truck. (Photo courtesy Roger Myers)*

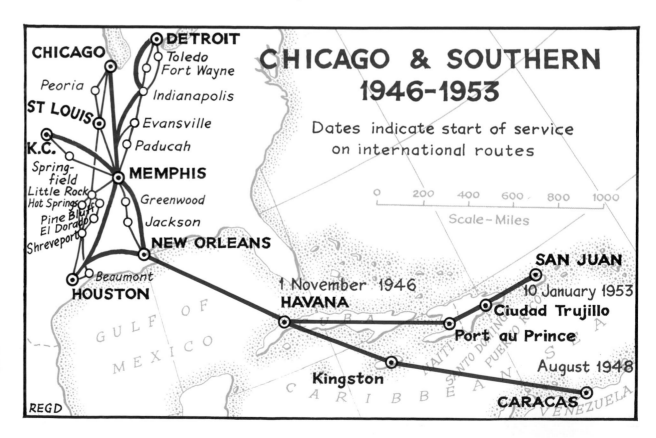

CHICAGO & SOUTHERN
1946–1953

Dates indicate start of service on international routes

DETROIT
Toledo
Fort Wayne
CHICAGO
Peoria
Indianapolis
ST LOUIS
Evansville
K.C.
Paducah
Springfield
MEMPHIS
Little Rock
Hot Springs
Greenwood
Pine Bluff
El Dorado
Jackson
Shreveport
NEW ORLEANS
Beaumont
HOUSTON

1 November 1946
HAVANA

SAN JUAN
10 January 1953
Ciudad Trujillo
Port au Prince
August 1948

Kingston

GULF OF MEXICO

CARACAS
VENEZUELA

Scale – Miles
0 200 400 600 800 1000

REGD

Lockheed 649A Constellation

57 SEATS ■ 320 mph

This aircraft is fitted with a speedpak, described on page 59.

Wright 749C-18BD-1 (2,500hp) x 4 ■ 94,000 lb. max. gross take-off weight ■ Range 2,200 miles ■ Length 95 feet ■ Span 123 feet ■ Height 24 feet

CHICAGO & SOUTHERN'S LOCKHEED 649A CONSTELLATIONS

MSN	Regn.	Name	Delivery Date	Remarks
2642	N86521	City of Houston, then Ciudad Trujillo	12 Aug. 50	Sold to TWA 1 Apr. 54
2653	N86522		27 Sep. 50	Sold to TWA 1 Jun. 54
2659	N86523	City of Detroit, then City of Caracas	21 Oct. 50	Leased, then sold to Pacific Northern, Mar.-Apr. 55
2660	N86524	City of San Juan	6 Feb. 51	
2662	N86525	City of Kingston	15 Feb. 51	
2673	N86535		18 May 51	Sold to TWA 20 Apr. 54

First five aircraft were delivered new from Lockheed as Model 649A-79-60s and converted to Model 749As after Chicago & Southern merged with Delta on 1 May 1953; N86535 was delivered as a Model 749A. Fleet Numbers last three of registration.

Almost every major airline, including Chicago & Southern, began four-engined service with the Douglas DC-4.

CHICAGO & SOUTHERN'S DOUGLAS DC-4 FLEET

MSN	Regn.	Name	Delivery Date	Remarks
18350	NC86574		23 Nov. 45	Sold to Resort Airlines, 2 Mar. 51
18338	NC88708	City of Caracas	13 Dec. 45	Sold to Brown & Brown, 14 Oct. 50
10448	NC88819	City of Kingston		Sold to Resort Airlines, 6 Mar. 51
27250	NC54361	City of San Juan		Sold to Brown & Brown, 14 Oct. 50
7467	NC53102	City of New Orleans		Sold to Brown & Brown, 15 Dec. 50
18353	N88818		29 Jan. 49	Obtained from Delta; sold to Airline Trspt. Carriers, Inc., 6 Jul. 50

Fleet Numbers C-41 to C-46; all ex-USAAF C-54s converted to DC-4 standard at Baltimore, Md. by Glenn L. Martin.

10306	NX53487		8 Apr. 46	To Penn. Central Air Lines, 29 May 46

Ex-U.S. Navy R5D-1; leased from War Assets Administration for crew training.

THE LOCKHEED CONSTELLATIONS

Model	Engine/hp (ea) (Wright R-3350) hp (ea)	Dimensions ft. Length	Span	Gross Weight (lb)	Typical Seats	Cruise Speed (mph)	Range (st.miles)	First Service Date	First Service Airline	No. Built
49	2,200	95	123	98,000	54	310	3,000	14 Jan. 46	Pan Am	88 [1]
749	2,500	95	123	107,000	64	300	3,000	17 Jun. 47	Pan Am	145 [1]
1049	2,700	114	123	120,000	88	279	2,450	17 Dec. 51	Eastern	104 [2]
1049G	3,250	114	123	137,500	99	335	4,620	1 Apr. 55	TWA	157 [3]
1649A	3,400	116	150	156,000	99	350	5,280	1 Jun. 57	TWA	44

Notes: 1. inc. military; 2. inc. C, D, E Models; 3. inc. H Model.

Twins to Quads

A Trunk Route at Last

When **Delta Air Lines** emerged from World War II, it underwent a complete transformation. This was because, after having spent its entire life as a regional airline of the South, and only during the war having broken out of its east-west axis to reach medium-sized cities such as Cincinnati and New Orleans, the Civil Aeronautics Board suddenly smiled at Delta and gave it two handsome routes. In July 1945 it granted access from Atlanta to Miami, via Jacksonville, and in December of the same year, it extended the Cincinnati route to Chicago, the second largest city in the United States and hub for substantial feeder traffic in the Great Lakes Area.

By this time Delta had also received eight impressed civil **Douglas DC-3s**, militarily designated as **C-49s**, and now declared surplus to requirements by the United States Army Air Force. By the fall of 1947 this number had been augmented to 15 — half as many aircraft again as Delta's total fleet at the outbreak of war. With such a profusion of capacity, Delta began its entry into the big leagues of the airline business by starting direct Chicago — Miami service, albeit with six stops en route, with the now-converted DC-3s, on 1 December 1945, at a frequency of four round-trips per day.

Trunkline to Sunshine

Late in 1945, Delta had received the first of seven **Douglas C-54B Skymasters** from the USAAF and these were modified by Douglas at Santa Monica to civilian DC-4s between October 1945 and May 1946. The first converted aircraft arrived at Atlanta on 16 February. Delta's Art Ford designed new ramp equipment for the new 44-seaters, while chief engineer J. F. Nycum designed the galley, which Douglas thought good enough to be the standard for all DC-4s coming off the modification line.

On 18 December 1945, the name **Delta Air Lines**, which hitherto had been only the operating title — the so-called "doing business as" or "dba" — became the official name of the airline, replacing the former corporate name Delta Air Corporation.

Reviving its old custom of naming its most important services, Delta listed the entry of the DC-4 to its system on 6 March 1946 as *The Rocket*, which operated between Chicago and Miami, and a few weeks later, with the same four-engined equipment, on 1 April, as the Atlanta — Dallas *Comet*. Delta dreams, as Catherine Fitzgerald remarked, were coming true. Only a dozen years previously, it had struggled back to its feet, with obsolescent aircraft. Now it was operating 44-seat four-engined airliners from the second biggest city in

Douglas DC-3, in Delta's postwar colors.

North America to the biggest sunshine resort in Florida. And in November, with CAB approval, the DC-4s began to fly the route nonstop.

Delta's first DC-4, delivered in February 1946.

Douglas DC-4

44 SEATS ■ 215 mph

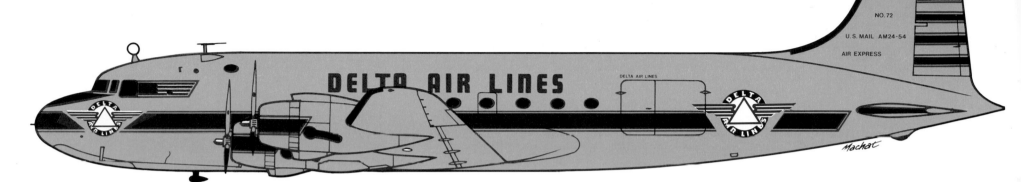

Pratt & Whitney Twin Wasp R-2000 (1,450hp) x 4 ■ 73,000 lb. max. gross take-off weight ■ Range 2,000 miles

Like all success stories, there were setbacks on the way. On 22 April 1947, eight Delta top company officials were killed when a private airplane struck a Delta DC-3 at Columbus, Georgia; and on 10 March 1948, a DC-4 crashed at Chicago. The 1947 incident was a dual setback, as the fatalities comprised a substantial element of Delta's senior management.

Prudently, late in 1947 it had canceled an order for ten Martin 2-0-2s, intended as a replacement for the DC-3; but Delta had a bigger problem. Eastern Air Lines, also on the Chicago — Miami route, did not take kindly to Delta's challenge, and put pressurized Constellations on its services to counter Delta's unpressurized DC-4s. The heat was on, but Delta had no intention of getting out of the kitchen.

LENGTH 94 feet
SPAN 118 feet
HEIGHT 28 feet

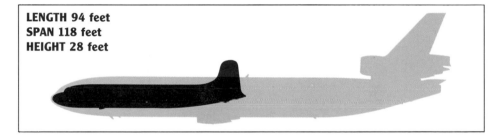

A Delta DC-4, in later "white crown" color scheme.

DELTA'S DOUGLAS DC-4 FLEET

MSN	Regn.	Delivery Date	Remarks
10444	NC37472	12 Feb. 46	Sold to Irving Herman, owner of Super Coach, 6 Feb. 53
10513	NC37473	17 Mar. 46	Leased to Northwest Jun.-Aug. 50, sold to Northwest, 4 Aug. 52
27238	NC37474	1 Mar. 46	Sold to Consolidated Airline Equipment, 22 May 53
27242	NC37475	2 Apr. 46	Sold to Pacific Northern 27 Feb. 53
10502	NC37476	11 May 46	Sold to Pacific Northern 26 Apr. 53
18333	NC37477	27 Apr. 46	Sold to North American Airlines, 15 Jun. 53
18390	NC37478	2 May 46	Crashed, Chicago, 10 Mar. 48
18353	NC88818	14 Apr. 48	From Braniff Airways; sold to Chicago & Southern Airlines, 29 Jan. 49

Fleet Numbers 72-79; all aircraft were originally delivered to the USAAF as C-54s, Jun. 44 - Jan. 45, and converted to DC-4s by Douglas at Santa Monica, 1945-46.

Delta Spreads Its Wings

Eastern Competition

The late 1940s were the exhilarating years of equipment competition between the two leading manufacturers of four-engined airliners, Douglas and Lockheed. Of the Big Four, American and United favored Douglas, TWA and Eastern Lockheed. Of the Other Trunks (as the Civil Aeronautics used to describe the other airlines as a term to separate the giants from those of lesser stature) one of the Douglas customers was **Delta Air Lines**. With DC-3s and DC-4s already in the fleet, C.E. Woolman, who was to strike up a relationship with Donald Douglas, Sr., that went beyond a business connection, must have had good reports from his engineers and pilots; for he went to Santa Monica for his next airplane.

He had been forced to do so because of intense competition from **Eastern Air Lines**. Headed by the ebullient **Eddie Rickenbacker**, who only a few years previously had dominated, almost as a monopoly, the eastern scene with his Great Silver Fleet of DC-2s and DC-3s, Eastern now sought to maintain its authority with the charismatic Constellation. It was much faster than the DC-4; it was pressurized, which the DC-4 wasn't; and although the maintenance men disliked its mechanical complexity, it was certainly much prettier. Delta was clearly outclassed on those routes with which it had to compete with Eastern, specifically the Chicago — Miami "trunkline to sunshine." So Woolman had to act promptly.

Delta ordered five **Douglas DC-6s** in February 1948, and when it put them into service on 1 December of the same year, it did so with style. The DC-6 was Delta's first pressurized type, and it was promoted as the fastest airliner of its day: the "300-Plus Deltaliners." It set new standards of comfort with the Skylounge in the rear of the cabin. And the "Airline of the South" advertised boldly "None Faster, None Finer to and thru' the South." Competing successfully with Eastern's Constellations, Delta built up its fleet of DC-6s to eleven within the next decade.

Interchange Services

As the volume of commercial air traffic in the United States expanded rapidly during the first decade following World War II, the Civil Aeronautics Board was, on the one hand, anxious to stimulate competition, but on the other, was reluctant to encourage too much, because it would be self-defeating for the airlines to suffer low load factors (and thus financial losses) over battles for market shares brought up-on by scheduling excess capacity. It hit upon a workable compromise and at the same time, found a solution to the problem of providing direct service between distant points that could not yet generate enough traffic to justify single-airline service.

Between 1948 and 1955, every airline in the trunk system, except Northeast, paired off to establish interchange agreements, by which, in rotation, the airline pairs would take turns in providing the aircraft on through services between points on each other's routes. This was similar to railroad practice, in which through trains were often given permission to run on the tracks of two or more companies.

Delta Air Lines promptly seized the opportunity. Recognizing that such operations would provide access to regions of the United States hitherto denied to it, and a chance to make itself known to communities that had never heard of it, it was the first to start an interchange service. Jointly with **TWA**, through services began between Detroit and Atlanta, via the interchange point at Cincinnati, on 1 June 1948. Delta then participated in a second interchange, from Atlanta to California, jointly with American Airlines, starting on 25 September 1949.

Delta joined one more interchange partnership and inherited another during the early 1950s. The first was with National Airlines and American Airlines, starting on 1 May 1951. This gave Delta the opportunity to show its colors in new markets, all the way from Florida to California, and spreading its image throughout the southwest and southeast.

The fourth Delta interchange route was inherited with the Chicago & Southern merger, making Delta the leading interchange participant. On 1 April 1953, Chicago & Southern had linked up with TWA so as to offer through service from New York to Houston, via Pittsburgh and Indianapolis. This was terminated as redundant after the Delta-C & S merger. The routes of these interchange agreements, and their importance to Delta in widening its horizons, are shown on the map on page 58.

This was Delta's first pressurized aircraft, a Douglas DC-6, delivered in October 1948. The legend on the fuselage proclaims "The Airline of the South."

Douglas DC-6

56 SEATS ■ 328 mph

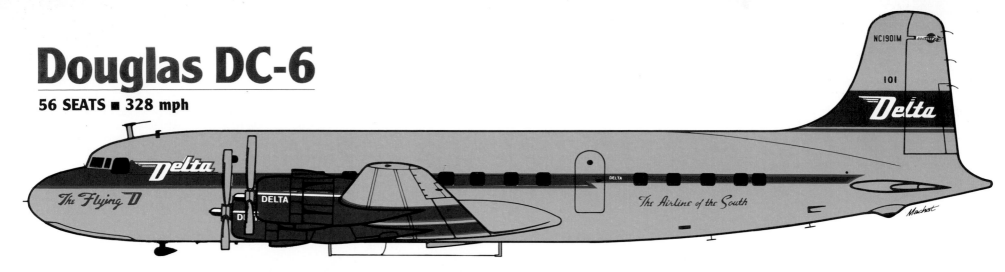

Pratt & Whitney Double Wasp R-2800 (2,100hp) x 4 ■ 97,200 lb. max. gross take-off weight ■ Range 2,200 miles

Although the **Douglas DC-4** had first flown on 14 February 1942, and had become the standard wartime logistics transport, as the **C-54** with the USAAF and the **R5D** with the Navy; and had helped dozens of airlines to resume or begin trunk line service after World War II, it had been outclassed by the Lockheed Constellation. Douglas's answer was the **DC-6** (the DC-5 had been a twin-engined type), seven feet longer than the DC-4, and most important, pressurized, to provide the comfort as well as the speed of the Connie.

As mentioned opposite, **Delta** introduced the DC-6 on 1 December 1948 on its trunk routes. At first, the DC-6s were crewed by two pilots (with two cabin crew) but shortly after entering service CAA regulations dictated that a flight engineer be added to the cockpit complement. Delta's DC-6s — the first was christened *The Flying D* —had seating for 50 passengers, in pairs each side of the aisle, although there were an additional six seats in the Skylounge which were not for sale, but for the use of passengers during the flight.

When, on 1 November 1946, Delta started service on the Chicago—Miami route it was the first nonstop in this market. Initially, DC-4s operated the flights, but with the introduction of DC-6s Delta was able to compete effectively with Eastern.

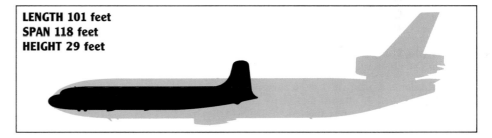

LENGTH 101 feet
SPAN 118 feet
HEIGHT 29 feet

DELTA'S DOUGLAS DC-6 FLEET

MSN	Regn.	Delivery Date	Remarks
43139	N1901M	1 Oct. 48	Sold to Aero Tech., 4 Dec. 68
43140	N1902M	21 Oct. 48	Sold to Aeromotive Enterprises, 12 Aug. 68
42897	N1903M	6 Nov. 48	Sold to Aero Tech., 27 Nov. 68
42898	N1904M	2 Nov. 48	Sold to All Sports, Inc., 31 Aug. 68
42899	N1905M	24 Dec. 48	Sold to All Sports, Inc., 29 Aug. 68
43142	N1906M	3 Dec. 49	Nose gear collapsed, Chattanooga, 15 Feb. 68; sold to Aeromotive Enterprises, 6 Mar. 68
43219	N1907M	4 Jan. 51	Sold to Aero Tech. 25 Nov. 68
43015	N37526	20 Jul. 59	First leased; then purchased from United Air Lines, 1960-61; sold to Aero Tech., 11 Dec. 68
43016	N37527	12 Jan. 59	
43020	N37531	28 Dec. 58	
43027	N37539	28 Dec. 58	

Fleet Numbers 101-107 (later 601-607) and 621-624; one other aircraft (43000/N37510 No. 625) was leased from United, 9 Apr. 59 to 9 Apr. 60.

Miss Laura Wizark (left), Delta's first flight attendant. A registered nurse, she started her duties on 15 March 1940, on a Douglas DC- 2. During the immediate postwar period, Delta had pursers (right) who were attired in maritime fashion.

Upgrading DC-3 Service

A Tough Act to Follow

The **Douglas DC-3**, which first made its appearance in 1936, had become so much a part of the aviation scene the world over, and had been such an outstanding success that no-one seemed to wish to part with it. While it was slow, compared with the Douglas and Lockheed pressurized types that now plied the oceans and across the continent, it was totally reliable, its purchasing costs had long been written off (and in most cases these were negligible, as they had been purchased at bargain prices from war-surplus stocks), and because its operating costs were so low, it had the habit of making money. Furthermore, the pilots loved it as a "forgiving airplane" in that, with an engine failure, a forced landing was little more than a minor inconvenience. But like a beloved pair of tattered old slippers that eventually has to make way for a sleek new Christmas gift, the old Gooney Bird finally had to go.

Easier Said than Done

Two U.S. manufacturers developed modern, tricycle-geared twin-engined airliners to meet the market need for a successor to the DC-3. Martin and Convair, both having many years of manufacturing experience, turned to the challenge of building a "DC-3 Replacement," a machine that was measurably bigger, in line with the traffic growth; but small enough to operate on the feeder routes that connected the lesser cities, many of which were in danger of losing service, now that, in the postwar era, the airlines had a tendency to skip them in the effort to compete between the major population centers.

Martin was first to show its colors, its **Model 2-0-2** making its first flight on 22 November 1946, four months before that of its rival Convair 240. However, Convair had flown a smaller twin, the Model 110, which assisted the development of the 240, in July 1946.

Substantial orders for the "Two-O-Two" were placed, but a structural deficiency in the wing, revealed by a fatal accident, plus other problems, forced Martin back to the drawing boards, to produce a pressurized variant, the **Model 4-0-4**. United Air Lines (followed by Northwest and Braniff) had also ordered the **Model 3-0-3**, which first flew on 3 July 1947, but this was never put into production following United's cancellation of its order.

Convair Scoops the Pool

Of the Big Four airlines, which customarily were expected to sponsor new commercial aircraft by placing the first large orders, TWA, Eastern, and United all favored Martin at first, although Northwest Airlines was the first to operate the Model 2-0-2, in August 1947. **American Airlines** (followed by Western, Continental and Pan American) chose Convair, and in 1945 placed what was then considered to be a huge order for 100 **Convair 240s**. When American put it into service on 1 June 1948, it was an immediate success in its own right, carrying 40 passengers at a better comfort level than the DC-3's 21, and cruising at 240mph, 80mph faster than the DC-3.

Although Martin exerted every effort to stay in the race, it was an uphill battle. TWA finally put the **Martin 4-0-4** into service on 5 October 1951, and Eastern followed in January 1952. By this time, Convair had developed the **Model 340**, 54in longer than the 240, and with greater wing span and power for improved high-elevation performance to attract United, now disillusioned by its flirtation with Martin, which put the **Convair-Liner** (as it had become known) into service on 16 November 1952.

Delta Air Lines, which had once tentatively agreed to buy ten Martin 2-0-2s, ordered ten Convair 340s in June 1951 and eventually had a fleet of 20, of which ten were from Chicago & Southern's initial

A Delta-C& S Convair 340.

order. It placed the first one into service on 1 March 1953, not long after United. The 340s replaced the DC-4s and DC-3s, although the last Gooney Bird was not retired until 1960, and Delta used them to promote its "Owl" aircoach services on its southern routes. Subsequently, in November 1955, it ordered eight more Convair-Liners, the **Model 440 Metropolitan**, the same size as the 340 but with improvements to reduce the cabin noise level and increased operating weights. Delta put its first Metropolitans, fitted with 52 coach-class seats, into service in 1956 and had its Convair 340s retroactively modified to 440 standard.

DELTA'S CONVAIR-LINERS

MSN	Regn.	Delivery Date	Remarks
Convair 340			
30	N4801C	18 Dec. 52	Sold to North Central Airlines, 1960-62
38	N4802C	20 Jan. 53	
39	N4803C	20 Jan. 53	
51	N4804C	26 Feb. 53	
60	N4805C	25 Mar. 53	
74	N4806C	6 May 53	
84	N4807C	11 Jun. 53	Sold to Ransome Sales, 1969
92	N4808C	16 Jul. 53	
95	N4809C	1 Aug. 53	
100	N4810C	13 Aug. 53	Sold to North Central, 1961
101	N4811C	12 Aug. 53	
105	N4812C	1 Sep. 53	
106	N4813C	28 Aug. 53	
107	N4814C	9 Sep. 53	Sold to Ransome Sales 1969-70
117	N4815C	7 Oct. 53	
118	N4816C	10 Oct. 53	
123	N4817C	25 Oct. 53	
124	N4818C	26 Oct. 53	
138	N4819C	21 Dec. 53	
152	N4820C	18 Feb. 54	Crashed, Evansville, 20 Mar. 68

Fleet Numbers 401-420; all converted to Model 440 standard, 1956-57.

MSN	Regn.	Delivery Date	Remarks
Convair 440			
359	N4821C	28 Aug. 56	Nose gear collapsed, Macon, 10 Jun. 69, and sold to Westernair, Albuquerque
377	N4822C	21 Nov. 56	Sold to North Central, 1964
378	N4823C	29 Nov. 56	Sold to Ransome Sales, 1970
379	N4824C	4 Dec. 56	Sold to North Central, 1966
380	N4825C	7 Dec. 56	
391	N4826C	12 Jan. 57	Sold to Ransome Sales, 1970
410	N4827C	20 Mar. 57	Sold to Allegheny Airlines, 1964
411	N4828C	26 Mar. 57	Sold to Ransome Sales, 1970

Fleet Numbers 421-428.

Convair 440

44 SEATS ■ 284 mph

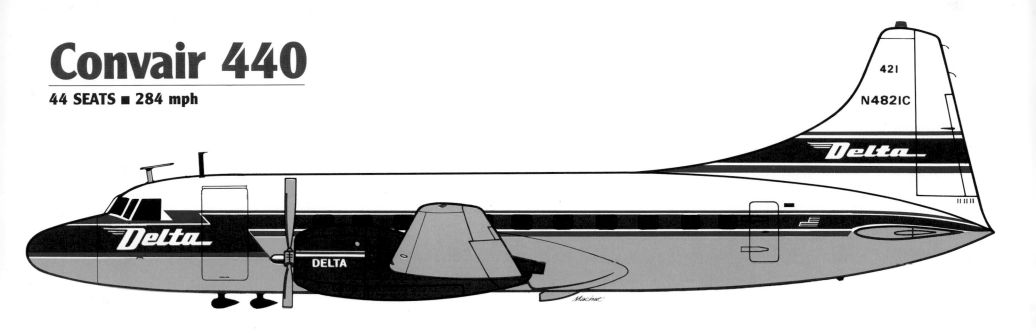

Pratt & Whitney Double Wasp R-2800 (2,400hp) x 2 ■ 47,000 lb. max. gross take-off weight ■ Range 580 miles

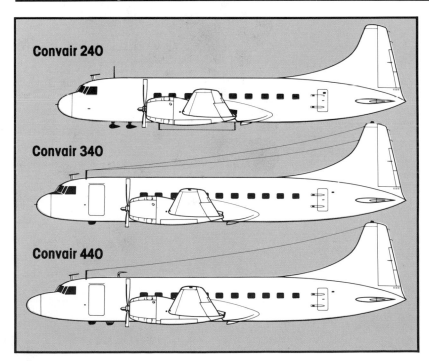

Convair 240

Convair 340

Convair 440

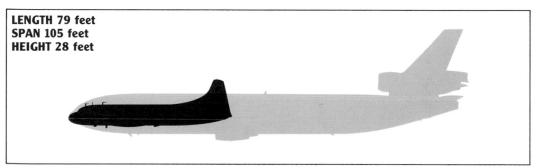

LENGTH 79 feet
SPAN 105 feet
HEIGHT 28 feet

THE CONVAIR-LINER FAMILY

Model	Engines Type	Dimensions (ft)			First Service Date	Airline	No* Built	Remarks
		hp	Lgth	Span	Seats				
240	P & W R-2800-CA18	2,400	75	92	40	1 Jun. 48	American	566	—
340	P & W R-2800-CB16	2,400	79	105	44	16 Nov. 52	United	311	—
440	P & W R-2800-CB17	2,500	79	105	52	8 Mar. 56	Continental	199	Known as the Metropolitan
540	Napier Eland	3,400	79	105	44	1 Jul. 59	Allegheny	10	Turboprop version of 340
580	Allison 501	3,750	82	105	52	1 Jun. 64	Frontier	(170)	Turboprop conversion of 340/440
600	Rolls-Royce Dart 10	3,000	75	92	52	30 Nov. 65	Central	(38)	Turboprop conversion of 240
640	Rolls-Royce Dart 10	3,000	79	105	56	23 Dec. 65	Hawaiian	(31)	Turboprop conversion of 340/440

* Includes military variants and Canadian production. Numbers in parentheses refer to conversions of earlier airframes.

Delta-C & S

An Ideal Merger

The merger between **Delta Air Lines** and **Chicago & Southern Air Lines** (or Airlines — both styles were used) may not have been conceived in heaven, but it was as close to an ideal marriage as was possible during the sparring for control of large market areas during the inevitable struggle for survival of the fittest that occurred during the first two decades of the postwar era. Quite a number of small airlines that had managed to obtain mail contracts in 1934 had been absorbed by their bigger and smarter brethren. Most of these amalgamations had taken place before World War II and the airline industry had settled down to a postwar environment in which the Civil Aeronautics Board which was content with the system that it had inherited in 1938.

After 1945 and back to postwar normality, Braniff Airways had absorbed Mid-Continent Airlines in 1952, and later in 1956, Eastern Air Lines was to engulf Colonial Airlines. Later still, in 1961, United Air Lines was to take over the irritating Capital Airlines to become the largest U.S. domestic airline. But these were all cases of a large airline swallowing up a smaller one, more to eliminate competition than to encourage it, to dominate rather than to share.

The Delta-C & S merger of 1953 was different, more of an alliance of equals than an example of a clear-cut takeover. Although C & S was only about half the size of Delta in productivity, it was twice the size of the late Mid-Continent and much larger than, say, Colonial or Northeast. Most important, it had direct access to the Caribbean and thus opened up a new world to Delta-C & S.

The Sum of the Parts

The two airlines hardly overlapped or duplicated any routes, whereas they came together at many common points, some of which were not always good traffic generators, although many of them were. Chicago & Southern, in fact, could boast more cities with large populations than could Delta. Excluding the commonly-served Chicago and New Orleans, C & S's Detroit, St. Louis, Kansas City, Houston, Memphis, and Indianapolis combined for about ten million potential travelers, compared with only about half that number in Delta's Atlanta, Cincinnati, Miami, and Dallas/Fort Worth.

This was a case of the sum of the parts being potentially much greater than the whole, especially bearing in mind the value of connections to Havana, San Juan, and Caracas as an international bonus to the merger.

The Delta-Chicago & Southern merger, the most important up to that time in the history of U.S. domestic air transport, was completed on 1 May 1953. Until September 1955 the airline was known as **Delta-C & S**, for name recognition in the former C & S markets.

One of the ex-Chicago & Southern Lockheed 649As in the short-lived colors of the merged Delta-C & S airline in 1953.

DELTA'S LOCKHEED CONSTELLATIONS

MSN	Regn.	Delivery Date	Remarks
2055	N88855	3 Sep. 56	Purchased from Pan American; withdrawn from service by 1 Jul. 58 and sold to American Flyers, 1 Apr. 60
2067	N88868	5 Jul. 56	
2053	N90923	29 Jun. 56	
2063	N90925	2 Aug. 56	

Fleet Numbers 501-504; all were built as Model 49s; the first two listed were subsequently upgraded to Model 149s.

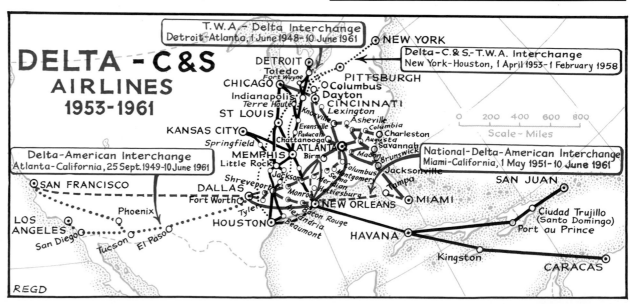

DELTA - C&S AIRLINES 1953-1961

T.W.A. - Delta Interchange
Detroit-Atlanta, 1 June 1948-10 June 1961

Delta-C.&S.-T.W.A. Interchange
New York-Houston, 1 April 1953-1 February 1958

Delta-American Interchange
Atlanta-California, 25 Sept. 1949-10 June 1961

National-Delta-American Interchange
Miami-California, 1 May 1951-10 June 1961

Scale - Miles
0   200   400   600   800

Lockheed 749 Constellation

72 SEATS ■ 327 mph

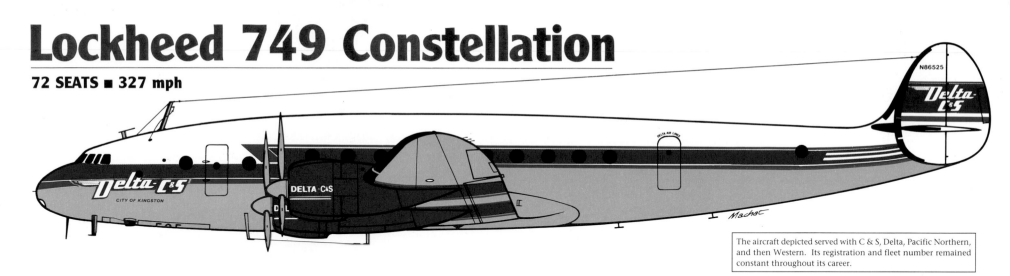

The aircraft depicted served with C & S, Delta, Pacific Northern, and then Western. Its registration and fleet number remained constant throughout its career.

Wright 749C-18BD-1 (2,500hp) x 4 ■ 102,000 lb. max. gross take-off weight ■ Range 1,800 miles

The Connie

The **Lockheed Constellation** had its origins in the late 1930s with the requirement for a pressurized airliner with a nonstop transcontinental capability. The "Connie," as it came to be known, made its first flight on 9 February 1943. Designated by Lockheed as the Model 49, 14 were delivered to the USAAF by the end of World War II as military C-69s. Progressive development of the original model resulted in the Model 649 and 749 aircraft and Connies were operated by **Chicago & Southern Air Lines**, **Delta Air Lines** and **Western Air Lines**, and **Pacific Northern Airlines**.

The Model 649A

After several speculative project variants, the Model 649 made its first flight on 19 October 1946, and obtained full CAA certification on 14 March 1947. The first to be designated solely for civilian service, with no military compromises, it was powered by four Wright R-3350 double row Cyclone radial engines, which had been upgraded to 2,500hp each, permitting a gross weight of 94,000lb. No sooner had the Model 649 made its debut when Lockheed produced a further development, by reinforcing the wing panels and installing a heavier landing gear, to increase the weight to 98,000lb. No different from the Model 49 in size, it was designated the Model 649A. The extra weight permitted 4,000lb more payload, and this was the version delivered to **Chicago & Southern Air Lines** (see page 51).

The Model 749

Certification of the gross weight to 102,000lb provided the flexibility of adding more payload or more fuel, or a combination of both. Compared with the Model 49, this was a full 8,000lb extra, translated into 40 passengers or several hundred miles of range. This model, designated 749, was first delivered in June 1947. Commercial deliveries totaled 60 and some were delivered to the U.S. Air Force as the C-121. An even later variant, the Model 749A, weighed in at 107,000lb. Sales totaled 59, of which 32 were for domestic use in the U.S.

Speedpak

Chicago & Southern opened Constellation service on 1 October 1950, and nine weeks later, on

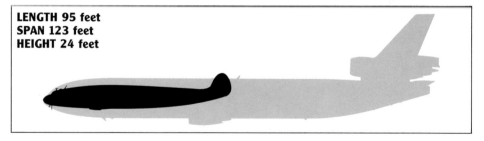

LENGTH 95 feet
SPAN 123 feet
HEIGHT 24 feet

11 December, it received its first speedpak. The speedpak was a removable container which incorporated an electrically driven winch, attached to the underside of the fuselage, and it could be raised into position or lowered to the ground in approximately one minute. Besides offering additional baggage and cargo space, the speedpak simplified the cargo loading procedure as its contents were easily accessible. Chicago & Southern used speedpak-equipped Constellations between New Orleans and Caracas, among other cities (see page 51).

One of Delta's early Model 149 Constellations, purchased from Pan American Airways in 1956 to provide service from the South to New York.

Delta to the Northeast

Introducing the DC-7

Continuing its allegiance to Douglas, **Delta Air Lines** ordered ten **Douglas DC-7s** in April 1952, and put them into service in fine style on 1 April 1954, between Chicago and Miami. A further development of the great Douglas line of four-engined piston airliners, following the DC-4, DC-6, and DC-6B, the DC-7 was notable in having the Wright R-3350 turbo-compound engines. These were later to gain an unenviable reputation for poor reliability and noise; but they were certainly powerful, deriving extra horsepower by an ingenious turbine mechanism that was driven by exhaust gases.

The DC-7 was three feet longer than the DC-6B and eight feet longer than Delta's previous Douglas, the DC-6. Delta's cabin layout included an eight-seat luxury Sky Room, and a five-seat Sky Lounge, in addition to two main cabins, for a total capacity of 69 passengers. The whole aircraft was furnished to provide an air of affluence. Meal service and onboard amenities were intended to match, and these included a typewriter for the workaholics and a shaver for the last-minute arrivals.

On 22 September 1958 the Douglas DC-7 introduced Delta's Royal Service *(see page 62).*

The inaugural on 1 April 1954 involved three services, all from Chicago to Miami, and in keeping with a now well-established tradition, they were named, respectively, the *Royal Biscayne,* the *Royal Poinciana,* and the *Owl Comet,* the last being an overnight "red-eye" service. More DC-7 *Golden Crown* services were added during the next months and on 1 April 1955 the *Royal Caribe* brought the new standard of excellence to the Caribbean as far as San Juan and Caracas — the first intercontinental DC-7 service.

To the Big Apple

Transcending even this demonstration of pride and confidence was an addition to the route network that even surpassed the expansion of routes from Chicago that the Delta-C&S merger had made possible. In the stilted language of the CAB's procedural vocabulary, the Additional Southwest-Northeast Service Case did not sound too dramatic; but when, after lengthy wrangling, with counter-submissions by all the interested parties that went on for months, the verdict was reached on 20 January 1956, the effect on Delta was electric. In receiving permission to operate from Atlanta to New York (even though at first the designated terminus was Newark) the airline could cease striving to elevate itself above the category of Other Trunks. For it could now serve New York, biggest commercial city of the western hemisphere, possibly of the world, which now seemed to be at its feet.

Douglas DC-6 *Daycoach* and *Golden Crown* DC-7 service started on 1 February 1956, with three daily services to the south, as far as Dallas-Ft. Worth and New Orleans, all named services of course, and serving the federal capital, Washington, as a bonus. On 1 April, additional services were added to include Charlotte, Baltimore, and Philadelphia, and direct service to the main southern destinations was soon further augmented. On 15 May, the New York terminus was transferred from Newark to Idlewild (later to be named John F.

Kennedy) International Airport, and Tampa was added in September as an additional Florida destination. For marketing reasons, the company name reverted to **Delta Air Lines**. It had arrived.

Last Fling of the Connie

Business was so brisk with all the new services added with the New York route award that Delta had to quickly obtain some more aircraft to cope with the demand. On 1 February 1956 — the same day as the great New York inaugural — it bought four **Lockheed 49/149 Constellations** from Pan American Airways. In rationalizing the fleet mix at the time of the merger, the Chicago & Southern Constellations had been sold, the last one departing as recently as June 1954. Perhaps C.E. Woolman did not dare to count his New York chickens before they hatched. In any event, the ex-Pan Am aircraft sufficed to tide Delta over until reinforcements arrived from Douglas, and the Connies were retired by 1 July 1958.

More Inaugurals

Not to be outdone by all this bravado up north, another inaugural took place in the Deep South. On the very same day that Delta made its debut in New York, complete with the latest Douglas DC-7 technical refinements, another Douglas aircraft, of a different generation, launched a new service from Houston to New Orleans, a less publicized and less glamorous affair, but notable in that the airplane that had the honor was none other than the veteran **DC-3**. In the process, it linked Houston directly with Atlanta by a new route, via points in Mississippi, Alabama, and Georgia (see map on page 58). That an aircraft that started its service life in 1936 should still be opening a new service for a trunk airline in 1956 was a remarkable tribute to the longevity of the veteran Douglas tail-sitter.

Douglas DC-7

69 SEATS ■ 360 mph

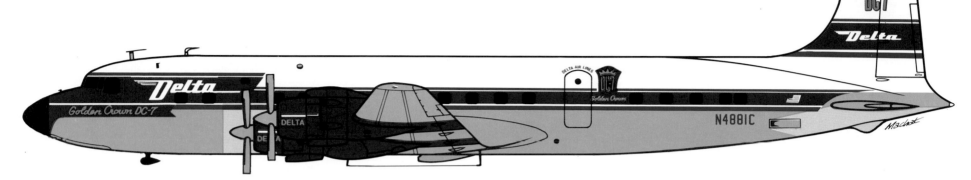

Delta joined the ranks of several U.S. trunk carriers which marked their aircraft of this era with actual metalic gold foil for such design accents as the *Golden Crown* logo.

Wright Double Cyclone R-3350 (3,250hp) x 4 ■ 122,200 lb. max. gross take-off weight ■ Range 2,760 miles

A Delta-C & S DC-7 in the delivery color scheme.

LENGTH 109 feet
SPAN 118 feet
HEIGHT 29 feet

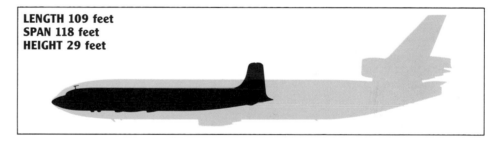

THE DOUGLAS "BIG PROP" FAMILY

Series	Engines Type	hp	Dimensions (ft) Lgth	Span	Seats	First Service Date	Airline	No. Built*
DC-4	P & W R-2000	1,450	94	117	44	7 Mar. 46	American	1,244
DC-6	P & W R-2800	2,100	101	117	56	27 Apr. 47	United	175
DC-6A	P & W R-2800	2,500	100	117	-	16 Apr. 51	Slick	74
DC-6B	P & W R-2800	2,500	106	117	66	11 Apr. 51	United	288
DC-7	Wright R-3350	3,250	109	117	70	29 Nov. 53	American	105
DC-7B	Wright R-3350	3,250	109	117	70	13 Jun. 55	Pan Am	112
DC-7C	Wright R-3350	3,400	112	127	84	1 Jun. 56	Pan Am	121

* Includes military versions.

DELTA'S DOUGLAS DC-7 FLEET

MSN	Regn.	Delivery Date	Remarks
44261	N4871C	3 Mar. 54	*Royal Biscayne*, written off in ground accident, Chicago, 16 Dec. 61
44262	N4872C	22 Mar. 54	
44263	N4873C	29 Mar. 54	
44264	N4874C	12 Apr. 54	
44679	N4875C	24 Nov. 54	Sold to BMR, Ontario, Calif. 1966-1968
44680	N4876C	16 Dec. 54	
44681	N4877C	23 Dec. 54	
44682	N4878C	25 Jan. 55	
44683	N4879C	17 Feb. 55	
44684	N4880C	26 Mar. 55	
44435	N4881C	10 Dec. 55	

Fleet Numbers 701-711. N4881C built as prototype DC-7B but delivered as DC-7.

Great Lakes - Southeast

The Douglas DC-7B

By the mid-1950s the relationship between **C. E. Woolman**, President and General Manager of Delta Air Lines, and **Donald Douglas, Sr**., Chairman of Douglas Aircraft Company, had reached a stage whereby any new Douglas airliner could automatically be assumed to have the Delta name on it, sooner or later. Thus, when the DC-7 was followed by the higher gross weighted DC-7B, Delta was quick to order 11 of them. Oddly, this number was reduced to ten, as Delta took delivery of the first production model, but this was certificated as a DC-7. Delta had a total of 21 of the two DC-7 series, and promoted them as"America's Fastest and Finest Airliner," after record-breaking 6 1/2-hour transcontinental delivery flights. Although the DC-6s outlived them by several months in Delta service, the Seven was chosen to introduce the **"Royal Service"** standard of catering, introduced to Delta passengers on 22 September 1958 to improve the competitive impact of the Atlanta airline against its more powerful rivals from the north.

The Royal Service standard was possibly unmatched by that of any other airline. An additional stewardess provided the flexibility to serve beverages separately from the meals, which featured a choice of the main course, and free champagne, accompanied by taped music – quite an innovation in those days.

On the ground, baggage handling was sharpened up, and special airport agents were available to welcome the clientèle – a feature still to be observed frequently at Delta's terminals today.

The Great Lakes-Southeast Case

In March 1958, the Civil Aeronautics Board made another important decision. Although not apparently so far-reaching as, for instance, the one that gave Delta access to New York (see page 60) because it added no new points to the route map, it was nevertheless significant. It enabled the Atlanta-based airline to consolidate many new nonstop routes from Chicago and Detroit directly to Florida and also to establish Atlanta as an even more important hub than before. By the end of the year, Delta had intensified its services throughout the system. The route map bore no resemblance to the predominantly east-west pattern of 1945, which was now difficult to identify in the web of intersecting trunk lines in a closely-woven network that embraced the Great Lakes, the Mississippi Valley, Texas, the Atlanta hub, Florida, and the Caribbean.

Ms. Catherine FitzGerald (left), Delta's first female employee, joined the predecessor company in 1926, rose to become assistant treasurer and secretary to the president, and was the first female executive of a major U.S. airline. C.H. "Charlie" Dolson (right) succeeded C.E. Woolman as president in 1965 and served in that capacity until 1970, and as chairman from 22 January 1970 until 1 November 1971.

A Golden Crown DC-7B immediately after take-off.

Douglas DC-7B

Although outlived in service life by the DC-6, the fleet of DC-7s and DC-7Bs outperformed their earlier relative. The DC-7B shown above served Delta until 1967.

When TWA, always carrying the Lockheed banner, put the improved **Super Constellation**, the **Model 1049G**, into service on 1 April 1955, there was no immediate response this time from the transcontinental rivals, United Air Lines and American Airlines. It was left to Pan American to sponsor the **Douglas DC-7B**, a slightly improved "Seven" (see page 60), that permitted more range, with optional saddle fuel tanks in the engine nacelles, or more payload with increased gross weights. Pan American introduced the new type on 13 June 1955, on the Atlantic route. A total of 112 DC-7Bs were built for eight customers, but none of the other U.S. operators, American Airlines, Continental, **Delta Air Lines**, Eastern Air Lines, National Airlines, and PANAGRA, installed the saddle tanks as extra range was not the prime requirement.

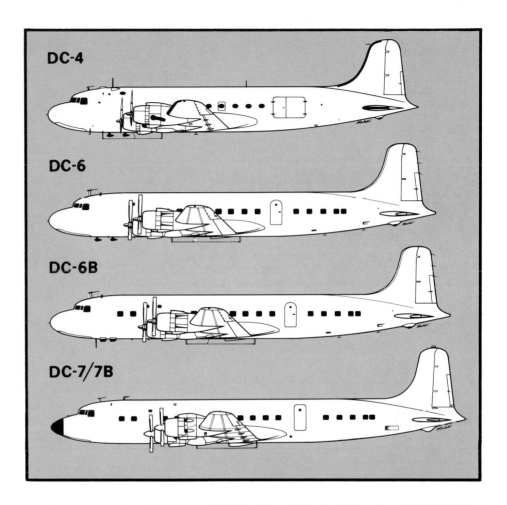

DELTA'S DOUGLAS DC-7B FLEET

MSN	Regn.	Delivery Date	Remarks
45311	N4882C	14 Jun. 57	
45312	N4883C	19 Jul. 57	
45313	N4884C	14 Aug. 57	
45314	N4885C	21 Sep. 57	Sold to BMR, Ontario, Calif.
45350	N4886C	11 Nov. 57	1967-68
45351	N4887C	27 Nov. 57	
45352	N4888C	5 Dec. 57	
45353	N4889C	29 Dec. 57	Sold to Skylark Enterprises, Inc. Jun. 66
45354	N4890C	7 Jan. 58	Sold to BMR, Ontario, Calif., 1967
45355	N4891C	15 Jan. 58	Crashed in Gulf of Mexico, 15 Nov. 59
Fleet Numbers 712-721.			

This DC-7 in Delta C&S colors is named Royal Biscayne.

Air Freight Specialists

The First All Cargo Service

Delta's first experience with all cargo aircraft came during World War II when it operated cargo flights for the U.S. Army Air Force via its Military Transport Division (see also page 48). Delta began dedicated cargo operations in July 1947, utilizing a fleet of two ex-USAAF **Douglas C-47s**. Initial service was offered between Atlanta and Chicago, via Cincinnati, and during March 1949 a third C-47 was added to the fleet. The C-47s performed their role well, but by the mid-1950s they could not offer the capacity needed to remain competitive.

Delta's C-46s

In October 1957, Delta placed the **Curtiss C-46** into service as a cargo transport. All five aircraft had been delivered from Civil Air Transport (CAT) of Taiwan, where they had been part of a fleet of 150 owned by the Chinese Nationalist government, and flown out there in the summer of 1948 by Transocean Air Lines, which had fitted them with long-range tanks for the Pacific crossing. So often disparagingly compared with the DC-3, Delta managed to make the "ugly duckling" C-46 quite attractive, although never entirely able to provide it with the plumage of a swan.

Growth of Air Freight

After World War II, Delta built up a measurable air freight market base with its C-47 "Air Freighters" and later its C-46s. Although from time to time there were bursts of enthusiasm in forecasting enormous volumes of air freight, the theories were not translated into long-term growth trends of more than a percentage point or two compared with the passenger traffic. Also, in the early 1960s, large numbers of passenger jets entered service, and these had as much capacity in their underfloor freight holds as the piston-engined predecessors had in their entire main floor decks.

The Curtiss C-46, product of the wartime years, had twice the capacity of the Douglas DC-3.

One of three ex-USAAF C-47s acquired by Delta for all-cargo services at Atlanta in 1955.

DELTA'S CURTISS C-46 FLEET

MSN	Regn.	Delivery Date	Remarks
22359	N9873F	26 Sep. 57	Sold to Aviation Assoc. of Georgia 31 Jan. 67
22363	N9874F	18 Sep. 57	
33153	N9883F	5 Oct. 57	
33132	N9884F	31 Aug. 57	
32878	N9885F	25 Oct. 57	Damaged beyond repair, Baton Rouge, 24 Nov. 64

Fleet Numbers 101-105; all ex-USAAF C-46Ds, then Civil Air Transport (Taiwan), and sold to Delta via Robert Hewitt Assoc.

DELTA'S LOCKHEED L-100 FLEET

MSN	Regn.	Delivery Date	Remarks
4147	N9268R	18 Aug. 66	Sold to Saturn Airways, 7 Dec. 73
4170	N9258R	17 Sep. 66	Sold to Air Finance Inc., 26 Oct. 73
4176	N9259R	14 Oct. 66	Sold to Air Finance Inc. for Alaska International Air, 30 Mar. 74

Fleet Numbers 301-303; purchased from Lockheed as Model 382Bs (L-100s) subsequently modified to Model 382E (L-100-20) standard by Lockheed, Georgia.

| 4234 | N7999S | 19 Jul. 68 | Model 382B |
| 3946 | N1130E | 28 Aug. 67 | Model 382E |

Fleet Numbers 300 and 304; short-term leases from Lockheed; another two unidentified aircraft were also leased in from Sep. to Dec. 68 and in Sep. 69.

| 4248 | N9262R | 5 Jun. 70 | Model 382B |

Leased for one week from National Aircraft Leasing, Miami; Fleet Number 310.

Lockheed L-100-20 Hercules

50,700lb PAYLOAD ■ 361 mph

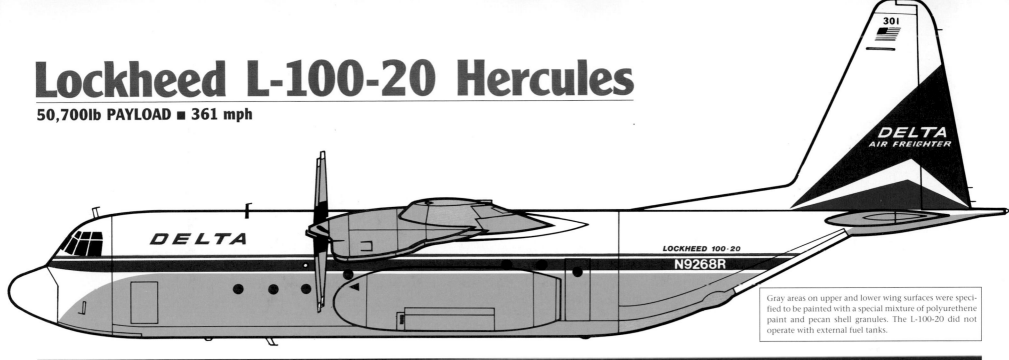

Gray areas on upper and lower wing surfaces were specified to be painted with a special mixture of polyurethene paint and pecan shell granules. The L-100-20 did not operate with external fuel tanks.

Allison 501-D22 (4,050ehp) x 4 ■ 155,000 lb. max. gross take-off weight ■ Range 1,800 miles

The Hercules

For a replacement of the aging Curtiss C-46, and after careful analysis, **Delta Air Lines** turned to its own backyard, and chose the **Lockheed L-100**, the commercial version of the military **C-130 Hercules**, that could land on unimproved short strips, yet carry bulky loads and military vehicles. The **Model 382** (its official designation) was a product of the **Lockheed Georgia Company** of Marietta, Georgia. The C-130 was, and still is, the workhorse of scores of air forces and civil operators all over the world. More than 1,800 have been sold to date.

The C-130 Hercules military transport was also operated commercially with the designation L-100.

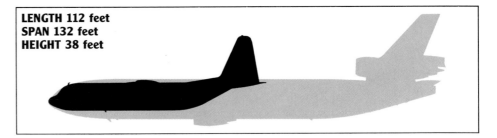

LENGTH 112 feet
SPAN 132 feet
HEIGHT 38 feet

On 15 September 1966 Delta became one of the first commercial operators of the Hercules. Delta used three L-100-10s in scheduled all-freight service and for ferrying engines and spare parts throughout its system. After two years of service, Delta began to return its fleet to Lockheed Georgia for a fuselage stretch of 8.3 feet and these were then re-designated L-100-20. During this time Delta leased several L-100s from Lockheed while its own aircraft were out of service for modification (see table below). By 1973, Delta was operating a fleet of ten wide-bodied Boeing 747s and McDonnell Douglas DC-10s with enormous under-floor cargo capacity. This capability eliminated the need for a fleet of specialized cargo aircraft, and accordingly, L-100 service came to an end on 1 September 1973.

THE CURTISS C-46 IN PERSPECTIVE

Aircraft	Dimensions			Gross Weight (lb)	Payload (lb)	Typical Seats	Normal Range	First Service		No. Built
	Length	Span	Height					Date	Airline	
DC-3	64'5''	95'0''	16'11''	24,400	3,840	21	1,000	25 Jun. 36	American	13,500
C-46	76'4''	108'0''	21' 9''	48,000	10,000	50	1,200	1 Oct. 42	Eastern	3,180
Convair 240	74'8''	91'9''	26'11''	41,790	9,350	40	1,800	1 Jun. 48	American	566

Western's Postwar Struggle

A Good Route and a Big Aircraft

For all the additions of extra states on its route map, as **Western Air Lines** zig-zagged across mid-America during the early 1940s, the significant step forward came when the Civil Aeronautics Board granted a route certificate on 13 August 1943 to operate between the two great Californian conurbations of Los Angeles and San Francisco. Service started in May 1944 with the meager resources of **Douglas DC-3s** left over from the trunk route to Salt Lake City.

Western was able to take delivery of the first postwar-built **DC-4**, the civil version of the wartime four-engined C-54, and started service on 18 January 1946, the first airline in the world to do so with this important airliner. By September of the same year, Western was operating twelve nonstop round-trips between Los Angeles and San Francisco, setting a fine pace and offering, for the first time, some effective competition to powerful airlines such as United and TWA.

Nonstop to Denver

The CAB also appeared to have shown some sympathy for Western's predicament in its distinctly odd route network across the western states (see map on page 37). The airline had managed to gain a foothold at the strategically-placed Denver, but the way it got there was not quite in orthodox style. Its acquisition of National Parks Airways (page 34) in 1937, and of Inland Air Lines (page 36) in 1943, provided a good route for an adventurous tourist, but hardly one for a businessman who would see no point in calling in at Salt Lake, Yellowstone, and Great Falls en route to Denver.

The award of a direct Los Angeles — Denver route on 20 March 1945, therefore, must have been another shot-in-the-arm for Western, coming hard on the heels of the California Corridor route, and cutting off the circuitous pair of regional itineraries that had hitherto been scenically attractive but no substitute for a real trunk air route.

The Convair 240

Less apparent than the additions to the route network and the introduction of four-engined equipment (the DC-4s) was an order placed in 1947 for ten **Convair 240s**. This twin-engined airliner had 40 seats — almost as many as the DC-4's 44 — and, more important, was pressurized. It was to be Western Air Lines' flagship equipment from its entry into service on 1 September 1948 until the arrival of the Douglas DC-6Bs in 1953 (see page 57 for full details of the Convair 240 and subsequent developments).

A Western Convair 240 in an updated color scheme.

North American AT-6 Texan (right) used on Western's Inland Division as an air mail carrier in 1946 and 1947.

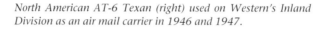

This view of Los Angeles Airport (below) was photographed in 1952. A Western Convair 240 is in the foreground.

THE WESTERN AIR LINES CONVAIR 240 FLEET

MSN	Regn.	Delivery Date	Remarks
3	N8401H	30 Dec. 48	Sold to Lockheed Aircraft, 5 Jun. 58
7	N8402H	11 Oct. 48	Sold to Lockheed Aircraft, 5 Jun. 58
12	N8403H	28 Jun. 48	Sold to Kern Co. Land Co, 30 Jun. 59
17	N8404H	16 Jun. 48	Sold to Air Carrier Service, 1 Apr. 61
22	N8405H	30 Dec. 48	Crashed, Palm Springs, 13 Feb. 58
27	N8406H	24 Dec. 48	Sold to Air Carrier Service, 1 Apr. 61
37	N8407H	2 Oct. 48	Crashed, Wright, Wy., 26 Feb. 54
47	N8408H	5 Oct. 48	Sold to Han Jin Transport, 6 Feb. 61
58	N8409H	29 Jul. 48	Sold to Chandler Leasing, 31 Mar. 60
70	N8410H	28 Jun. 48	Sold to Hughes Aircraft Co., 23 Feb. 61

All aircraft purchased new from Convair; Fleet Numbers 801-810.

*Western Air Lines operated two **North American AT-6 Texan** trainers (71-4371/NC63082 and 78-6659/NC63083) from February 1946. The second aircraft crashed at Rapid City, S. Dak. on 17 March 1947, the other was retired on 9 December 1947. A third (NC63084) was used for spares.*

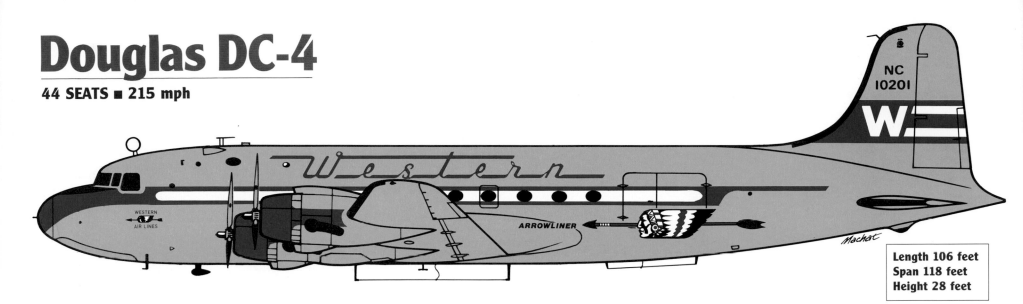

Douglas DC-4

44 SEATS ■ 215 mph

NC 10201

Length 106 feet
Span 118 feet
Height 28 feet

Pratt & Whitney Twin Wasp R-2000 (1,450hp) x 4 ■ 73,000 lb. max. gross take-off weight ■ Range 2,000 miles

Early Four-engined Pioneering

During the mid-1930s, the only large four-engined airliners to see extensive passenger service were the big flying boats such as Pan American's Sikorskys, Martins, and Boeings, and the Shorts "Empire" boats of Imperial Airways. Deutsche Lufthansa introduced the Fw 200 Condor and the Junkers-Ju 90 landplanes in 1938, but war intervened to halt the civil development of these promising aircraft.

A "white-top" DC-4 receives a Western reception upon arrival at Las Vegas, Nevada.

The Douglas DC-4

Douglas flew its experimental 60-seat **DC-4E** in June 1938, but it was too large. Refined into the 44-seat **DC-4**, the Big Four (except for Howard Hughes and TWA) and Pan American ordered a total of 61 44-seat **Douglas DC-4s** on 26 January 1940. But these contracts were canceled as the growing demands for the military **C-54** version placed the emphasis on supplying the armed forces. The C-54 first flew on 14 February 1942, and 1,163 were built. Unpressurized though it was, the DC-4 laid the foundation for a great generation of Douglas airliners.

THE WESTERN AIR LINES DOUGLAS DC-4 FLEET

MSN	Regn.	Delivery Date	Remarks
42904	NC10201		Sold to Waterman Air Lines, 7 Nov. 46
42917	NC10202	Mar. 46	Sold to Australian National { 28 Feb. 47
42918	NC10203	Apr. 46	Airlines (ANA) { 9 Jul. 47
42982	NC10204	2 May 46	Sold to United Air Lines, 1947
42983	NC10205	18 May 46	Sold to Alaska Air Lines, 2 Feb. 56
Fleet Numbers 201-205; purchased new from Douglas.			
10479	NC86568	} 16 Oct. 46	} Sold to United Air Lines, 1947
10512	NC86581		
10457	NC86578		Sold to Alaska Airlines, 6 Aug. 51
27249	NC88816		Sold to Guest Aerovias, Mexico 18 Dec. 56
10474	NC88701	8 Aug. 46	Purchased through War Assets Admin.; sold to United, Aug. 47
18336	NC88702		Sold to Loide Aero Nacional, Brazil, 1957
10458	NC88721	} 16 Oct. 46	Sold to Sobelair, Belgium, 15 Feb. 56
10494	NC88722		Sold to Alaska Airlines, 18 Jan. 56
18383	NC86573	19 Mar. 54	Purchased from Braniff; sold to Loide Aero Nacional, 31 May 57
Fleet Numbers 206-212, 214-215; all ex-USAAF C-54Bs.			

Western Consolidates

Belt-Tightening Again

When the postwar travel boom subsided, the airlines at the second level, of which **Western Air Lines** was one, had to lead a hand-to-mouth existence, unless they happened to benefit from an especially lucrative route award from the Civil Aeronautics Board.

In 1946, Western gained an extension of its Canadian foothold route at Lethbridge to Calgary and Edmonton, fast-growing cities of oil-rich Alberta; and a route from Los Angeles to Mexico City. Western had to wait several years for operating permission from both countries (see page 70).

On 1 January 1947, **Terrell C. Drinkwater** was elected president of Western, and although, on 19 May of that year, the CAB awarded a West Coast route to Portland and Seattle, the traffic and revenue base of the existing route structure was not enough to keep Western's body and soul together. Accordingly, Drinkwater had to make an agonizing decision: to sell one of the best routes to a rival. The Los Angeles — Denver route certificate was sold to United Air Lines on 1 August for $3,750,000. Four DC-4s also went with the sale, which brought in enough to pay off defaulted bank loans and to restore creditworthiness.

Steady Recovery

During the late 1940s, Western took steps that preserved its image as a respected airline of the West, and strengthened its economic base. As mentioned on page 66, one of the most important of these was to deploy the **Convair 240** widely over a route network for which the long range of a four-engined aircraft was superfluous. For a while, as an economy measure, food service was discontinued, from 10 December 1948. On-board catering was gradually resumed, and in June 1954, Western introduced its famous Champagne Flights to wipe out the image of low catering standards.

Route Strengthening

The route to the Pacific Northwest was inaugurated on 1 August 1947 and a few small cities added (see page 37). On 9 April 1952, the CAB approved the consolidation with **Inland Air Lines**, which operated as a Western subdivision since 1944. This paved the way for Western to eliminate the meandering V-shaped route pattern with a direct Salt Lake City — Rapid City segment, granted in December 1952, permitting a one-carrier service between Los Angeles and Minneapolis that was acceptable to the public.

A Great Flagship

Now that Western had two trunk routes of more than regional range, it could move into a program of fleet improvement consistent with its new aspirations as a trunk airline and with the assets to go along with the description on its Certificate of Public Convenience and Necessity. Early in 1953 it put into service, on the West Coast and California — Minneapolis routes, five **Douglas DC-6Bs**, purchased at a cost of $6,000,000. These proved to be so successful that further orders followed, as shown in the table.

Equipped with this fine fleet, Western was able to make a good pitch to Washington in one of the most important decisions ever handed down by the CAB. In the famous **Denver Case**, the big transcontinental airlines all shared improved access to both of the major Californian cities; but Western also obtained a slice of the cake with an award of direct service from San Francisco to Denver, via Reno. Apart from the importance of the inter-city connection, Western now held the distinction of offering service to the two main gambling resort cities of the United States.

Along with the new flagship came service improvements. The passenger was given a positive welcome on boarding, and the cuisine was excellent. Champagne was served on both the Champagne and Fiesta flights, while in the morning, a Hunt breakfast was dispensed by a suitably attired flight attendant. Sound effects of a traditional English hunt, complete with tally-hos and bugle calls, were produced from a tape recorder mounted on the serving cart, but this was, for some unaccountable reason, banned by the FAA.

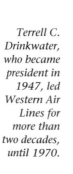

Terrell C. Drinkwater, who became president in 1947, led Western Air Lines for more than two decades, until 1970.

The airliner that wouldn't lie down. The legendary Douglas DC-3 remained in active service with Western Air Lines until the late 1950s.

THE WESTERN AIR LINES DOUGLAS DC-6B FLEET

MSN	Regn.	Delivery Date	Remarks
43822	N91302	24 Nov. 52	Sold to Northwest, 30 Sep. 58
43823	N91303	10 Dec. 52	Crashed, San Francisco Bay, 20 Apr. 53
43824	N91304	15 Dec. 52	Sold to Northwest, 30 Sep. 58
43825	N91305	15 Jan. 53	Sold to the FAA, 3 Aug. 63
43826	N91306	29 Jan. 53	Sold to Alaska Airlines, 9 Jun. 61
44429	N91307	24 Jul. 54	27 Jul. 54
44430	N91308	13 Aug. 54	Sold to Slick Airways 26 Jun. 61
44431	N91309	20 Sep. 54	30 Jun. 61
44434	N91310	6 Oct. 54	Sold to Los Angeles Dodgers, 28 Feb. 61
45063	N91311	27 Apr. 56	Sold to Braniff, 31 Mar. 58
45064	N91312	21 May 56	Sold to Slick Airways 26 Jun. 61
45065	N93114	21 Jun. 56	Sold to Lockheed, 6 Oct. 61
45066	N93115	26 Jun. 56	
45067	N93116	16 Aug. 56	Sold to Japan Air Lines, 27 Feb. 62
45060	N93117	10 Oct. 56	
45173	N93118	11 Apr. 57	Sold to Japan Air Lines, 6 Jul. 62
45174	N93119	25 Apr. 57	Sold to FAA, 5 Jul. 63
45175	N93120	27 Jun. 57	Sold to Purdue University, 14 May 65
45176	N93121	25 Jul. 57	Sold to Northeast, via F.B. Ayer, 7 Jun. 65
45177	N93122	26 Aug. 57	Sold back to Douglas, 26 Jul. 65
45178	N93123	27 Aug. 57	Leased to Canadian Pacific Air Lines, 1 Sep. 65; sold to Concare Leasing, May 69
45179	N93124	6 Sep. 57	Sold back to Douglas, 6 Jul. 65
45321	N93125	31 Jan. 58	Sold to Iran National Airways, 1 Oct. 65
45322	N93126	11 Feb. 58	Sold to Purdue University, 6 Oct. 66
45323	N93127	18 Mar. 58	Sold to Concare Leasing, 1969
45324	N93128	3 Apr. 58	Sold to Stevens Inc., 31 Jul. 67
45534	N93129	1 Aug. 58	Sold to LAN Chile, 9 Aug. 65
45535	N93130	19 Aug. 58	Sold to LAN Chile, 11 Aug. 65
45536	N93131	29 Aug. 58	
45537	N93132	24 Sep. 58	Sold to Dade Aviation Sales, 1969
45538	N93133	30 Sep. 58	Sold to Concare Leasing, 1969

All aircraft were purchased from Douglas Aircraft; Fleet Nos. 902-912, 914-933.

Douglas DC-6B

80 SEATS ■ 315 mph

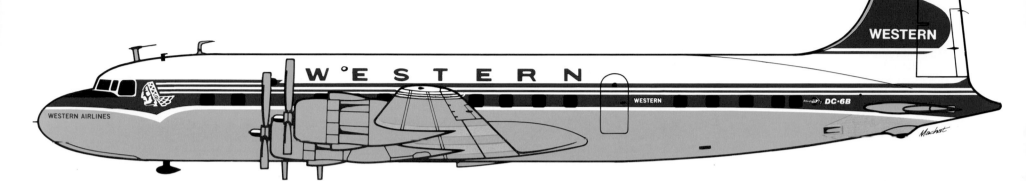

Pratt & Whitney R-2800 (2,500hp) x 4 ■ 107,000 lb. max gross take-off weight ■ Range 2,200 miles ■ Length 106 feet ■ Span 118 feet ■ Height 29 feet

The See-Saw Battle for Leadership

For ten years of scintillating competition, from the end of World War II until 1957, when the Starliner marked the last gasp of the four-engined piston landplane generation, Douglas and Lockheed were locked in combat. Kelly Johnson's design genius, stimulated by Howard Hughes's persistent search for perfection, produced the Constellation, the aircraft that cracked the hitherto unchallenged Douglas supremacy as the supplier of commercial airliners to America.

The early months of 1946 were truly revolutionary for the U.S. airlines. To underline the magnitude of the metamorphosis, consider the situation with United Air Lines: on 1 January 1946, its entire fleet consisted of 77 twin-engined Douglas DC-3s. When it put the pressurized **Douglas DC-6** into service on 27 April 1947, it was desperately trying to match TWA's **Model 49 Constellations**, introduced on 1 March 1946.

And so the competition went on, broadly-based and intensified throughout the U.S.A. and even overseas, where a healthy export market was now vigorously pursued by both manufacturers. Pan American brought in the improved **Model 749** "Connie" on 17 June 1947, but it took Douglas four years to match it with the **DC-6B**, again with United, on 11 April 1951. The battle continued. Eastern Air Lines launched the **Model 1049 Super Constellation** on 17 December 1951, still setting a hot pace; and Douglas replied with the **DC-7** on 29 November 1953. Later, on 1 April 1955, TWA's **1049G**; then on 13 June 1955, Pan Am, with the **DC-7B**; and finally, on 1 June 1957 — TWA again — the **Model 1649A Starliner**, took the Douglas-Lockheed rivalry to its ultimate conclusion before the Boeing 707 made it all irrelevant.

The Douglas DC-6B

There were bigger and better Douglas airliners during the 1950s but none gained the respect and confidence-inspiring reputation of the DC-6B. The proof of the pudding was in the eating, or more bluntly the sales figures. Including the DC-6A cargo version, 362 Douglas DC-6Bs were built. This was twice as many as the 175 DC-6s and more than the combined total of DC-7s, DC-7Bs, and DC-7Cs. As Winston Churchill once said of political judgment — "leave it to the people" — Douglas left it to the airlines. And most of them, including **Western** (see opposite page), and **Northeast** (see pages 81-82) chose the DC-6B.

The Douglas DC-6B was acknowledged as the thoroughbred airliner of the piston-engined era. Western operated a substantial fleet of them.

Turbine Power

Maintaining the Momentum

The year 1956 did not start well, with a 73-day strike from 9 January until 21 March, but **Western Air Lines** bounced back into the aviation news headlines when, in May, it announced the purchase of nine **Lockheed 188 Electras** at a price of $19,500,000, including spares. The timing of the order was important as although the Electra was a turboprop airliner, not a pure jet, it was destined to enter service well before United Air Lines, the main competitor, could introduce the Douglas DC-8.

The program was successful, at least until the spring of 1960, when a structural defect (see opposite page) compelled all Electras to be modified. Preceded by another crippling strike, lasting no less than 110 days, from 21 February until 10 June 1958, the turboprop airliner went into service with Western on 1 August 1958, first on the Los Angeles — San Francisco — Portland — Seattle route, and then from Los Angeles to Minneapolis and Phoenix, the latter city having been added to the network on 1 December 1957.

Changing the Route Structure

Western Air Lines had been frustrated from operating to Mexico because of the failure of the U.S. and Mexican governments to reach agreement on a bilateral accord. The Mexicans feared dominance by the powerful U.S. airlines and its only company of substance, Cia. Mexicana de Aviación (CMA) was controlled by Pan American. Five conferences were held between 1945 and 1951 and President Truman finally lost patience in 1952 and withdrew his approval of the inoperative international certificates awarded by the CAB to U.S. airlines, including Western, in 1946.

With the Republican administration in 1953, however, the climate changed. President Eisenhower reviewed the situation and canceled Truman's revocation in a letter to the CAB Chairman, James R. Durfee, on 8 March 1957. The bilateral agreement, signed on the same day, was effective on 5 June. Western Air Lines was first off the mark, starting DC-6B service from Los Angeles to México City on 15 July 1957, and introducing coach service on 1 December 1958.

Gaining confidence from this notable route addition, Western laid plans for further expansion. It mapped out a network to serve all the main cities of Texas and, on 12 March 1959, made its first application to the CAB for routes to Hawaii. The Texas routes were never more than a dream; but the Hawaii ones were the subject of interminable wrangling between politicians, administrators, and airline executives

for many years. Western's part in this saga of procrastination is summarized on page 92.

In a neat balance of route modification, Western took steps to terminate service at some of its smaller cities. As a result of the **Seven States Area Case**, thirteen points in the north central states were transferred to local service airlines in 1959, and the map took on a sharper appearance, consistent with Western's policies. Matching these operational and service changes, the fleet changed also. The last Douglas DC-4s were sold in 1957, the DC-3s were gradually phased out until the last one was retired on 31 March 1959, and the Convair 240's last flight occurred on 16 February 1961. Western Air Lines was ready for the jet age. The Electras, incidentally, continued to give good service, and the last one was not sold until 24 October 1972.

WESTERN'S LOCKHEED 188A ELECTRA FLEET

MSN	Regn.	Delivery Date	Remarks
1046	N7135C	20 May 59	Sold to Concare Acft. Lsg., 27 Nov. 70
1070	N7136C	10 Jul. 59	
1074	N7137C	29 Jul. 59	
1087	N7138C	4 Sep. 59	
1094	N7139C	26 Sep. 59	Sold to Intl. Jet Air, 29 Nov. 73
1118	N7140C	21 Jan. 60	Sold to Reeve Aleutian, 25 Nov. 72
1127	N7141C	24 Mar. 61	Sold to Pacific Western { 24 Oct. 72 / 18 Jan. 74
1128	N7142C	17 May 61	
1129	N7143C	24 May 61	Sold to Intl. Jet Air, 29 Nov. 73
1140	N9744C	3 Feb. 61	Sold to Reeve Aleutian, 26 Sep. 70
1143	N9745C	15 Feb. 61	Sold to Nordic Air, 16 Aug. 72
1145	N9746C	9 Feb. 61	

Fleet Numbers 135-146; all aircraft purchased new from Lockheed.

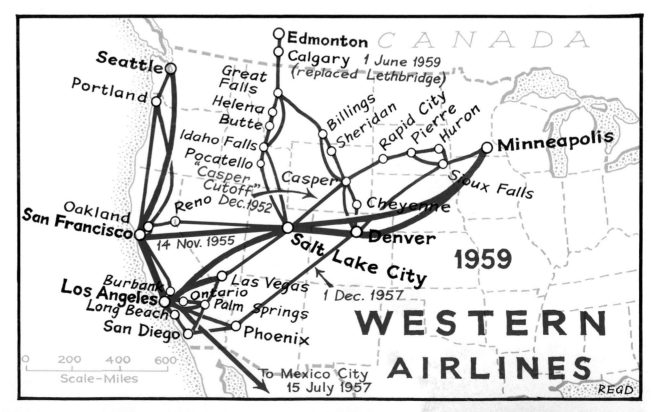

Lockheed 188 Electra

66 SEATS ■ 370 mph

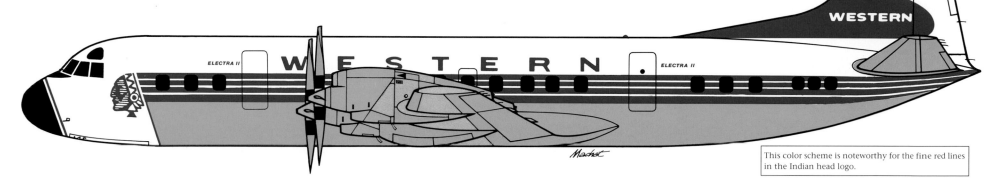

N7145C

WESTERN

ELECTRA II
ELECTRA II

Machat

This color scheme is noteworthy for the fine red lines in the Indian head logo.

Allison 501-D13 (3,750ehp) x 4 ■ 113,000 lb. max. gross take-off weight ■ Range 1,600 miles

Toprank Turboprop

When Capital Airlines opened service on 26 July 1955 with the Vickers Viscount, most of the other U.S. domestic airlines took prompt steps to counteract the threat of a severe loss of market share. Unimpressed with the British Bristol Britannia's rather hesitant debut, the U.S. industry opted for the 60/85-seat **Lockheed 188 Electra**. American Airlines placed the first order on 10 June 1955 — less than a week before Capital received its first Viscount — and Eastern Air Lines followed on 27 September, for 35 and 40 respectively, and from that time, the Britannia, which had been ordered by Northeast Airlines (see page 82) and the other British contender, the Vickers Vanguard, never had a chance.

Lockheed delivered the first Electra to American on 5 December 1958, but a pilots' strike enabled Eastern to be the first operator, starting New York   Miami service on 12 January 1959.

Crisis

Within little more than a year of service, there were two crashes caused by an unexplained in-flight structural failure. The FAA ordered an immediate investigation by Lockheed and it was discovered that the cause was "whirl mode." An outboard engine could begin to vibrate continuously if its mounting was weakened and jolted by turbulence; the vibration was then transmitted to the wing which would fail at the fuselage join area in less than a minute. Lockheed had to undertake an enormous and costly modification program. Fortunately for Lockheed, "Pete" Quesada, the FAA Administrator, permitted the Electras to continue in service, but with reduced cruising speed — from 400 to 260mph — until the problem was solved. The restriction was in force from 25 March to 31 December 1960.

The first **Electra II** (as it was now referred to by Western and other customers) returned to service on 24 February 1961, and although continuing to work well, they were, in the main, relegated to secondary routes and services. They were comfortable and dependable, and could use airfields that the jet airliners could not. Up to 1990, it was still the chosen instrument of the world's first air shuttle service, the Brazilian Ponte Aérea between Rio de Janeiro and São Paulo, able to use downtown airports otherwise restricted for the jets.

LENGTH 105 feet
SPAN 99 feet
HEIGHT 33 feet

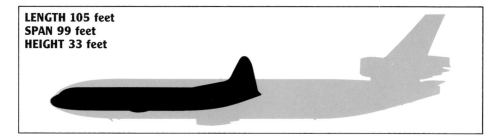

Western entered the turbine-engined era with the Lockheed 188 Electra.

The Jet Age - First of a Delta Trio

First with the Douglas DC-8

Traditionally, new aircraft types had always been sponsored, by the pledge of a large order, by one of the Big Four airlines, as these had habitually been the only ones with enough capital resources or creditworthiness among their prime lenders to be able to guarantee the substantial investment required. In its prompt order for the DC-8, **Delta Air Lines** provided evidence that the gap between the Big Four and the "Other Trunks" was narrowing, and that its stature could be measured by business policies that allowed for no special pleading. Eastern Air Lines decided to go for a more powerful version of the DC-8. By this decision, Eastern's president, Eddie Rickenbacker, gave his major competitor, Delta, several months of pure-jet operation against his turboprop Electras when deliveries of the improved DC-8s were delayed.

Delta on a Jet Roll

By putting the 119-seat DC-8 into service on the New York — Atlanta route on 18 September 1959, Delta Air Lines was the first airline in the world to launch the big Douglas jet. True, United Air Lines, whose order was much bigger, started service on the same day, but because of the difference in time zones, Delta was off the mark by a margin of only a few hours. Still, like a photo-finish race, there was no gainsaying the achievement. Furthermore, the New York — Atlanta run was no isolated token service. DC-8s were also deployed on Delta's domestic trunk routes, and on its interchange serv- ices. And this was only the beginning. Eight months later, the **Convair 880s** joined the Douglas fleet (see page 74); and in 1965, Delta launched one of the world's most successful short-haul jets, the **Douglas DC-9** (see page 78).

When the early jets, such as this Delta DC-8 Series 11, were taking off, they left a trail of black smoke caused by water-injection to provide sufficient thrust. This was rectified by the use of more powerful fan-jet engines, such as on the DC-8-51 (above), caught retracting its landing gear after take-off.

Douglas DC-8-11

119 SEATS ■ 590 mph

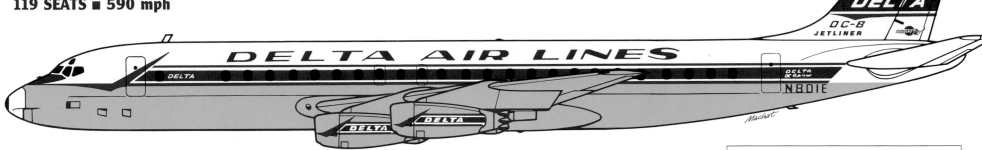

This color scheme has the distinction of being used on only one aircraft in all of Delta's jet fleet.

Pratt & Whitney JT3C-6 (13,500 lb) x 4 ■ 137 tons max. gross take-off weight ■ Range 2,740 miles

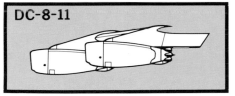

DC-8-11

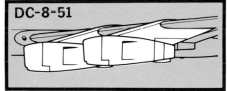

DC-8-51

LENGTH 151 feet
SPAN 142 feet
HEIGHT 42 feet

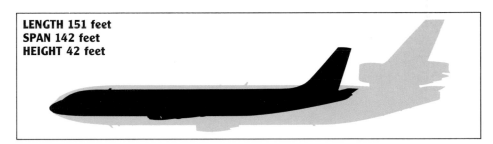

DELTA'S DOUGLAS DC-8 FLEET

Regn.	MSN	Delivery Date	Regn.	MSN	Delivery Date
DC-8-51			N819E	45806	11 Dec. 65
N8008D	45252	2 Oct. 67	N820E	45815	21 Jan. 66
N801E	45408	22 Jul. 59	N821E	45877	25 Aug. 66
N802E	45409	14 Sep. 59			
N803E	45410	10 Oct. 59			
N804E	45411	28 Oct. 59			
N805E	45412	5 Nov. 59			
N806E	45413	12 Nov. 59			
N807E	45645	27 Apr. 62			
N808E	45646	15 May 62			
N809E	45649	20 Jun. 62			
N810E	45650	12 Dec. 62			
N811E	45672	13 Nov. 63			
N812E	45673	4 Dec. 63			
N813E	45688	15 May 64			
N814E	45687	29 Oct. 64			
N815E	45689	5 Nov. 64			
N816E	45690	24 Mar. 65			
N817E	45807	28 Oct. 65			
N818E	45808	23 Nov. 65			

Fleet Numbers 800-821; N801E - N806E delivered as DC-8-11, upgraded to DC-8-12, and later to DC-8-51 standard. All but the first (ex-Trans International Airlines) were purchased from Douglas; N801E was sold to Douglas, 6 May 77; N802E crashed New Orleans, 30 Mar. 67; the remainder sold to F.B. Ayer, 1976-81.

DC-8-33

Regn.	MSN	Delivery Date
N8038A	45256	
N8148A	45267	
N8166A	45269	31 Dec. 68
N8170A	45270	
N8184A	45271	
N8016	45254	31 Aug. 69
N8027	45255	7 Aug. 69

Fleet Numbers 831-837; purchased from Pan American; withdrawn from service Jan. 74 and sold to Boeing.

One of seven ex-Pan Am DC-8-33s used on the Delta-Pan Am interchange services to Europe and selected long-haul domestic routes.

First with the Convair 880

The World's Fastest

Third of the big American jetliners was the **Convair 880 (Model 22)**, developed by Convair at San Diego as an effort to stay in the business of building commercial airliners, now that the Convair-Liner was showing signs of obsolescence. Originally called the Skylark 600, then Golden Arrow, it set out to be the fastest of all the four-engined jets. It was sponsored by Trans World Airlines (TWA), still under the control of Howard Hughes, who subsequently had much to do with the Convair 880's fortunes (and misfortunes). The Convair 880 was officially launched with orders signed by TWA (for 30) and by **Delta Air Lines** (for ten) on 10 September 1956.

The Convair 880, as the Model 22 was renamed in 1957, made its first flight on 27 January 1959, and, because of financial complications experienced by TWA, first entered service with Delta on 15 May 1960.

An Eventful Month of May

Delta's first Convair 880 services were to Atlanta, Houston, and New Orleans, each served nonstop from New York (Idlewild),in an all-first class 84-seat layout. The airliner seemed to offer the prospect of being a good running mate for the Douglas DC-8, which had joined the fleet only eight months previously. Also, although Delta was elated with the Douglas Jets, just before the Convair 880 debut it announced that the DC-8s were to be sent back to the factory at Long Beach for minor modifications, to be fitted with new wing tips, new wing slots, and improved windshields. DC-8 operations to Florida were to be maintained, but the improvements to each aircraft would take between four and six weeks; and so it was fortunate that the Convair 880s were coming on line to fill the gaps in the schedules. Delta was encouraged to order three more 880s in June 1960, to bring the total to 17.

Farewell to a Veteran

In common with all the U.S. trunk airlines entering the jet age, Delta realized that, excellent performers though they were, and potential money-makers on the long- and medium-haul routes, the four-engined flagships could not be economically deployed on the short-haul segments. Pondering over its choice for a short-haul jet, it also began to look carefully at the feeder routes on its system, and at the traffic results from some of the smaller points served. Thus, some of the communities in the south, such as Hattiesburg and Selma, which had proudly been added to the Delta map in 1956 lost service.

This was largely the result of a decision — like old age, it comes to all of us — finally to retire the **Douglas DC-3**, the twin-engined 21-seater that had served so well since 1940. The last Delta DC-3 taxied onto the ramp at Atlanta, after a flight from Knoxville, on 29 October 1960.

Aristocrat of Jets

One of Delta's Convair 880s at Dallas-Love Field with a Delta DC-8 in the background. (Photo by Mel Lawrence)

DELTA'S CONVAIR 880 FLEET

Regn.	MSN	Delivery Date
N8801E	22-00-4	13 Dec. 60
N8802E	22-00-7	10 Feb. 60
N8803E	22-00-11	4 May 60
N8804E	22-00-16	6 May 60
N8805E	22-00-17	2 Jun. 60
N8806E	22-00-21	5 Jul. 60
N8807E	22-00-29	5 Aug. 60
N8808E	22-00-36	1 Oct. 60
N8809E	22-00-38	22 Oct. 60
N8810E	22-00-41	22 Oct. 60
N8811E	22-00-50	9 Sep. 61
N8812E	22-00-51	20 Sep. 61
N8813E	22-00-52	24 Oct. 61
N8814E	22-00-62	17 Jul. 62
N8815E	22-00-63	2 Jul. 62
N8816E	22-00-64	13 Jul. 62
N8817E	22-00-65	20 Jul. 62

All Model 22-2; Fleet Numbers 901-917. N8804E crashed, Atlanta, 23 May 60; N8807E written off, Chicago, 20 Dec. 72 in a ground collision; the remainder sold to Boeing, Nov. 73 - Jan. 74.

Convair 880

84 SEATS ■ 586 mph

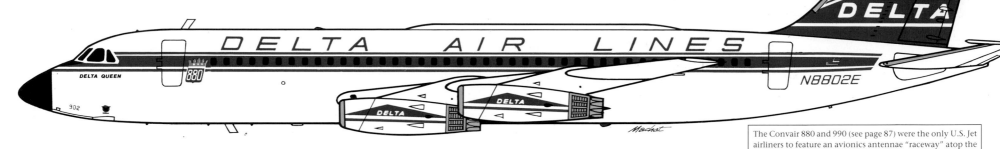

The Convair 880 and 990 (see page 87) were the only U.S. Jet airliners to feature an avionics antennae "raceway" atop the fuselage.

General Electric CJ-805-3B (11,200 lb.) x 4 ■ 92 tons max. gross take-off weight ■ Range 2,600 miles

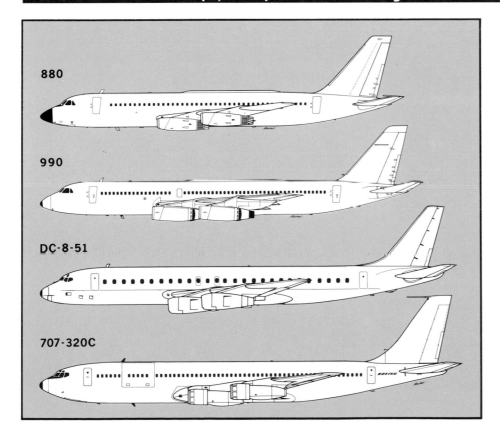

880

990

DC-8-51

707-320C

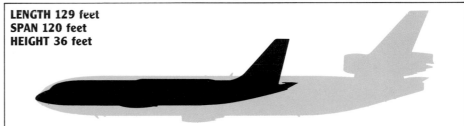

LENGTH 129 feet
SPAN 120 feet
HEIGHT 36 feet

A Delta Convair 880 in "widget" colors.

Southern Transcontinental

Culmination of a Dream

When C. E. Woolman first started the Delta Air Service route from Dallas to Jackson, Mississippi, way back in 1929 (page 10) he may have glanced westwards and wondered if a route to California was more than a dream. But it was a beginning, even if the Delta domain was only a fifth of the total distance of a southern transcontinental route. At that time, his dream, in any case, would have been unfulfilled, as the American Airways group was given the favored nod from Washington. After the Air Mail Scandals, Delta was able to extend to the Atlantic, at Charleston, S.C., so that its route was now spanning half the distance between the two oceans (page 26).

Twenty-seven years were to pass before the other half was added. In an historic decision, on 11 March 1961, the Civil Aeronautics Board awarded to **Delta Air Lines**, in company with National, another airline seeking fresh fields to conquer, route certificates from Los Angeles to Miami in the **Southern Transcontinental Route Case**. All existing interchange agreements (see page 54) were now redundant and were terminated.

Exactly three months after the award, on 11 June 1961, Delta Air Lines made its first Atlanta — Los Angeles flight on a schedule that was not dependent on the interchange device.

Atlanta's importance as a major traffic hub was strengthened as Delta fed traffic from the west coast to Florida cities, adding Orlando (serving Cape Canaveral at that time but, as yet, not DisneyWorld), in October 1961. At the western end, it was even permitted, on 1 May 1962, to carry local traffic from Las Vegas to San Francisco. Taking full advantage of the expanded scope of its own network, it obtained permission to operate through services from California to foreign destinations in the Caribbean in April 1963, so that the citizens of Los Angeles or San Francisco could now add Jamaica, for example, to their traditional resorts in Mexico.

In an unrelated decision, the CAB approved, in December 1963, another important interchange agreement. This was a new departure in that it involved a domestic airline, **Delta**, and an international one, **Pan American Airways**. Through plane service was permitted from Delta stations New Orleans and Atlanta to Pan American points in Europe, via Washington, D.C., common to both airlines. Delta received its first taste of the North Atlantic route and Londoners were frequently surprised to see DC-8s in Delta colors at Heathrow.

The transcontinental route was the final achievement for Delta in fashioning a nationwide air network. While some areas, notably the northwest, were still beyond its immediate interest, the Atlanta airline now served, among other cities, the five giant metropolises of the United States: New York, Chicago, Los Angeles, Philadelphia, and Detroit. And it still served Monroe, Louisiana, where the story began.

The Douglas DC-8-61, the "Stretched Eight" was introduced on Delta routes in April 1967.

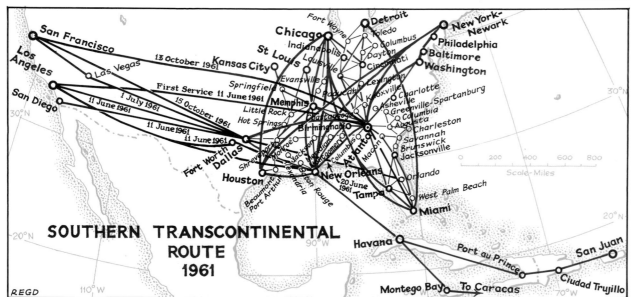

SOUTHERN TRANSCONTINENTAL ROUTE 1961

DELTA'S DOUGLAS DC-8-61 FLEET

Regn.	MSN	Delivery Date
N822E	45907	10 Apr. 67
N823E	45914	11 Jun. 67
N824E	45915	19 Jul. 67
N825E	45944	25 Jan. 68
N826E	45979	30 May 68
N1300L	46014	18 Oct. 68
N1301L	46018	19 Dec. 68
N1302L	46029	16 Jan. 69
N1303L	46030	23 Jan. 69
N1304L	46048	24 Jan. 69
N1305L	46072	8 Aug. 69
N1306L	46055	5 Nov. 69
N1307L	46056	6 Nov. 69

Fleet Numbers 861-873; all bought from Douglas. Converted to DC-8-71 standard with CFM56-2 engines Apr. 82 - Nov. 83; sold to United Parcel Service Dec. 86 and leased back until 1988-89.

Douglas DC-8-61

195 SEATS ■ 580 mph

The DC-8-61 was the only stretched DC-8 to retain engine pylons that extended over the top of the wing leading edge.

Pratt & Whitney JT3D-3 (18,000 lb.) x 4 ■ 162 tons max. gross take-off weight ■ Range 4,200 miles ■ Length 187 feet ■ Span 142 feet ■ Height 42 feet

The Stretched Eight

While Boeing "saw Douglas off in a big way" — as one English commentator remarked when the 707 outsold the DC-8 — and set a pace that Douglas found difficult to match, the California company could derive some satisfaction from putting on a great performance over the last development stage before both airliners were made obsolete by the wide-bodied generation. With all successful commercial types, the original version is quickly superseded by improved variants, with the main objective of lengthening the fuselage so as to offer more capacity and therefore lower operating costs. In this endeavor, **Douglas** won hands down.

The Boeing 707's wing was swept back more than the DC-8's and this limited the amount of "stretch" that could be made, as on take-off the tail would have scraped the ground if the fuselage had been lengthened by more than eight feet. In contrast, the DC-8 was far less restricted, and to Douglas's delight, was stretched by no less than 37 feet. The remarkable DC-8-61, looking like a long thin cigar, made its first flight on 14 March 1966, and went into service with United Air Lines on 24 February 1967. **Delta Air Lines** was not far behind, putting the first of 13 aircraft into service on 18 April 1967. While the long cabin could accommodate 252 seats in an all-economy layout, Delta's mixed-class choice allowed 195. Compared with the 119 seats of the standard DC-8, this was more than 60 per cent more capacity, yet the operating costs were no more than ten per cent higher. The Stretched Eight was a real winner, and a total of 261 of the Super Sixties were built, 88 -61s, 66 -62s, and 107 of the -63s.

THE DOUGLAS DC-8 FAMILY

| Series | Engines (P & W)* | | Dimensions (ft) | | Gross Weight (short tons) | Max Seats | Range (st.miles) | First Service | | No. Built |
	Type	Thrust (lb)	Length	Span				Date	Airline	
DC-8-10	JT3C-6	13,000	151	142	137	179	3,800	18 Sep. 59	Delta	29
DC-8-20	JT4A-3	15,000	151	142	140	179	4,000	24 Jun. 60	Eastern	34
DC-8-30	JT4A-11	17,500	151	142	157	179	4,500	27 Apr. 60	Pan Am	57
DC-8-40	Conway	17,500	151	142	163	179	4,800	1 Apr. 60	TCA	32
DC-8-50	JT3D-3B	18,000	151	142	163	179	4,800	30 Apr. 61	United	141
DC-8-61	JT3D-3B	18,000	187	142	164	252	4,500	25 Feb. 67	United	88
DC-8-62	JT3D-7	19,000	157	148	175	189	5,500	22 May 67	SAS	68
DC-8-63	JT3D-7	19,000	187	148	177	252	5,000	27 Jul. 67	KLM	107

*Except the Rolls-Royce Conway powered DC-8-40.

A Delta Fanjet DC-8-61 landing at Las Vegas. (Photo by John Wegg)

First with the Douglas DC-9

The Douglas DC-9

Delta Air Lines was more concerned with its short-haul jet program. In April 1963, it had placed the first order for the **Douglas DC-9**, no doubt resulting from a friendly chat between Donald Douglas Sr. and C.E. Woolman. On 8 December 1965 it began scheduled services with the **DC-9-14**. Delta had 17 of this early series, and supplemented them with no less than 63 of the later **DC-9-32s**. The first DC-9-32 went into service with Delta on 20 April 1967 and served Delta well for more than two decades, into the early 1990s.

Supersonic Diversion

On 28 April 1964, **Delta Air Lines** ordered three of the United States' supersonic airliners; or to be more correct, it put its name down on a list of prospective customers for a **U.S. SST**, if one was built by a yet-to-be-selected manufacturer that was to bid for that doubtful privilege. The names were being collected by the FAA which was still uncertain of what shape or size the SST would be, or who would pay for it; and hadn't the faintest inkling of the market prospects or even how to calculate them. Eventually, in February 1969 — five years after Delta's order — the **Boeing 2707** was selected as the U.S. entry for the supersonic airliner race, but the sands were running out in the face of insuperable problems of cost,

The trio of Delta stalwarts who took on the difficult task of succeeding C.E. Woolman. Left to right, C.H. "Charlie" Dolson, president from 1965 to 1970; W.T. "Tom" Beebe, 1970 to 1971; and David Garrett, 1971 to 1983.

sonic booms, noise, and, even to an all-powerful and immensely capable aircraft industry, construction. The U.S. SST was canceled when, on 24 March 1971, the Senate voted against any further funding.

THE DELTA DOUGLAS DC-9 FLEET

Regn.	MSN	Regn.	MSN
DC-9-14		N3334L	47175
		N3335L	47176
N3301L	45696	N3336L	47177
N3302L	45697	N3337L	47273
N3303L	45698	N3338L	47274
N3304L	45699	N3339L	47275
N3305L	45700	N3340L	47276
N3306L	45701	N5341L	47277
N3307L	45702	N5342L	47278
N3308L	45703	N1261L	47317
N3309L	45704	N1262L	47257
N3310L	45705	N1263L	47258
N3311L	45706	N1264L	47259
N3312L	45707	N1265L	47260
N3313L	45708	N1266L	47261
N3314L	45709	N1267L	47262
N8953U	45797	N1268L	47284
N8901E	45742	N1269L	47285
N8902E	45743	N1270L	47318
Fleet Numbers 201-217; delivered		N1271L	47319
Jul. 66 - Jan. 67. N3305L crashed,		N1272L	47320
Fort Worth, Tex., 30 May 72;		N1273L	47321
N8953U was a DC-9-15 leased		N1274L	47322
from Jet Intl., Aug. 67 - Oct. 71;		N1275L	47323
N8901E/8902E leased from		N1276L	47324
Eastern Air Lines, Jun. 70 - Apr.		N1277L	47356
71; remainder sold to Southern		N1278L	47357
Airways, 1972-73.		N1279L	47358
		N1280L	47359
DC-9-32		N1281L	47377
		N1282L	47378
N3315L	45710	N1283L	47379
N3316L	47025	N1284L	47380
N3317L	47026	N1285L	47381
N3318L	47027	N1286L	47426
N3319L	47028	N1287L	47427
N3320L	47029	N1288L	47443
N3321L	47030	N1289L	47444
N3322L	47031	N1290L	47445
N3323L	47032	N1291L	47466
N3324L	47103	N1292L	47529
N3325L	47104	N1293L	47486
N3326L	47105	N1294L	47516
N3327L	47106	N1295L	47525
N3328L	47107		
N3329L	47108	*Fleet Numbers 231-293;*	
N3330L	47109	*delivered Apr. 67 - Jul. 71;*	
N3331L	47172	*N3323L written-off,*	
N3332L	47173	*Chattanooga, Tn., 27 Nov. 73;*	
N3333L	47174	*thirty-two remain in service in*	
		1990, remainder sold 1976-81.	

Repeating its feats in 1959 with the DC-8 and in 1960 with the Convair 880, Delta introduced the world's first Douglas DC-9 service with a Series 14. One of Delta's early DC-9-14s (N3304L) was named Delta Prince *in keeping with the airline's royal theme. (Photo by Mel Lawrence)*

Douglas DC-9-14

65 SEATS ■ 560 mph

Note the underwing leading edge vortex generator designed to delay onset of stalls at high angles of attack, and the early blade-type antennae. Compare to MD-88 (page 105).

Pratt & Whitney JT8D-1 (14,000 lb.) x 2 ■ 91,500 lb. max. gross take-off weight ■ Range 1,700 miles

The Douglas DC-9

The world's first short-haul jet airliner was the French SE 210 Caravelle, first flown in 1955, and which entered U.S. service in 1961, with United Air Lines, the only North American customer. After a brief flirtation with the idea of building the Caravelle under license, Douglas announced its **DC-9** in April 1963.

The revival of an almost discarded project, there were many who thought that the Long Beach plant would be full of "white-tails" — aircraft off the production line for which there were no orders. As in the case of the Caravelle, the skeptics were wrong. Douglas's reputation was such that the DC-9 gained a substantial foothold in what became an enormous short-haul jet airliner market. The company placed great emphasis on design aspects aimed to reduce maintenance costs to a level never previously achieved by any other airliner. From the date of the first order for 15 aircraft from the launching customer, **Delta Air Lines,** Douglas never looked back. The **Series 10** Douglas DC-9 made its first flight on 25 February 1965, obtained its FAA certificate on 23 November 1965, and went into service with Delta before the year was out, as described on the opposite page.

Because of the then FAA restrictions on the maximum gross weight of a two-crew operated aircraft, the DC-9 had been weight restricted. However, Douglas had planned for substantial growth and when regulations were modified, offered the stretched Series 30, initially with a gross weight of 98,000lb, some 18,000lb more than the original Series 10. Delta chose the 108,000lb **Series 32** and the first was delivered on 9 April 1967. The 89-seat DC-9-32 entered service eleven days later and the fleet grew to a total of 63 by July 1971. A comparison of the various DC-9 models is given on page 105.

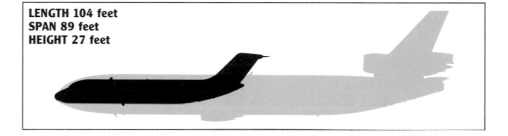

LENGTH 104 feet
SPAN 89 feet
HEIGHT 27 feet

Delta was also one of the earliest operators of the DC-9-32.

Northeast's Postwar Struggle

Atlas Corporation Control

When the Civil Aeronautics Board (CAB) was formed (for the first two years as the Civil Aviation Authority) on 7 July 1938, it perpetuated and even strengthened one of the provisions of the Black-McCarran Act of 1934 that eliminated control of an airline by an air transport manufacturer. As the **Boston and Maine Railroad** had, in effect established "grandfather rights" to the ownership of Northeast Airlines, the CAB, in an important decision in August 1943, did not insist that the railroad should pull out. But in a cynical maneuver, the Board let it be known that Northeast could not expect any new route awards.

Facing cold facts, the Boston and Maine decided to sell its interests and negotiated the sale of 90 per cent of Northeast stock. Most of this went to the **Atlas Corporation**, headed by the financier Floyd Odlum, who was married to Jacqueline Cochran, a famous pilot who thus acquired a seat on the board. The way should have been clear for route expansion, but other factors intervened.

An Opportunity Missed

If any airline deserved to receive a favorable nod from Washington for services rendered during World War II, then that airline should have been Northeast, whose exploits during those critical years are described on pages 42-43. Northeast's president, S.J. Solomon, fully recognized the potential, realizing that, geographically, Northeast was in an advantageous position. Accordingly, on 17 March 1943, he filed with the CAB an application for a package of routes to northern Europe, including most of the capital cities from London to Moscow. For good measure, he also requested a network of helicopter routes in New England. On 27 July 1943, he applied for two routes to Chicago — an ambition not realized for a quarter of a century — and in 1944 requested a route to New Orleans, via Atlanta.

All these ideas came to nought. The New Englanders took what can only be described as a parochial attitude, and their long-range sights were set no further than New York. On 12

NORTHEAST'S CURTISS C-46 FLEET

MSN	Regn.	Delivery Date	Remarks
419	N1381N	1 Apr. 54	Ex-USAAF; leased from L.B. Smith Acft. for one month
22490	N4718N	28 Apr. 57	Ex-USAAF; leased from Slick Airways until 1 Oct. 57

This Convair 240 was leased from Pan American by Northeast. The Convair-Liners were the flagships and the workhorses of the line for a decade. (Photo John Wegg Collection)

June 1944, the CAB approved a service from Boston to New York, via Worcester, New Bedford, and Waterbury, with nonstop authority, to fill the gap left by the defunct **Airline Feeder System**, and by **Mayflower Airlines**, which Northeast purchased in August of the same year (see page 39). Disillusioned, Solomon left to become the president of California Eastern Aviation.

The Crisis of the Short-Haul

Northeast Airlines quickly discovered that the Boston-New York route was not the answer to its problems. To challenge the largest airline in the country, American Airlines, which had hitherto had a monopoly, was one thing; but to take on Eastern Air Lines, and Eddie Rickenbacker's Great Silver Fleet, also the beneficiary of the 12 June 1944 award, was quite another.

Northeast proceeded to lose its shirt, in spite of increasing frequency in November 1945 to 16 round-trips per day. On 13 May 1946, **Douglas DC-4s** were put into service — hardly the right aircraft for such a short route — and some semblance of order restored by the introduction of **Convair 240s** early in 1949.

As the map shows, Northeast was more of a local service airline than one with the prestigious "grandfather rights" bestowed upon it by the CAB. But the New Englanders were introspective. The acquisition of some extra routes in New Hampshire, resulting from the demise of **Wiggins Airways**, warranted celebration. Even the deployment of **Curtiss C-46s** on the route to Montreal was newsworthy.

Floyd Odlum tried to solve the chronic problems by trying to bring about a merger with other trunk airlines, but the parties could never agree to an equitable association. Eventu-

ally, the issue of a merger became moot, as in 1951, Northeast Airlines applied for a route to Miami, and at last tried to break out from the self-imposed Herculean struggle of trying to operate as a trunk airline over a route network that would be viewed with scepticism by a commuter airline today.

Douglas DC-6B

80 SEATS ■ 315 mph

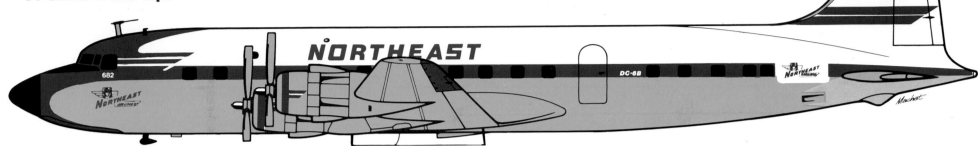

Pratt & Whitney R-2800 (2,500hp) x 4 ■ 107,000 lb. max. gross take-off weight ■ Range 2,200 miles ■ Length 106 feet ■ Span 118 feet ■ Height 29 feet

Northeast DC-6B in the delivery color scheme.

NORTHEAST'S DOUGLAS DC-4 AND DC-6B FLEET

MSN	Regn.	Delivery Date	Remarks
Douglas DC-4			
3115	NC86556	12 May 46	Ex-USAAF C-54; on lease from PCA until purchased, 1 Jun. 47; sold to Aircraft Investment Corp., 23 Aug. 50.
3123	NC88852	2 May 46	
3118	NC88844	26 May 46	
18391	N88904	52	Leased from PANAGRA during summer
Douglas DC-6B			
44678	N34954	57	Leased from Flying Tigers (DC-6A); crashed, Rikers Is., N.Y., 1 Feb. 57
44255	N6255C	5 Sep. 63	Leased from F.B. Ayer until Sep. 67
45210	N6500C	10 Jan. 57	
45217	N6581C	23 Feb. 57	
45218	N6582C	17 Mar. 57	
45219	N6583C	22 May 57	
45220	N6584C	12 Jul. 57	Purchased from Douglas; Fleet Numbers 680-689; sold to Fairchild Hiller, 1966-67
45221	N6585C	18 Jul. 57	
45222	N6586C	1 Aug. 57	
45223	N6587C	23 Aug. 57	
45224	N6588C	14 Sep. 57	
45225	N6589C	15 Oct. 57	
43738	N8221H	11 Sep. 63	
43739	N8222H	9 Sep. 63	Leased from F. B. Ayer until Sep. 67 (N8224H written off 24 Feb. 67, after in-flight damage)
43740	N8223H	5 Sep. 63	
43741	N8224H	9 Sep. 63	
43847	N90770	10 Aug. 64	
45176	N93121	15 Jun. 65	

NORTHEAST'S CONVAIR 240 FLEET

MSN	Regn.	Delivery Date	Remarks
140	N91237	25 Feb. 49	Sold to Wold Assoc., 9 Jan. 59
158	N91238	15 Mar. 49	Crashed, Flushing Bay, N.Y., 14 Jan. 52
159	N91239	18 Apr. 49	Crashed, LaGuardia Airport, 6 Feb. 53
160	N91240	18 May 49	Sold to Calif. Airmotive, 22 May 59
161	N91241	19 May 49	Crashed, Portland, Maine, 11 Aug. 49
162	N91241	2 Sep. 49	Sold to Mohawk Airlines, 10 Oct. 55

Model 240-13 purchased from Convair; Fleet Numbers 37-41, and 41.

MSN	Regn.	Delivery Date	Remarks
34	N90659	8 Mar. 54	Sold to VARIG, Jan.- Feb. 59
65	N90665	30 Apr. 54	
67	N90666	18 Jan. 54	
90	N90670	23 Apr. 54	Crashed, Nantucket, 15 Aug. 58

Model 240-2 leased, then purchased from Pan American; Fleet Numbers 59, 65, 66, and 70.

Northeast Breaks With Tradition

Breaking Out

During five years of endeavor in the quest for a long-haul route, **Northeast Airlines** barely kept body and soul together. Its only route of consequence, with dense traffic, was less than 200 miles long, and the competition comprised American Airlines, U.S. leader in passenger miles, and Eastern Air Lines, U.S. leader in passenger boardings. After introducing the Convair-Liners in 1949, three were lost in crashes — fortunately without passenger fatalities — within four years, and two DC-3s crashed also. And one Convair-Liner escaped miraculously when on 17 January 1956, only superhuman efforts by the crew, with a complete electrical failure, no instruments, not even a working compass, and in severe icing conditions, brought the aircraft safely into LaGuardia with five minutes of fuel remaining in the tanks.

When therefore, in September 1956, the CAB finally awarded to Northeast a parcel of routes from Boston and New York to Miami and Tampa, via intermediate points, it was like throwing a life belt to a drowning man.

The Florida Route

Northeast opened service from Boston to Miami, via New York, on 9 January 1957, with a **Douglas DC-6A**, converted for passenger use, and leased from Flying Tigers. This solitary long-range airliner was joined on 20 January by the first of ten **DC-6Bs**, ordered in March 1955. The elation of getting into the big leagues was dampened by a much-publicized inferno when the DC-6A was taking-off in a snowstorm from LaGuardia on 1 February and crashed at Rikers Island. And the media did not allow Northeast to forget it for many years. During 1957, service was opened to Philadelphia, Washington, and Tampa; but the bad luck continued, with two more fatal crashes in 1957 and 1958.

Flirtation with Britannia

In one big step for Northeast Airlines, five **Bristol Britannia Series 305** four-engined turboprop airliners were ordered, under the direction of George Gardner, who had taken over the presidency of Northeast in 1947, replacing Paul Collins. But as the DC-6Bs settled into service Northeast's interest waned. The order was deferred in October 1957, and definitely canceled in June 1958.

The Britannia was not the right airplane for Northeast. Even Boston — Miami nonstop was on the short side for the long-range Britannia, and Northeast turned to another British manufacturer to take a giant technical leap forward.

The Viscount

Within a month of the Britannia cancellation, Northeast ordered nine **Vickers Viscount 798D** four-engined short/medium-range turboprops. The first one entered service on 21 August. This was the initial departure from the old conservative image and the competitive effect was impressive. Northeast was able to achieve a substantial penetration of major markets, particularly the Boston — New York route, where its market share rocketed from a dismal eight per cent to a respectable 35 per cent.

More Problems

The late 1950s witnessed the arrival of the big jet airliners and these were all in the hands of the big airlines; so little Northeast was at a disadvantage. It overcame its handicap well, first by leasing a Boeing 707-331 from TWA on 17 December 1959 to cope with the Christmas rush to Florida. Northeast flew jets to Florida before Eastern did, and the schedule was integrated with TWA's North Atlantic services.

On 15 December 1960, Northeast introduced the first of six **Convair 880s**, leased from the Hughes Tool Company. The common denominator in all these equipment moves was **Howard Hughes**, still in control of TWA and eager to acquire Northeast, a merger plan that was approved by the latter airline's board in May 1960 but violently opposed, not surprisingly, by National and Eastern. Such were the corporate machinations at the time that the Atlas Corporation, Northeast's owner, in September 1961, had to turn down a joint offer by Eastern, National, and Mohawk Airlines, to take over the whole route structure, and eliminate an irritating competitor by dividing the spoils.

The Hughes Tool Company agreed to buy Northeast on 8 May 1962, and the CAB approved the deal on 19 June; Hughes paid $5 million for the shareholding (he had already lent $11.5 million to the airline). But when the Board denied renewal of Northeast's Florida route in August 1963, the billionaire announced that he would no longer cover further operating losses. The airline had, only a month previously, been obliged to agree to return most of the Viscount and Convair 880 fleets to the respective manufacturers, because it had not maintained its progress payments.

When Hughes Tool agreed to a plan, published in October 1964, to relinquish control of Northeast and transfer 55 per cent of the stock and the outstanding $23 million loan to a one-man trustee, L.J. Hector, the New England airline faced yet another crisis of survival. Northeast now needed a fairy godmother to wave its wand, preferably over Miami; but the

Northeast came close to acquiring the Bristol Britannia, and one was even painted in Northeast's colors at the factory in Bristol, England, in 1958. (Photo courtesy John Stroud)

almost impossible came to pass, and the airline from Boston was reprieved in colorful fashion.

NORTHEAST'S FLEET OF TURBOPROPS

MSN	Regn.	Delivery Date	Remarks
Vickers Viscount 798D			
232	N6590C	8 Aug. 58	Sold to Aloha Airlines, 4 Oct. 63
233	N6591C	8 Aug. 58	
234	N6592C	21 Aug. 58	Written off, Boston, 15 Nov. 61
286	N6593C	3 Sep. 58	Sold to Hawaiian Airlines, 14 Oct. 63
284	N6594C	22 Sep. 58	
230	N6595C	2 Oct. 58	
288	N6596C	31 Oct. 58	
391	N6597C	11 Dec. 58	
392	N6598C	8 Jan. 59	
226	N6599C	27 Feb. 59	

Fleet Numbers last three of registration. All but three aircraft noted repossessed by the Irving Trust Co. on 9 Sep. 63. Northeast also leased a Viscount 745D (198/N7442) from United Air Lines (ex-Capital Airlines) Jun.-Sep. 61.

MSN	Regn.	Delivery Date	Remarks
Fairchild Hiller FH-227B			
504	N374NE	13 Jul. 66	Sold to Air New England 1974-75. N379NE leased to Shawnee and Out Island Airways, 1971-72; and to Bahamasair (by Delta), 1974.
506	N375NE	31 Aug. 66	
507	N376NE	14 Sep. 66	
510	N377NE	15 Oct. 66	
512	N378NE	2 Nov. 66	
516	N379NE	12 Feb. 66	
517	N380NE	23 Dec. 66	Crashed, Lebanon, N.H., 25 Oct. 68

Fleet Numbers 274-280; 001-006 with Delta (except N380NE). One FH-227C (N7804M/509) leased from Mohawk, Jun. 68-Sep. 69.

Vickers Viscount 798D

48 SEATS ■ 312 mph

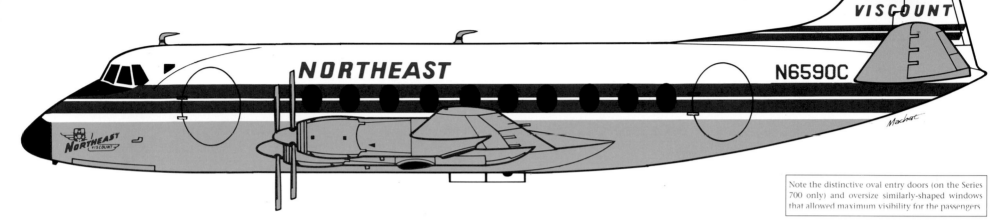

Note the distinctive oval entry doors (on the Series 700 only) and oversize similarly-shaped windows that allowed maximum visibility for the passengers

Rolls Royce R.Da. 6-510 (1,650ehp) x 4 ■ 64,500 lb. max. gross take-off weight ■ Range 1,150 miles

The world's first turboprop airliner, the 32-seat **Vickers V.630 Viscount**, made its first flight on16 July 1948. British European Airways (BEA) insisted on a larger model, the 40-seat Series 700, which went into service on 16 April 1953, and with variants, the Viscount went on to become the most successful airliner, measured by its sales of more than 430, in the history of the British aircraft industry. By the time Northeast received its first Viscounts, the aircraft was already established in the United States. Capital Airlines had ordered 75 and put the type into service on 26 July 1955, to challenge the Big Four airlines (United, TWA, American, and Eastern) with a clearly superior product.

Northeast's introduction of the British turboprop, the Vickers Viscount, in 1958, set new competitive standards on the Boston — New York high-density commuter route.

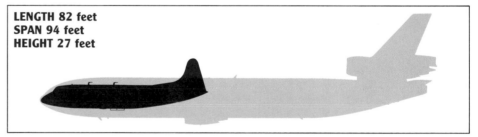

LENGTH 82 feet
SPAN 94 feet
HEIGHT 27 feet

Northeast's aircraft were Series 798Ds, the suffix "D" indicating a version with more powerful Dart 510 engines and extra fuel tankage, plus a number of modifications to meet U.S. certification requirements (the "98" was a customer number).Its tenth Viscount was the last of 289 Series 700 delivered. Northeast's fleet was fitted with 48 seats but some later Viscount variants developed the design to accommodate up to 80 passengers, in somewhat cramped style.

This Fairchild-Hiller FH-227B went into service with Northeast in 1966 (see page 84), passed to Delta with the merger, and was the only turboprop passenger type ever operated by the latter airline. (Photo by Karl Kraemer)

New England's Yellowbirds

Miami Tightrope

When the Civil Aeronautics Board awarded the Florida routes to **Northeast Airlines** in 1956 (see page 82) this action had been qualified as temporary, although few observers of the airline industry doubted that the decision would be confirmed as permanent. When, therefore, late in 1962, the CAB decided to terminate the authority, this came as a shock. If carried through, this action would, at the very least, weaken the company to the status of a local service airline; and now that Eastern Air Lines had, on 30 April 1961, started the famous Air-Shuttle service on Northeast's best route, from Boston to New York, the loss of the Florida routes would be the equivalent of receiving a death sentence.

In an unprecedented display of support for Northeast's cause by the entire New England community, a petition containing 250,000 signatures was presented to the U.S. Congress. The CAB procrastinated, but after interminable proceedings, it granted a permanent certificate on 2 March 1967.

George B. Storer

A silver lining — or perhaps a yellow ribbon — appeared on the Florida horizon to give Northeast Airlines yet another lease of life, rather like a cat going into its ninth. In June 1965, the Storer Broadcasting Company of Miami, headed by **George B. Storer**, took an option to purchase the 55 per cent of stock, formerly held by Howard Hughes, and now in the hands of a one-man trustee, L.J. Hector. Storer absorbed accumulated debts, interest charges, and other obligations, and tried to put the airline back on its feet.

On 10 August 1965, in a display of confidence, he ordered 33 new jet aircraft, worth about $100 million. The initial order consisted of 14 Douglas DC-9s, 12 Boeing 727s, of which six were the stretched-200 series, and seven Fairchild-Hiller FH-227B twin-engined turboprop feederliners.

The Yellowbirds

The first of the FH-227s was delivered on 13 July 1966 and promptly put into service in New England. In the latter part of 1969, many unprofitable routes were transferred to commuter airlines operating in the area.

During the summer of 1966, Storer introduced the Yellowbird image which was created by the reknowned industrial designer, Raymond Loewey, to revolutionize the old conservative styling (see page 87). One Yellowbird deserves special mention. When the first **Boeing 727-200** made its inaugural scheduled flight on 14 December 1967, from Miami to New York (Kennedy) this was the first in the world by one of the most successful commercial aircraft in history.

New Routes at Last

During 1968, new routes were opened from Boston and New York direct to Nassau and Freeport, resort cities in the Bahamas; from 14 March 1969, Bostonians could fly Yellowbirds straight to Bermuda. And on 28 April of the same year, Portland — Manchester — Detroit — Chicago service opened, quickly followed by Bangor — Burlington — Cleveland — Chicago on 31 May. S.J. Solomon (see page 80) would have been pleased.

Then the CAB awarded, on 23 September 1969, a route certificate for the southern transcontinental route, nonstop from Miami to Los Angeles. Oddly, this presented Northeast with a problem. Once again it was entering a heavily competitive route, with a well-established incumbent, namely National. So the route was opened, cautiously, on 1 October with the smallest aircraft that could fly the route, the **Boeing 727-95**.

Northeast ordered four L-1011 TriStars in 1968 for delivery in 1972, but these were cancelled two years later with the decision to merge with Northwest (see page 86).

NORTHEAST'S JET FLEET

Regn.	MSN	Regn.	MSN
Convair 880 (Model 22-1)		N1641	19446
		N1642	19447
N8478H	22-00-5	N1643	19448
N8479H	22-00-8	N1644	19449
N8480H	22-00-12	N1645	20139
N8481H	22-00-20	N1646	20140
N8482H	22-00-22	N1647	20141
N8483H	22-00-23	N1648	19994
		N1649	19995
Fleet Numbers 478-483; leased		N1650	20248
from General Dynamics, Nov. 60-		N11651	20249
Sep. 63.			
		Fleet Numbers 739-751 (Delta
N8492H	22-00-9	*439-451), delivered Dec. 67 - Oct.*
N8493H	22-00-18	*69. All were leased, then taken*
N8494H	22-00-34	*over by Delta. N1648/1649 -291.*
N8495H	22-00-39		
		DC-9-31	
Fleet Numbers 492-495; operated		N970NE	47053
Dec. 61-Feb. 68, leased from		N971NE	47054
Hughes Tool Co.		N972NE	47057
		N973NE	47058
Convair 990A (Model 30A-5)		N974NE	47066
		N975NE	47075
N5612	30-10-24	N976NE	47082
		N977NE	47095
Leased from F.B. Ayer, Jan. 67 -		N978NE	47096
Apr. 68, Flagship Rita		N979NE	47097
		N980NE	47134
Boeing 727-95		N981NE	47135
		N982NE	47136
N1631	18850	N983NE	47137
N1632	18858		
N1633	19249	*Fleet Numbers 970-983, later*
N1634	19250	*217-230 with Delta, delivered*
N1635	19251	*May 67 - Feb. 68; N975NE*
N1636	19252	*crashed, Boston, Mass., 31 Jul.*
N1637	19595	*73; remainder sold to Allegheny*
N1638	19596	*and Ozark, Aug. 72 - Jun. 75. In*
		addition, a DC-9-15 (N8953U/
Fleet Numbers 731-738 (Delta		*45797 Fleet Number 51) was*
431-438), delivered Oct. 65 - Oct.		*leased from Douglas Dec. 66-*
67. All taken over by Delta, then		*Jun. 67.*
sold May 73 - Dec. 77.			
Boeing 727-295			
N1639	19444		
N1640	19445		

The airline leased Convair 880s from Hughes Tool in 1960.

Boeing 727-295

138 SEATS ■ 605 mph

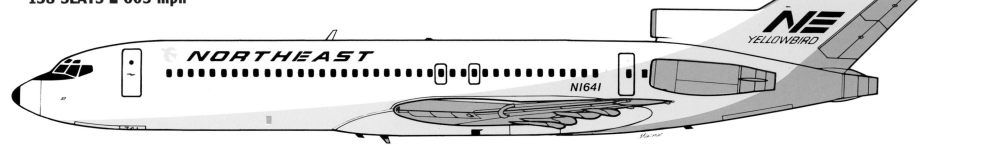

The depicted aircraft displays the final Yellowbird scheme. Yellow areas gradually gave way to bare metal finish. The original delivery scheme is shown on page 87.

Pratt & Whitney JT8D-7 (14,000 lb.) x 3 ■ 152,000 lb. max. gross take-off weight ■ Range 1,800 miles

When Boeing received its order for 20 Boeing 707s from Pan American in 1955, Douglas still had the edge, as was indicated by the same airline's order for 25 DC-8s on the same day. Certainly, Boeing had flown the Model 367-80 as a prototype on 15 July 1954 and had great confidence in the first 707 when it first flew on 20 December 1957. But at that time, even the enterprising engineers and project visionaries at Seattle could not have foreseen the amazing success that would follow in the trail of America's first jet airliner.

For on the same jigs and tools for the fuselage (the diameter of which is the one parameter that never changes during the development history of an airliner, once the basic design is signed and sealed by the head of the team) Boeing produced an entire family of airliners, three great series, each one of which would have been considered to have been the pinnacle of achievement for any other manufacturer, with the possible exception of Douglas.

In 1960, Boeing launched one of the most successful aircraft programs of all time. The first **Boeing 727-100** went into service with Eastern Air Lines on 1 February 1964. Including the longer-fuselage **-200** series, no less than 1,832 Boeing 727s came off the production line, a

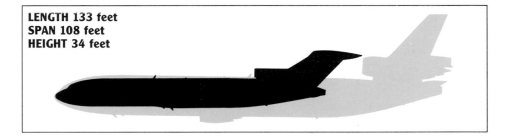

LENGTH 133 feet
SPAN 108 feet
HEIGHT 34 feet

record that was not to be broken until another of the types based on the 707 fuselage cross-section, the Boeing 737, broke the 2,000-order mark in 1986. Boeing assigned the customer number "95" for aircraft built for Northeast.

Northeast's first two 727-95s were delivered in the red, white and blue mid-1960s color scheme. All other Boeing 727s would wear Yellowbird plumage.

Delta Wins a Merger Battle

The Limits of Survival

Throughout its history **Northeast Airlines** seemed to be facing adversity of some sort. It was always handicapped by having to operate a small route network with a very short average stage length, thus increasing its operating costs. The winters were severe, and many of its airports were little more than local airfields, poorly equipped.

Sometimes, the solution was beyond Northeast's, or any airline's, control. The Civil Aeronautics Board, during the immediate postwar years and even into the early 1960s, seemed bent on restricting Northeast to New England with a "thus far and no further" attitude.

Ultimately, after crisis had succeeded crisis, the Storer control gave to Northeast all except the routes it needed; and although positive steps were taken, as described on page 84, the situation was beyond recall.

Delta - NEA Merger

The first suitor for Northeast in its re-Storered structure, was Northwest Airlines, which first proposed a merger on 11 November 1969. A year later, on 31 December 1970, the CAB approved, but stipulated that this would be conditional on the surrender of the Miami — Los Angeles transcontinental route. Northwest maintained a position of "all or nothing" and withdrew its offer on 10 March 1971.

Eastern Air Lines and TWA had also been eager to pick up the Northeast pieces and the former had even gone so far as to offer to buy the Storer Broadcasting Company as well. When the Northwest discussions fell through, the counter- claimants resumed negotiations, and Storer publicly acknowledged that **Delta Air Lines** was the likely favorite. And sure enough, on 23 April 1971, the merger was announced.

In May, the boards of both Northeast and Delta agreed in principle to merge and filed formal applications to the Civil Aeronautics Board. The sands were running out. Northeast announced a $6 million loss in the first six months of 1971. Such an amount may not seem much today, but it was a formitable figure then.

While Northeast did not seem much of a bargain, on paper, the prospects of adding and consolidating an entire market area to an existing nationwide network were attractive in that they would integrate two mutually supportive route networks into one. At least Eastern thought so. In a last-minute statement, born of desperation, it submitted, in a brief to the Board, that Storer Broadcasting would save $4 million in taxes, that it should not be allowed to abandon its certificate responsibilities, nor should it "walk away from the whole misadventure with a profit."

To no avail: on 19 May 1972, President Nixon approved the Delta-Northeast merger — the President's signature was required because foreign routes were involved and NEA was absorbed by Delta on 1 August. During the 1960s and 1970s, Delta's name had not been freely circulated during the many rumors and reports about airline mergers. But when it did make its move, it did so firmly and effectively; and the unofficial but nevertheless accepted term (even by the CAB itself) that referred to the "Big Four," fell into disuse. Delta Air Lines was now among the leaders of the industry.

On merger day, 1 August 1972, (left to right) Bill Michaels, W.T. Beebe, George B. Storer, Sr., and David C. Garrett, Jr., celebrate the joining of NEA and Delta.

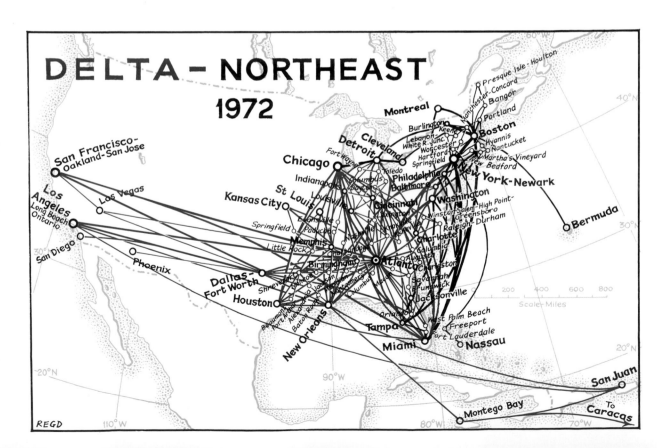

The Yellowbirds

NORTHEAST

Fairchild-Hiller FH-227

The **FH-227** was developed from the successful Dutch **Fokker F.27 Friendship** and built under license by Fairchild at Hagerstown, Maryland. **Northeast Airlines** was the second airline to introduce it, on 13 July 1966; the fleet passed to **Delta Air Lines** with the merger.

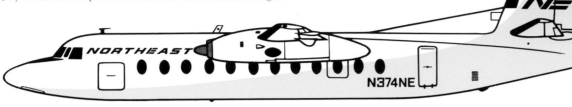

Douglas DC-9-31

Northeast Airlines introduced pure-jet service to its smaller New England cities with the **DC-9-31**. The DC-9s also replaced DC-6Bs on East Coast commuter routes.

Boeing 727-95

Northeast Airlines put the **Boeing 727-95** tri-jet into service in August 1965, and later used it on the transcontinental route from Miami to Los Angeles.

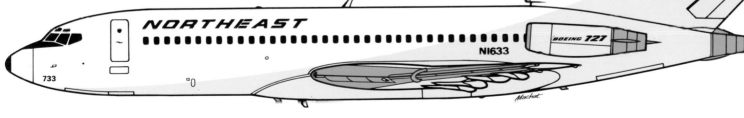

Convair 990A

In addition to its Convair 880s, Northeast leased an ex-American Airlines Convair 990A, christened *Flagship Rita*.

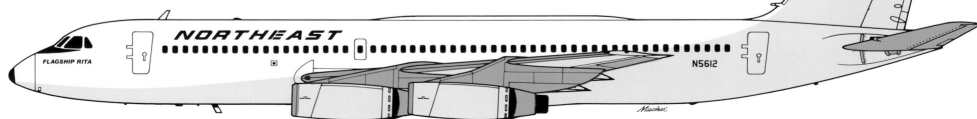

Western's First Boeing Jets

The First Jet

Western Air Lines ordered three **Boeing 720B** jet aircraft in February 1960 and took up its option for another one in July. Shortly afterwards, the Electra crisis occurred (see page 71) but to offset this setback, which severely affected operations and its public image until the following year, Western accelerated its jet introduction program, partly because of events beyond its control. On New Year's Day 1959, Fidel Castro's revolution in Cuba effectively canceled all outstanding aircraft orders with the West.

Cubana's two undelivered **Boeing 707s** were taken over on lease by Western and entered service on 1 June 1960. Equipped with 42 first-class seats, 71 economy class, and a four-place lounge, this was an unprecedented standard of luxury. The Boeing 707s were retained on lease until September 1962.

Cut-throat Competition

Alone among the trunk airlines of the United States, Western had to face competition not only from rival trunks but also from a vigorous and aggressive company that did not come under the jurisdiction of the Civil Aeronautics Board. The traffic generated between the two main cities of California, comprising the whole San Francisco Bay area and the enormous sprawl of the Los Angeles megalopolis, was not only the largest in the world; but from a regulatory point of view that was critical to the fortunes of the participating lines, it was under the control only of the California Public Utilities Commission (PUC). **Pacific Southwest Airlines (PSA)** took full advantage of the freedoms thus conferred upon it.

PSA set a cracking pace, based on a no-frills, low-fare policy. When it introduced Lockheed Electras in 1959, Western was forced to use the same equipment, superseding its DC-6B

A Boeing 737-247, in Western's improved color scheme.

Coachmaster service, which it had been able to sustain at a 20 per cent higher fare. The Douglases were then used to promote the *Thriftfair* economy fare, which by February 1964 had been reduced to an amazing $11.43 for the one-way San Francisco-Los Angeles trip.

Further competition from **United Air Lines** (*Jet Commuter* Boeing 727, 27 Sept. 1964, $14.50) and PSA (727, 9 April 1965, $13.50) were met by Western's *Fanjet Commuter* on 2 April 1965, at PSA's fare, with 146-seat Boeing 720Bs.

The competitive pressures led to desperate measures. Western swallowed its orthodox pride and came up with its popular *Flub Stub* campaign in May 1966, with the offer: "it's worth a buck if we goof." This remarkable promotion lasted for more than a year. A passenger could trade a stub for a drink, and was quite popular, in spite of its droll name.

The alleviation, if not the complete solution of Western's problems came with a level-headed aircraft choice. On 11 June 1968, the first **Boeing 737-200** entered service. Combining the attraction of the Boeing jet series that had started with the Boeing 707 (and had been forced upon it by Douglas) the 737's performance, size, and resultant economy, stemming from low operating costs and high load factors, led to Western making it one of the mainstays of its fleet, as the accompanying table shows.

Western ordered five Boeing 707-347Cs in May 1967.

WESTERN'S BOEING 737-200 FLEET

Regn.	MSN	Regn.	MSN
737-247		N239WA	23187
		N242WA	23516
N4501W	19598	N243WA	23517
N4502W	19599	N244WA	23518
N4503W	19600	N245WA	23519
N4504W	19601	N373DL	23520
N4505W	19602	N374DL	23521
N4506W	19603	N375DL	23602
N4507W	19604	N376DL	23603
N4508W	19605	N377DL	23604
N4509W	19606	N378DL	23605
N4510W	19607	N379DL	23606
N4511W	19608	N380DL	23607
N4512W	19609	N381DL	23608
N4513W	19610	N383DL	23609
N4514W	19611		
N4515W	19612	*First eight delivered to Western,*	
N4516W	19613	*Nov. 84 - Dec. 86; remainder*	
N4517W	19614	*delivered directly to Delta from*	
N4518W	19615	*Feb. 87; N236WA-N375DL*	
N4519W	19616	*originally Fleet Numbers 236-248,*	
N4520W	19617	*changed to 360-375 with Delta.*	
N4521W	20125		
N4522W	20126	**737-2S3 Advanced**	
N4523W	20127	N367DL	21774
N4524W	20128	N368DL	22279
N4525W	20129	N369DL	21776
N4526W	20130		
N4527W	20131	*Fleet Numbers 251-253, changed*	
N4528W	20132	*to 367-369 with Delta; leased*	
N4529W	20133	*from GPA, ex- EI-BPY/BRB/BPW.*	
N4530W	20134		
		737-2T4 Advanced	
Fleet Numbers 201-230; delivered		EI-BOM	22368
new from Boeing Jun. 68 - Jun.		EI-BON	22369
69; N4527W crashed, Casper,		N4569N	22701
Wy., 31 Mar. 75; N4502W/03W/			
05W/07W/ 09W/11W-14W/16W/		*Fleet Numbers 261-262, 231*	
18W-21W taken over by Delta		*(changed to 370-371, 355 with*	
with Fleet Numbers 341-354.		*Delta); first two leased from*	
		GPA, other from Alaska Intl. Air.	
737-284 Advanced			
		737-2T2 Advanced	
N70721	21500	N4571N	22793
N70722	21501		
		Fleet Number 232 (356 with	
Fleet Numbers 284-285; leased		*Delta); leased from Alaska*	
from Aloha Airlines 1983.		*Intl. Air.*	
737-247 Advanced		**737-2J8 Advanced**	
N236WA	23184	N235WA	22859
N237WA	23185		
N238WA	23186	*Fleet Number 235 (359 with*	
		Delta); leased from Boeing.	

(See page 101 for Western's Boeing 737-300 fleet.)

Boeing 720-047B

140 SEATS ■ 600 mph

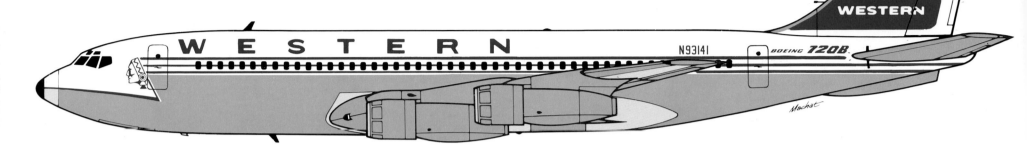

Pratt & Whitney JT3D (18,000 lb.) x 4 ■ 117 tons max. gross take-off weight ■ Range 4,500 miles ■ Length 136 feet ■ Span 131 feet ■ Height 38 feet

When the Boeing 707 was launched, the Boeing design team spared no effort to break into the commercial airline market that had so long eluded them. Unusually, when the conventional course of airliner development is to "stretch" the fuselage by increasing engine power, permitting higher payload and more fuel for greater range, Boeing did the reverse. It "shrunk" the fuselage of the 707 to produce special versions for specific customers — anything was justified if it prevented the sale going to Douglas or Convair, whose DC-8s and Convair 880s, respectively, were providing powerful competition.

After limited success with short-bodied models of the 707-100, Boeing refined the idea with the **720.** Similar in appearance to the 707, except for an eight-foot shorter fuselage, the 720 incorporated extensive changes, including a refined wing optimized for short-field performance which also offered an increase in maximum cruising speed. Although the 720 did not sell in great numbers — at least not in the numbers that Boeing would become accustomed to — it filled a gap: an airliner smaller than the DC-8, suitable for medium-stage routes of lower traffic density.

The **720B** was fitted with the new Pratt & Whitney JT3D fan engines, and, curiously, for a short while, had the privilege of having the longest range of any commercial jet. A total of 154 Boeing 720s and 720Bs were built, in addition to 763 Boeing 707s, excluding military derivatives.

Pacific Northern started Boeing 720 service on 1 May 1962 (see page 90) and **Western** Boeing 720B service on 15 May 1961 (see opposite page). PNA's non-fan 720s were subsequently taken-over by Western with the merger. Western

operated a total of 27 Boeing 720Bs for over 18 years, and it was an ideal aircraft because of its sparkling performance at "hot and high" airports such as Denver and México City, both important markets for Western. In pre-fuel economy days, Western was able to advertise the 640mph 720B as the fastest jet in the world for a brief period.

A Boeing 720-047B, in Western's red and white "swizzle-stick" colors. (Photo by John Wegg)

WESTERN'S BOEING 720-047B FLEET

Regn.	MSN	Delivery Date	Regn.	MSN	Delivery Date
N93141	18001	8 Apr. 61	N93157	18830	17 Jun. 65
N93142	18062	9 May 61	N93158	18963	21 Jul. 65
N93143	18063	7 Jun. 61	N3159	19160	26 Jan. 66
N93144	18167	11 Jul. 61	N3160	19161	12 Mar. 66
N93145	18451	26 Jul. 62	N3161	19207	30 Jul. 66
N93146	18452	9 Aug. 62	N3162	19208	30 Jul. 66
N93147	18453	29 Aug. 62	N3163	19413	13 May 67
N93148	18588	3 Apr. 63	N3164	19414	28 Jun. 67
N93149	18589	23 Apr. 63	N3165	19438	13 Aug. 67
N93150	18590	2 May 63	N3166	19439	7 Sep. 67
N93151	18749	21 May 64	N3167	19523	20 Sep. 68
N93152	18818	25 Sep. 64			
N93153	18820	21 Jan. 65	*All bought from Boeing; Fleet Numbers 341-367. N3166 crashed, Ontario, Calif., 31 Mar. 71 (pilot training); remainder sold Jan. 74 - Jan. 80.*		
N93154	18827	10 Mar. 65			
N93155	18828	19 May 65			
N93156	18829	2 Jun. 65			

WESTERN'S BOEING 707 FLEET

Regn.	MSN	Delivery Date
707-139		
N74613	17903	4 May 60
N74614	17904	13 May 60
Leased from Boeing until Sep. 62.		
707-347C		
N1501W	19963	22 Jun. 68
N1502W	19964	25 Jul. 68
N1503W	19965	29 Jul. 68
N1504W	19966	10 Sep. 68
N1505W	19967	19 Sep. 68
Fleet Numbers 401-405; sold May 80 - Jul. 81.		

Pacific Northern Airlines

Woodley Airways

On 10 April 1932, **Arthur G. Woodley** started a one-man, one-plane charter service between Anchorage and points in southwest Alaska. Two years later, he was awarded a Post Office contract to carry the mails, and he was able to establish a reputation for reliability in some of the world's worst operating conditions, of climate as well as of terrain, to the extent that, in 1938, he was able to obtain permanent certificates for routes to Kodiak and to the Bristol Bay and Kuskokwim River regions.

After a sequence of complicated corporate maneuvers, **Woodley Airways** emerged as **Pacific Northern Airways (PNA)** on 23 August 1945, the first airline in Alaska to be certificated by the Civil Aeronautics Board, and became **Pacific Northern Airlines** two years later. By then, Woodley had progressed from single-engined Travel Airs, Bellancas, and Wacos to the **Boeing 247D** and the **Douglas DC-3**, with which the route network had taken a significant step southwards, to Juneau. Pacific Northern then looked for fresh fjords to conquer.

Pacific Northern Goes South

PNA introduced **Douglas DC-4s** in 1947, proudly opening nonstop service on 1 October from Anchorage to Seattle, later adding Portland, Oregon, to its map. In 1955, Woodley acquired three **Lockheed Constellations** from Delta Air Lines —a harbinger of things to come. During the same year, the route to Juneau was extended to the south; but the local routes around Anchorage, except the one to Kodiak, were handed over to Bristol Bay Airlines.

Direct Seattle-Kodiak flights started on 1 May 1959, and Woodley demonstrated his intent to keep in the front running by starting **Boeing 720** jet service on the Anchorage, Juneau, and Ketchikan links with the Pacific Northwest on 27 April 1962.

Arthur Woodley received a severe blow on 29 March 1965, when he lost a virtual monopoly on the best route to Alaska, Seattle-Anchorage. The CAB awarded the route to Northwest in compensation for losing the Seattle — Fairbanks route to Pan American. PNA became the sole carrier on the Ketchikan — Juneau route, with Pan American withdrawing, but authority to serve Portland was suspended for seven years.

At the end of the year, the CAB made a generous offer of a lump sum in lieu of the past three years' subsidy, linked with a proposal to drop subsidy altogether. And then, on 31 October 1966, Arthur Woodley agreed to merge with **Western Air Lines**. The merger was completed on 1 July 1967. For a short while, Arthur Woodley was Western's biggest individual shareholder.

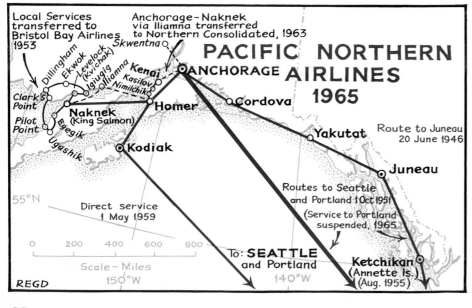

Arthur Woodley (1906-1990).

THE FLEET OF WOODLEY AIRWAYS & PACIFIC NORTHERN AIRLINES

MSN	Regn.	Delivery Date	Remarks
Stinson A			
9104	NC14566	31 Jan. 40	From Frank Reynolds; crashed, Juneau, 19 Jan. 43
9115	NC15155	1 Jan. 45	From USAAF; sold to Straton & Thomas, 7 Mar. 46
Boeing 247D			
1691	NC13310	Aug. 44	Ex-USAAF C-73s; withdrawn
1734	NC13352	22 Jul. 44	from use Feb. 46

*Woodley Airways also used a number of smaller aircraft, including two **Travel Air S-6000s** (one was NC14975); **Lockheed 10-A** NC17391 (1101); and **Consolidated Fleetster 20A** NC13209 (2).*

MSN	Regn.	Delivery Date	Remarks
Douglas DC-3			
42955	NC37465	25 Jan. 46	Sold to Air Ivoire, 15 Jun. 64
42959	NC37469	7 Feb. 46	Sold to Connie Air Lsg., 1 Oct.63
42960	NC37470	1 Mar. 46	Ex-Colonial Airlines
42966	NC34970	27 Feb. 46	Sold to Caribair, 1963
43074	NC33676		
6098	NC49277		From Gull Airways (ex-USAAF); sold to All American Av., 19 May 48
26676	NC49319	29 May 46	From Reconst. Fin. Corp. (ex-USAAF); sold to Western, Dec. 53
13395	N41341	49	From Canadian Govt. (ex-USAAF) for spares use

*The first four were DC-3s (postwar production), the remainder converted C-47s. Pacific Northern also used **Lockheed 12-A** NC69033 (1265).*

MSN	Regn.	Delivery Date	Remarks
Douglas A-26B Invader			
28038	NC956		Ex-USAAF (44-34759 and 44-34770);
28049	NC67814	24 Oct. 46	used for route surveying
Douglas DC-4			
27243	N3934C	Jul. 51	From Aerovias Guest; sold to Chile, 28 May 62, Fleet Number 34C
27242	N37475	27 Feb. 53	From Delta; sold to Overseas National
10502	N37476	26 Apr. 53	From Delta; sold to California Eastern
10395	N41341		Ex-U.S. Navy R5D-1; sold to Boreas Corp.
Lockheed 749A Constellation			
2659	N86523	1 Apr. 55	Damaged beyond repair, Kenai, 6 Jun. 66
2660	N86524	15 Mar. 55	
2662	N86525	1 Apr. 55	
2505	N1552V	30 Nov. 58	Purchased from BOAC
2556	N1593V	6 May 56	
2655	N6017C	17 Aug. 60	Leased from TWA, purchased from Connie Leasing, 1 Oct. 63
2668	N6022C	30 Jun. 66	From TWA

*The first three aircraft were leased from Delta, then purchased 2 March 1956. The six surviving Constellations passed to **Western Air Lines** with the merger on 1 July 1967, were withdrawn by December 1968, and were sold to Concare International on April 11, 1969 except for N1552V — donated to the city of Kenai (and later broken up). Fleet Numbers 523-525, 552, 593, 517, and 522.*

MSN	Regn.	Delivery Date	Remarks
Boeing 720			
18376	N720V	23 Mar. 62	Series -062
18377	N720W	18 Apr. 62	Series -062
18042	N7081	20 Jun. 66	Series -048

*Fleet numbers 301-303; first two bought from Boeing, the other from Braniff. All three passed to **Western** and were later sold to Alaska Airlines.*

Boeing 720

140 SEATS ■ 590 mph

PNA

THE ALASKA FLAG LINE

N720V

PACIFIC NORTHERN

BOEING *720*

| LENGTH 136 feet |
| SPAN 131 feet |
| HEIGHT 38 feet |

Pratt & Whitney JT3C-7 (12,500 lb.) x 4 ■ 115 tons max. gross take-off weight ■ Range 3,600 miles

In the Alaskan bush country, wheels are often exchanged for floats or skis. This Travel Air S-6000 is pictured during the summer in a quiet backwater. All pioneer airlines had DC-3s and Pacific Northern was no exception.

When PNA received its route award to Seattle on 24 May 51, it started service with DC-4s.

This Pacific Northern Constellation (fitted with a speedpak, see pages 51 and 59), is shown here in a typical summertime Alaskan setting, at Kodiak Island.

Into the Big Leagues

The Boeing 727

When **Western Air Lines** ordered the **Boeing 727**, it specified the "stretched" -200 series, and from the first deliveries on 16 October 1969, it proceeded to augment the fleet steadily. Except for the 12 Lockheed Electras, Western's jet fleet was all-Boeing until the McDonnell Douglas DC-10 entered service in May 1973.

It's a Long Way to Honolulu

As long ago as 1959 (and page 70 of this book) Western had made its first application to the Civil Aeronautics Board for a route to Hawaii, where an American and United Air Lines shared a huge and lucrative air market. The ensuing deliberations ebbed and flowed in an exercise of political and industrial in-fighting that only Pan Am and United could have enjoyed.

On the face of it, Western had a strong case and did all the right things that were normally expected of an aspirant for a new route award. When Hawaii achieved statehood on 12 March 1960, Drinkwater once again applied for the route, which had now become a straightforward domestic issue. Hopes were high as the CAB announced the award to Western on 19 January 1961; but a stay order delayed it, ending further investigation, and president Eisenhower disapproved. In an agonizing sequence of events, the case dragged on. Under the Kennedy administration, the CAB re-opened the proceedings on 27 July 1961 on the international phase of the Transpacific Route Case but mainland — Hawaii service was excluded. The CAB lifted its stay order on 8 June 1962. The Transpacific Route Case was terminated on 8 November 1963, whereupon Western filed a petition for reconsideration on 29 November. This was denied on 3 March 1964, but Western argued its case before the Court of Appeals on 12 May.

By this time truckloads of documents and dossiers were pouring into the CAB as 18 airlines sought a piece of the action in the **Transpacific Route Investigation**. In the fall of 1966, Western's proposals, concentrating on Hawaii, were unique, in that they specified not only three other main islands of the Hawaiian group, as well as Honolulu (on Oahu); but also proposed the use of satellite airports in the San Francisco and Los Angeles metropolitan areas.

Hawaii Here We Come

Finally, on 4 January 1969, the CAB announced the award. Western was granted almost every point and route it had asked for, including the satellite airports such as San Jose and Long Beach, plus San Diego, Phoenix, Denver, and the Twin Cities, even Anchorage as well. But, in the see-saw of politics, the incoming president, Richard Nixon, deferred the awards, almost as his first executive action, on 24 January 1969. On 11 April he disapproved the use of the satellite airports, a negative step that seemed to run against the tide of traffic demand and the need to diffuse airport hub congestion.

After ten years of struggle, Western Air Lines finally won through. On 22 July 1969, the routes to Hawaii were confirmed, subject to a long-haul restriction that required service to a point east of California as a condition of scheduling practice.

Merger Talks with American

While the Hawaii debate continued, much else was happening. In the **Pacific Southwest Local Service Case**, Western acquired several new non-stop authorities to consolidate its position in the southwestern states, effective on 24 April 1962; and it expanded to Alaska by the acquisition of **Pacific Northern Airlines**, announced on 26 October 1966 and finally confirmed on 1 July 1967 (see page 90).

Some important moves affecting Western's ownership and its survival were made late in 1968. **Kirk Kerkorian**, financier and former owner of the supplemental airline Trans International Airlines (TIA), purchased 28 percent of Western's shares, for $61.7 million and established contact with George Spater, Chairman of **American Airlines**. After several high-level meetings, both the Western and the American shareholders voted simultaneously on 19 March 1971 to merge. J. Judson Taylor, Western's president, stated that American had been chosen above Continental because both were in the Hawaiian market, but the real reason was believed to be Kerkorian's ambition to become the largest shareholder in American. Eventually, the merger fell through, because the Department of Justice disapproved, in January 1972, and the CAB in July of the same year. Arthur Kelly was appointed president of Western, with Dominic Renda as executive vice-president. By the end of the year, Kerkorian had reduced his shareholding.

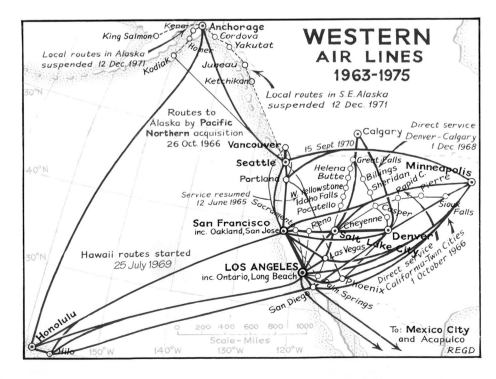

Boeing 727-247

135 SEATS ■ 605 mph

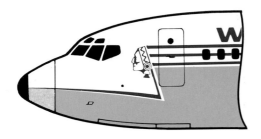
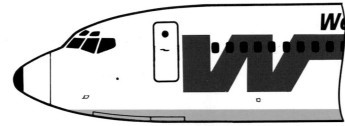
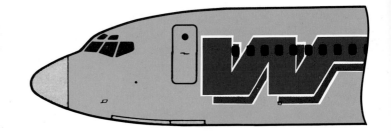

These Boeing 727 noses depict the evolution of Western's color scheme. The 727 and 737 were the only types in the Western fleet to feature all three variations.

Pratt & Whitney JT8D-7 (14,500 lb.) x 4 ■ 104 tons max. gross take-off weight ■ Range 1,600 miles ■ Length 133 feet ■ Span 108 feet ■ Height 38 feet

Invariably, during the life of a successful airliner, the original design is modified so as to develop an even better aircraft. Most of the improvements stem from engine refinements that increase the power or produce leaner fuel consumption, or a combination of both. This permits, as a rule, the classic "stretch" in which extra sections can be inserted in the fuselage, fore and aft of the wing to preserve balance, so as to take advantage of the extra weight that can be lifted with the augmented power. The larger fuselage provides room for more seats and cargo space, thus improving the unit costs (expressed as cost per seat-mile or per ton-mile) and the power increase also allows more fuel to be carried, usually in the wing, and thus adds range. The **Boeing 727-200** series was one of the most successful of such developments. Of the 1,832 727s built, 1,260 were of the "stretched" model. They were sold to almost every airline in the United States and to almost every airline of stature all over the world.

WESTERN'S BOEING 727-247 FLEET

Regn.	MSN	Delivery Date	Regn.	MSN	Delivery Date
N2801W	20263	16 Oct. 69	N2824W	21329	9 Mar. 77
N2802W	20264	16 Oct. 69	N2825W	21330	3 May 77
N2803W	20265	16 Oct. 69	N2826W	21331	24 May 77
N2804W	20266	14 Nov. 69	N2827W	21392	15 Dec. 77
N2805W	20267	14 Nov. 69	N2828W	21393	21 Dec. 77
N2806W	20268	14 Nov. 69	N2829W	21481	20 Jun. 78
N2807W	20579	12 May 72	N830WA	21482	9 May 78
N2808W	20580	13 Jun. 72	N831WA	21483	31 May 78
N2809W	20581	16 Jun. 72	N282WA	21484	12 Jul. 78
N2810W	20648	4 Aug. 72	N283WA	21485	13 Jul. 78
N2811W	20649	16 Aug. 72	N284WA	21697	24 Apr. 79
N2812W	20868	29 Mar. 74	N286WA	21698	1 May 79
N2813W	20869	2 Apr. 74	N287WA	21699	29 May 79
N2814W	20870	26 Apr. 74	N288WA	21700	7 Jun. 79
N2815W	20871	29 May 74	N289WA	21701	19 Jun. 79
N2816W	20872	25 May 74	N831L	21826	27 Jul. 79
N2817W	20873	5 Jun. 74	N290WA	22108	5 Mar. 80
N2818W	20874	25 Jul. 74	N291WA	22109	11 Mar. 80
N2819W	21057	3 May 75	N292WA	22110	6 Mar. 80
N2820W	21058	29 May 75	N293WA	22111	9 May 80
N2821W	21059	3 Jun. 75	N294WA	22112	19 May 80
N2822W	21327	9 Mar. 77	N295WA	22532	29 May 81
N2823W	21328	9 Mar. 77	N296WA	22533	5 Jun. 81
			N297WA	22534	22 May 81

Fleet Numbers 801-847, changed to 551-589 with Delta (N2818W, 2827W, 2828W, 284WA-289WA not taken over by Delta); N2807W and subsequent aircraft are Advanced models; N831L Series 2Q8 Advanced leased from International Lease Finance Corp., N2823W named City of Boston with Delta.

A Western Boeing 727-247 in the updated "swizzle-stick" livery. (Photo by Ronald C. Miller)

Western Revolution

The DC-10

On 29 September 1971, **Western Air Lines** moved further into the ranks of the industry leaders by assuming responsibility for four of the **McDonnell Douglas DC-10s** for which American Airlines held options. Although these were the -10, or domestic version, they were fitted with over-water equipment, as nonstop mainland — Hawaii services were contemplated. The first DC-10 was delivered on 19 April 1973 and reinforced Western's schedules on all its longer main routes, especially those to Hawaii, which accounted for a substantial percentage of its traffic and revenue.

Western Expands its Horizons

Even after embracing Hawaii, as far away from the California base as was the east coast of the United States, Western was still regarded primarily as an airline whose only concern was serving the West, an assumption that was quite reasonable, bearing in mind the name of the airline. But times had changed. Regional identities, once considered to be an important identification with the catchment area and traffic base, no longer applied.

During the 1970s, the interest in Alaska, implicit in the acquisition of Pacific Northern (page 90) had diminished when on 12 December 1971, the CAB suspended Western's authority to serve the southeastern Alaskan cities of Juneau and Ketchikan. Although Western protested the decision, which it described as "clearly a revocation in disguise, contrary to FAA regulations, and therefore illegal," the die was cast. Western continued to serve Anchorage and Kodiak only, nonstop from Seattle, and in 1980 even the latter point was dropped, along with some other cities on the Western network.

Since the Pacific Route Case (see page 92) Western had filled in a remote segment of the world airline map with a nonstop route from Anchorage to Honolulu. On 9 October 1980 it utilized its single foothold in Alaska rather ingeniously by opening a unique **trans-Atlantic service**: Honolulu — Anchorage — London. Providing as it did an opportunity for Londoners to take a winter break in Hawaii or a summer one in Alaska, and for affluent Hawaiians to enjoy a London theater during a free weekend, this route perhaps deserved to do well; but it had to be suspended in October 1981. The same fate awaited Western's other trans-Atlantic venture. Service from Denver to London opened on 25 April 1981 but it too had to be withdrawn on 1 January 1982.

In the late 1970s and early 1980s, Western's route expansion was more circumspect, and Zihuatanejo in Mexico represented the extent of Western's ambitions in that direction.

Mergers On and Off

During the turmoil of the Western-American negotiations, one of the disappointed candidates — and one that would have made a far more logical partner for a California-based operator — was **Continental Air Lines**. After a lapse of several years, the idea was revived, and accord was reached in principle on 1 August 1978, but a year later the agreement was withdrawn as the CAB opposed the idea. On 8 August 1980, a second Western-Continental agreement was proposed, but by this time other moves were afoot and Continental found itself embroiled in another merger and ended up as part of Frank Lorenzo's Texas Air empire.

Western had some strange suitors. On 20 July 1981, **Air Florida** submitted a plan for control, having already acquired about 12 per cent of the stock. Western shareholders protested, and the CAB, while approving the plan in principle, required the holdings to be placed in a voting trust. On 29 January 1982, the CAB approved the takeover but would not consolidate the action with a quite separate negotiation in which an attempt was being made for Western to acquire **Wien Air Alaska**. This latter deal had been promoted by **Neil Bergt** of Alaska International Air (AIA), who had made a strong offer to buy Wien and trade the stock for Western preferred shares and the position of chairman of Western.

In July 1982, the CAB approved Bergt's proposal but stipulated that he must isolate himself from AIA. Western approved, but Bergt did not, and the merger activity was eventually terminated on 29 October 1982.

The Salt Lake City Hub

Bergt had rocketed to success during the oil boom on the Alaska North Slope, and was a man of decisive action. Though his sojourn with Western was brief, he was able, as a relative outsider, to take drastic and unpalatable steps to save Western from its then precarious financial position, laying off 500 of the middle management, eliminating a dozen top executives, negotiating wage reductions, and then turning his eyes to the operational problems.

He was highly critical of the way in which Western had handled the route structure and the scheduling practice. Reminiscent of Walter F. Brown's comments on small airlines back in 1930, he described Western as an airline that went from nowhere to nowhere, or worse had no cohesive plan.

As an antidote to this haphazard approach to route planning, he embarked on a major restructuring of the network, highlighted by the establishment of a route hub at **Salt Lake City**. This was a shrewd step and long overdue. All the airlines in the United States were bent on establishing hubs in middle America, channeling passengers to and from east and west coast destinations and achieving maximum load factors by careful integration of schedules and aircraft capacities.

Salt Lake City was selected not solely because it was the original point served by Western Air Express in 1926, although this was a happy coincidence for the traditionalists. Denver was already dominated by United and Continental; and all the other places such as Chicago, St. Louis, Kansas City, Dallas, Houston, and Minneapolis were firmly under the control of other airlines. In addition to opening service to eight new destinations, Western increased Salt Lake City departures, on 1 May 1982, from 29 to 59 daily, reducing those at Denver from 33 to 22. The fleet utilization increased by 22 per cent as a direct result of the restructuring.

On 7 September 1983, Western expanded its Los Angeles services to create it as more of a hub than as a terminus and intensified the connections to Salt Lake. By 1 June 1985, there were 115 departures a day from this Rocky Mountain hub, and the concentration was intensified on 27 January 1986, when Western entered into an operating agreement with a prominent regional (formerly commuter) airline, Skywest, to add feeder lines from a number of small cities in the west, some of which had formerly been served by Western itself.

"Wally Bird" was a feature of Western's advertising from the mid-1950s to the wide-bodied era.

McDonnell Douglas DC-10

294 SEATS ■ 552 mph

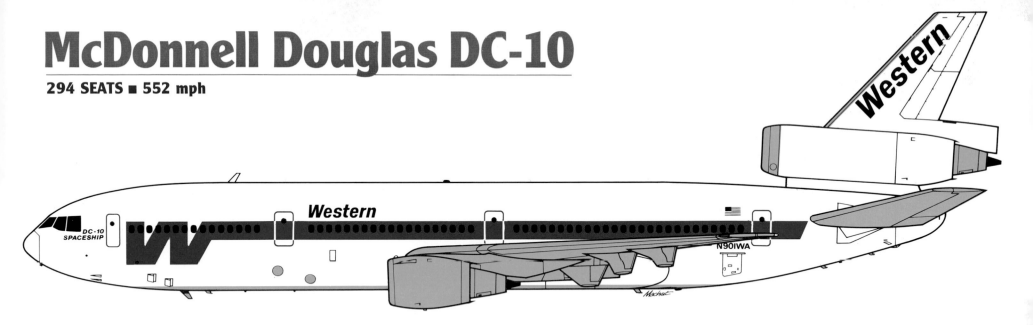

General Electric CF6-6D (40,000 lb.) x 3 ■ 220 tons max. gross take-off weight ■ Range 2,700 miles ■ Length 181 feet ■ Span 155 feet ■ Height 58 feet

Transcontinental Wide-Body

In the late 1960s, several U.S. airlines showed interest in a smaller aircraft than the capacious Boeing 747, but still retaining its wide-body passenger appeal. Any aircraft supplementing the Boeing 747 had to have transcontinental range and it had to split the size difference between the 180-seat narrow-bodied jets and the 360-seat 747, as the total market would not support another front-line airliner the size of the big Boeing. The competition quickly resolved itself into a tri-jet battle between two old adversaries, **Douglas** and **Lockheed**.

McDonnell Douglas's **DC-10-10**, first flew on 24 October 1970, three weeks before Lockheed's **L-1011 TriStar**. American Airlines put the DC-10 into service on 5 August 1971, by which time Douglas, with an eye to the world-wide market, had produced a longer-range version, the DC-10-30, with a higher gross weight to give it much longer range. An extra set of main landing gear wheels, mounted midway along the fuselage, was essential for the extra weight, a feature that the rival TriStar could not adopt without major structural changes, and which severely handicapped Lockheed's efforts to win overseas markets on a large scale.

Western Air Lines marked its long-sought access to the Atlantic seaboard by introducing DC-10s on the Los Angeles — Miami route on 1 October 1976, and on routes to London, from Anchorage from 9 October 1980, and from Denver from 25 April 1981. Both of these trans-Atlantic crossings were terminated after little more than a year's service, and the DC-10 "Spaceships" settled down as Western's flagship on the main U.S. trunk routes for the 1980s.

WESTERN'S McDONNELL DOUGLAS DC-10-10 FLEET

Regn.	MSN	Delivery Date	Regn.	MSN	Delivery Date
N901WA	46908	19 Apr. 73	N908WA	46977	13 Mar. 78
N902WA	46928	12 Jun. 73	N909WA	46983	18 May 78
N903WA	46929	27 Jun. 73	N912WA	46645	19 Jul. 79
N904WA	46930	25 Jul. 73	N913WA	46646	26 Jul. 79
N905WA	46938	20 May 74	N914WA	47832	12 May 80
N906WA	46939	6 Jun. 74	N915WA	47833	5 Jun. 80
N907WA	46946	22 Jun. 76	N821L	47848	9 Apr. 81

Fleet Numbers 901-913. N903WA crashed, México City, 31 Oct. 79; N821L was a DC-10-30 leased from International Lease Finance Corp., Apr. 81 - Sep. 83 with Fleet Number 950.

DC-10-10 at Salt Lake City in the revised Western colors. (Photo by John Wegg)

Delta Wide-Bodies

The Boeing 747

When Pan American Airways launched the airline world into the wide-bodied, or Jumbo-Jet era with Boeing 747 service to London on 22 January 1970, the U.S. domestic airlines were hard on its heels. The first battle for equipment superiority was on the transcontinental route from the northeast, specifically New York, to California. TWA opened service on 25 February, American on 2 March, and United on 23 July. Continental started Chicago—Honolulu service, via Los Angeles, on 26 June, and Northwest linked the Windy City with Tokyo, via Seattle, on 1 July, and by the end of the year Eastern and Braniff had brought the total of U.S. domestic operators of the 747 to nine. Both **Delta Air Lines** and National Airlines, sharing the southern transcontinental route, had opened 747 service on the same day, 25 October. Delta's route was Atlanta — Dallas — Los Angeles.

By 12 November 1971, Delta had moved strongly to acquire **Northeast Airlines** (see page 86) to strengthen its position in the northeast and to obtain direct routes from New York and New England to Florida, the so-called "gravy-run." But neither these nor its existing network was ideal for the huge Boeing. Operations of an aircraft with 370 seats, in mixed class, needed large volumes of traffic to maintain load factors that were sufficient on a year-round basis, during the tough periods as well as the peaks, to maintain operational and financial viability. Furthermore, the route segments were simply not long enough for maximum efficiency. As yet, the trans-Atlantic routes were still a distant prospect, although the CAB was cautiously sympathetic, and Delta was still denied direct Miami — Los Angeles nonstop authority. It had hoped also to receive a Chicago — Atlanta — Jamaica route, it had served all these points since the merger with Chicago & Southern in 1953, but the privilege went to Eastern and Pan American.

Faith in the Tri-Jet

Delta had studied its options for entry into the wide-bodied era very carefully. It decided that the size and the range of the Boeing 747 were not essential for its route structure. Its order was restricted to five, and the last one was retired on 23 April 1977. Bearing in mind the close relationship between Delta and Douglas however, its tri-jet decision came as something of a surprise to industry observers, when, in April 1968, it ordered 24 **Lockheed L-1011 TriStars**, powered by three Rolls-Royce RB.211 engines.

When, in the fall of 1970 and the early part of 1971, the prestigious British Rolls-Royce company was facing bankruptcy, and the engine program was falling desperately behind schedule, the TriStar, with no alternative engine variant in the series, was itself in jeopardy. And so were its customers. As an insurance against possible delays, or even non-delivery of its fleet, Delta ordered five **McDonnell Douglas DC-10s** on 18 March 1971. These were then sold to United Air Lines before they were delivered and then leased back from November 1972 until May 1975.

A Delta Boeing 747-132 at London-Heathrow Airport on the Pan American interchange service from Washington. (Photo by Bob Sage)

DELTA'S WIDE-BODY FLEET

Regn.	MSN	Regn.	MSN
Boeing 747-132		N729DA	193C-1180
		N730DA	193C-1199
N9896	19896	N1731D	193C-1200
N9897	19897	N1732D	193C-1213
N9898	19898	N733DS	193C-1224
N9899	20246	N1734D	193C-1225
N9900	20247	N735D	193C-1226
		N736DY	193C-1227
Fleet Numbers 101-105, delivered		N737DA	193C-1228
Sep. 70 - Nov. 71. Traded-in to		N1738D	193C-1234
Boeing, Sep. 74-Apr. 77.		N1739D	193C-1237
		N740DA	193C-1244
McDonnell Douglas DC-10-10		N741DA	193C-1245
N601DA	47965		
N602DA	47966	*Fleet Numbers 701-741; all Model*	
N603DA	47967	*L-1011-385-1 delivered new from*	
N604DA	47968	*Lockheed, Oct. 73 - May 83.*	
N605DA	47969	*N726DA crashed, Dallas, 2 Aug.*	
		85; aircraft 736-741 subsequently	
Fleet Numbers 601-605, leased		*converted to TriStar 250 (L-1011-*	
from United Air Lines from Oct. 72		*385-15), aircraft 724 del. as TriStar*	
to May 75.		*100 then converted to TriStar 200.*	
Lockheed L-1011 TriStar 1		**Lockheed L-1011 TriStar 500**	
N701DA	193C-1041		
N702DA	193C-1046	N751DA	193W-1166
N703DA	193C-1052	N752DA	193W-1172
N704DA	193C-1057	N753DA	193W-1189
N705DA	193C-1071	N754DL	193Y-1181
N706DA	193C-1074	N755DL	193Y-1184
N707DA	193C-1077	N756DR	193Y-1185
N708DA	193C-1078	N759DA	193Y-1176
N709DA	193C-1081	N760DH	193Y-1194
N710DA	193C-1084	N761DA	193Y-1208
N711DA	193C-1086	N762DA	193Y-1210
N712DA	193C-1088	N763DL	193Y-1197
N713DA	193C-1089		
N714DA	193C-1090	*Fleet Numbers 751-756, 759-763.*	
N715DA	193C-1092	*First three Model L-1011-385-3*	
N716DA	193C-1095	*delivered new from Lockheed,*	
N717DA	193C-1096	*May 79 - Aug. 80; remainder*	
N718DA	193C-1097	*Model L-1011-385-3 built for Pan*	
N719DA	193C-1135	*Am; aircraft 754-756 bought from*	
N720DA	193C-1136	*Pan Am Sep. 84 - Jan. 85, others*	
N721DA	193C-1139	*purchased from United Airlines*	
N722DA	193C-1147	*1988.*	
N723DA	193C-1150		
N724DA	193C-1151	**Lockheed L-1011 TriStar 200**	
N725DA	193C-1162		
N726DA	193C-1163	N31028	193B-1108
N727DA	193C-1167	N31029	193B-1109
N728DA	193C-1173		
		Fleet Numbers 798-799; Model	
		L-1011-385-1 leased from TWA,	
		Apr. 78 - Apr. 80.	

Lockheed L-1011 TriStar 1

250 SEATS ■ 552 mph

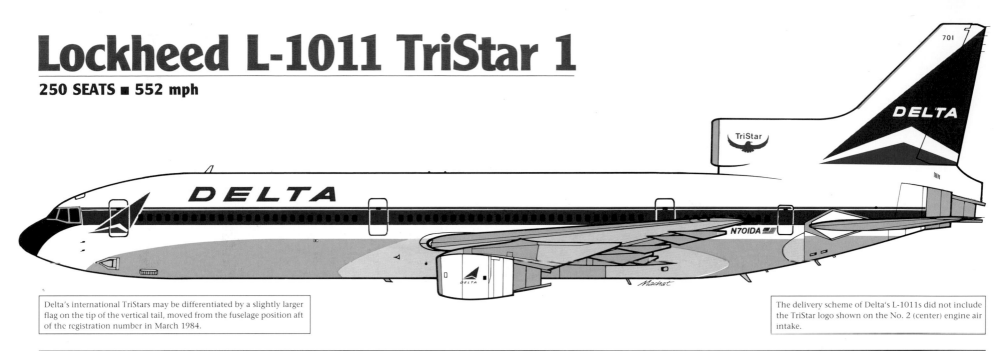

Delta's international TriStars may be differentiated by a slightly larger flag on the tip of the vertical tail, moved from the fuselage position aft of the registration number in March 1984.

The delivery scheme of Delta's L-1011s did not include the TriStar logo shown on the No. 2 (center) engine air intake.

Rolls-Royce RB.511-22B (42,000 lb.) x 3 ■ 215 tons max. gross take-off weight ■ Range 3,000 miles

The first of Delta's 250-seat L-1011 TriStar 1s went into service in December 1973, and the fleet was eventually to total 54 of all variants. Because of the "insurance" order for the McDonnell Douglas DC-10, Delta was the first airline to enjoy the unusual distinction of operating all three wide-bodied aircraft types at the same time.

Trans-Atlantic Service

On 21 December 1977, the Civil Aeronautics Board and the President awarded a trans-Atlantic route to Delta Air Lines, in an unusual manner. Traditionally apprehensive that the new contenders might not reach the traffic levels confidently predicted, it was obliged nevertheless to grant new authority because of the provisions of "Bermuda II" — the new round of bilateral routes between the U.S.A. and the United Kingdom. It neatly hedged its bets. For selected city pairs, it granted rights to the designated carriers of the two nations who would then alternate for the honor of inaugurating the new service. Thus, British Caledonian Airways was given a two-year monopoly between Houston and London (Gatwick) and the U.S. carrier, (Continental), joined in the fray two years later, by which time, the CAB estimated, traffic would have built up sufficiently to accommodate two competitors. **Delta Air Lines** drew the lucky card for Atlanta — London (also Gatwick) and opened service on 30 April 1978. British Caledonian (now British Airways, after a takeover) came in after the two-year stipulated period.

No sooner had the CAB award been made when Delta ordered three **Lockheed TriStar 500s**, in January 1978. These were long-range versions of the basic aircraft, several seat rows smaller because — in contrast with the DC-10-30 with its extra main landing gear leg — payload had to be traded off for the extra fuel required. Nevertheless, with 241 seats, they were well suited to the traffic potential on the London route from Atlanta.

Anxious to get going, Delta leased two TriStar 200s from TWA and opened up to London on 30 April 1978. The TriStar 500s augmented the service on 17 June 1979 with the inauguration of the Atlanta — Frankfurt service.

LENGTH 179 feet
SPAN 155 feet
HEIGHT 55 feet

Delta adopted the Lockheed L-1011 TriStar as its choice for the first wide-bodied era. This is a long-range TriStar 500 at Frankfurt-Main. (Photo by John Wegg)

Delta In Full Stride

Tidying Up The Fleet

When **Delta Air Lines** took over **Northeast Airlines** on 1 August 1972 (see page 86) it did not need all the latter's aircraft, as integration of the two route networks permitted substantial economies by careful scheduling. Of the Northeast fleet, the early Boeing 727-95s were phased out, the 13 DC-9-31s sold to Allegheny Airlines and Ozark, and the FH-227Cs sold to Air New England. It kept the Boeing 727-295s, however, to augment its own fleet. Delta had placed its first order for 14 **Boeing 727-232 (Advanced)** models on 29 March 1972. During the next decade, Delta built up its 727-200 fleet to 129, at the time the biggest in the world of this, one of the most successful commercial aircraft in air transport history. As a matter of interest, the number included the first of the -200s to be placed in airline service (by Northeast), the 500th 727 (for Northeast) and the 1,000th 727 (for Delta) to come off the line.

Meanwhile, to standardize the fleet, the last Convair 880 departed in January 1974, and, as already mentioned (page 96) the last Boeing 747 went too. The DC-9 fleet was being reduced progressively, as the Boeing 727 became a jack-of-all-work. As described on the page opposite, however, Delta had not finished with its DC-8-61s (the earlier DC-8-51s had been retired), and embarked on an enterprising conversion program to extend the life of these veterans of the air.

In the fall of 1983 Delta traded eleven TriStar 1s to Boeing in a deal that netted Delta 33 Boeing 737-232s. This versatile twin-jet allowed Delta to expand its domestic routes considerably, and enabled it to expand rapidly at the Dallas/Fort Worth hub.

When problems arose at a critical stage of the Lockheed L-1011 development, Delta leased some DC-10-10s from United Air Lines. (Photo by Peter R. Keating)

More Atlantic Service

On 30 April 1978 Delta Air Lines inaugurated trans-Atlantic service with an Atlanta – London route. In its characteristic style, Delta fashioned its Atlantic network at its own pace, planning carefully and marketing astutely with new U.S. gateways, to supplement the Atlanta base, at Dallas, Orlando, and Cincinnati. The Atlantic would be the training ground for wider horizons across another ocean (see page 110).

One of Delta's Boeing 727-232 (Advanced) models. (Photo by John Wegg)

DELTA'S BOEING 727-232 (ADVANCED) FLEET

Regn.	MSN	Regn.	MSN
N452DA	20634	N415DA	21257
N453DA	20635	N416DA	21258
N454DA	20636	N417DA	21259
N455DA	20637	N418DA	21271
N456DA	20638	N419DA	21272
N457DA	20639	N420DA	21273
N458DA	20640	N421DA	21274
N459DA	20641	N501DA	21303
N460DA	20642	N502DA	21304
N461DA	20643	N503DA	21305
N462DA	20644	N504DA	21306
N463DA	20645	N505DA	21307
N464DA	20646	N506DA	21308
N465DA	20647	N507DA	21309
N466DA	20743	N508DA	21310
N467DA	20744	N509DA	21311
N468DA	20745	N510DA	21312
N469DA	20746	N511DA	21313
N470DA	20747	N512DA	21314
N471DA	20748	N513DA	21315
N472DA	20749	N514DA	21430
N473DA	20750	N515DA	21431
N474DA	20751	N516DA	21432
N475DA	20752	N517DA	21433
N476DA	20753	N518DA	21469
N477DA	20754	N519DA	21470
N478DA	20755	N520DA	21471
N479DA	20756	N521DA	21472
N480DA	20860	N522DA	21582
N481DA	20861	N523DA	21583
N482DA	20862	N524DA	21584
N483DA	20863	N525DA	21585
N484DA	20864	N526DA	21586
N485DA	20865	N527DA	21587
N486DA	20866	N528DA	21702
N487DA	20867	N529DA	21703
N488DA	21018	N530DA	21813
N489DA	21019	N531DA	21814
N490DA	21020	N532DA	22045
N491DA	21060	N533DA	22046
N492DA	21061	N534DA	22047
N493DA	21062	N535DA	22048
N494DA	21074	N536DA	22049
N495DA	21075	N537DA	22073
N496DA	21076	N538DA	22076
N497DA	21077	N539DA	22385
N498DA	21142	N540DA	22386
N499DA	21143	N541DA	22387
N400DA	21144	N542DA	22391
N401DA	21145	N543DA	22392
N402DA	21146	N544DA	22493
N403DA	21147	N545DA	22494
N404DA	21148	N546DA	22677
N405DA	21149		
N406DA	21150		
N407DA	21151		
N408DA	21152		
N409DA	21153		
N410DA	21222		
N411DA	21223		
N412DA	21232		
N413DA	21233		
N414DA	21256		

Fleet numbers 452-499, delivered Jan. 73 - Sep. 75; 400-421, delivered Sep. 75 - Feb. 77; 501-546, delivered May 77 - Nov. 81. N473DA crashed, Dallas/Ft. Worth, 31 Aug. 88; N530DA written off in ground fire, Salt Lake City, 14 Oct. 89.

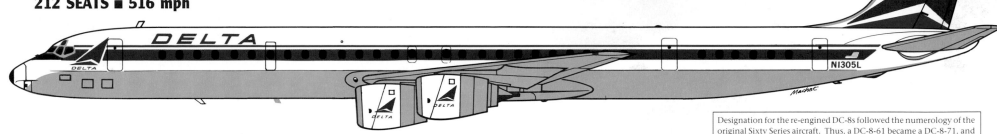

McDonnell Douglas DC-8-71

212 SEATS ■ 516 mph

Designation for the re-engined DC-8s followed the numerology of the original Sixty Series aircraft. Thus, a DC-8-61 became a DC-8-71, and the -62 and -63 becoming the DC-8-72 and -73 respectively.

CFM International CFM56-2-C1 (24,000 lb.) x 4 ■ 162 tons max. gross take-off weight ■ Range 3,735 miles

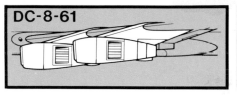

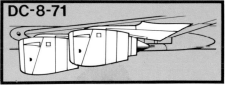

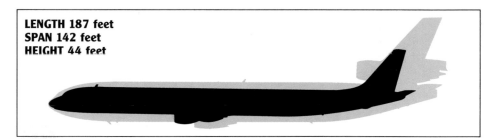

LENGTH 187 feet
SPAN 142 feet
HEIGHT 44 feet

Beyond the Limits

Just as the aviation world thought it had closed the book on what were by now being described as narrow-bodied jets, the Douglas line of DC-8s were given one more lease of life in 1977. Jackson McGowan, who had led Douglas through its successful selling period during the 1960s, set up a company at El Segundo, near Los Angeles Airport, to perpetuate the life of the **DC-8-60 Series**. The **Cammacorp** company's idea was to replace the Pratt & Whitney JT3D engines with the highly efficient CFM56 engines, produced jointly by the General Electric and the French SNECMA manufacturers. This gave the DC-8-60s more power with reduced noise, better economy, and a new lease of life, especially for carrying cargo, which was not so fussy as passengers in insisting on wide-bodied comfort.

Another First for Delta

Possibly McGowan had inherited, or at least remembered, the close relationship between his former chief, Donald Douglas, Sr., and C.E. Woolman. In any event, the first airline he approached was **Delta Air Lines**. All except the first of Delta's 13 DC-8-61s — which was modified by Cammacorp at Tulsa — were converted at Delta's own base in Atlanta, from kits supplied by Cammacorp. The most important changes were the installation of the engines, a new pressurization system, and considerable upgrading of the avionics. The first **DC-8-71** — the Cammacorp conversions were all designated as the -70 Series — went into service on 24 April 1982 on the somewhat improbable choice for an inaugural route, Atlanta — Savannah.

The DC-8-71 fleet was sold to the United Parcel Service (UPS) on 2 September 1986, a "paper" transaction initially, as they were promptly leased back to Delta for three years. After three decades of service, the last of Delta's family of DC-8s was retired with due ceremony on 1 May 1989. Delta converted a total of 48 DC-8-60s to the new standard and altogether, 110 Seventy series were produced.

Western Joins Delta

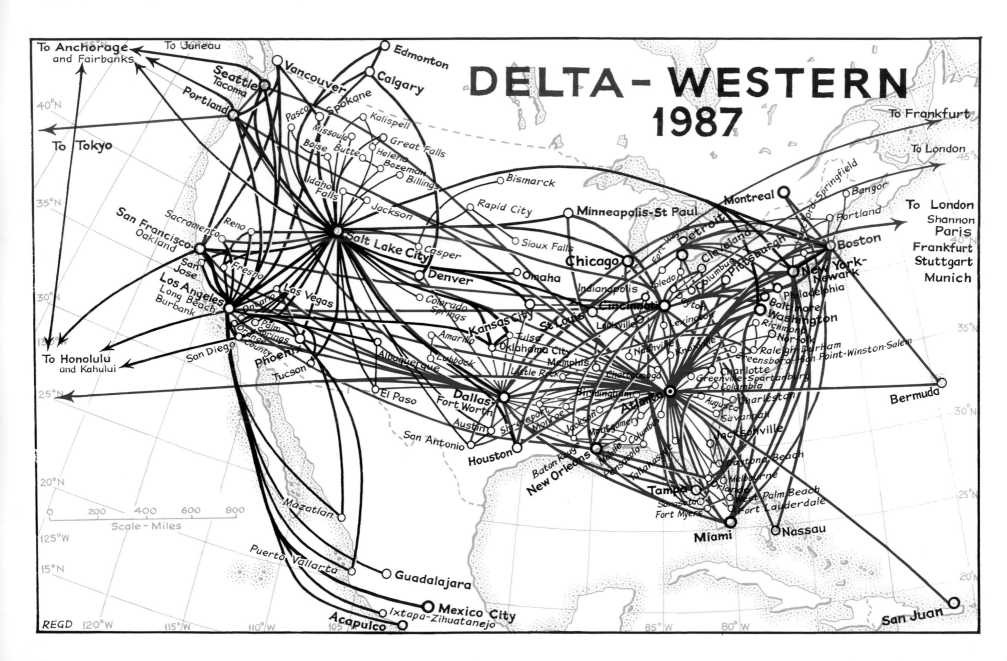

DELTA-WESTERN
1987

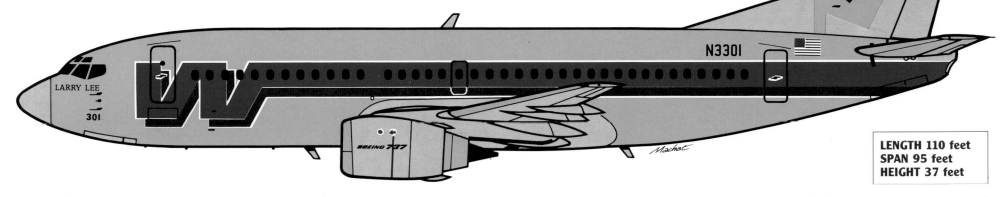

Boeing 737-347

128 SEATS ■ 560 mph

N3301

LARRY LEE
301

BOEING 737

LENGTH 110 feet
SPAN 95 feet
HEIGHT 37 feet

CFM International CFM56-3 (20,000 lb.) x 2 ■ 135,500 lb. max. gross take-off weight ■ Range 2,250 miles

Decisive Decision

Western Air Lines had many suitors for its hand in merger-marriage (see page 94). These had fallen through for a variety of reasons, not the least of which was less than stellar financial performance during the 1970s. Primarily two factors, which occurred in the mid-1980s changed Western's fate. First, beginning in 1983, Western's management was able to obtain significant wage concessions and work rule changes from its unions. Second, Western reworked its flight schedule and established a strategic highly successful hub in Salt Lake City. These decisive changes not only made Western an attractive merger candidate, but also saved the carrier from almost certain bankruptcy. Under the leadership of **Neil Bergt**, **Larry Lee**, and later **Gerald Grinstein**, Western underwent a complete metamorphosis in the 1980s.

On 5 August 1985, Western announced a comfortable profit estimated to be $45 million for the first 7 months of the year, and that future prospects were good. Whether or not that meant the prospects were good for a takeover was not explained. But within a year's time, one of the nation's oldest airlines became the subject of a benevolent takeover by another of America's pioneer airlines, **Delta Air Lines**. Delta bought Western for $860 million, thereby becoming the fourth largest airline in the U.S. and the fifth largest in the world. Western became a wholly-owned subsidiary of Delta on 19 December 1986, and was operationally merged into the Delta system on 1 April 1987.

Gerald Grinstein, CEO and Chairman of Western from 1984 until its merger with Delta.

A Western Boeing 737-347 with Delta titles at Salt Lake City shortly after the merger. (Photo by George Hamlin)

DELTA'S BOEING 737 FLEET

Regn.	MSN	Regn.	MSN
737-232 Advanced		N330DL	23102
		N331DL	23103
N301DL	23073	N332DL	23104
N302DL	23074	N334DL	23105
N303DL	23075		
N304DL	23076	*Fleet Numbers 301-333; delivered*	
N305DL	23077	*Oct. 83 - Dec. 84.*	
N306DL	23078		
N307DL	23079	**737-347**	
N308DL	23080		
N309DL	23081	N3301	23181
N310DA	23082	N302WA	23182
N311DL	23083	N303WA	23183
N312DL	23084	N304WA	23345
N313DL	23085	N305WA	23346
N314DA	23086	N306WA	23347
N315DL	23087	N307WA	23440
N316DL	23088	N308WA	23441
N317DL	23089	N309WA	23442
N318DL	23090	N2310	23596
N319DL	23091	N311WA	23597
N320DL	23092	N312WA	23598
N321DL	23093	N313WA	23599
N322DL	23094		
N323DL	23095	*Delivered to **Western**, Mar. 85 -*	
N324DL	23096	*Jun. 86; Fleet Numbers 301-313,*	
N325DL	23097	*changed to 201-213 with Delta.*	
N326DL	23098	*N3301 named Larry Lee, N302WA*	
N327DL	23099	*Wally Bird, and N303WA Salt*	
N328DL	23100	*Lake City. **Delta** has 50 737-332s*	
N329DL	23101	*on order, plus another 50 options.*	
		Deliveries will start in 1993.	

The New Delta

Pacific Service

Delta had already entered the Pacific arena on 14 December 1984, when it started a TriStar service from Atlanta to Honolulu, via Dallas/Fort Worth, adding nonstop service from Atlanta to Hawaii on 1 June 1985. Concurrently with the Western Air Lines merger, it was able to consolidate and expand its Pacific involvement, not only absorbing Western's substantial West Coast — Hawaii network but by adding, on 2 March 1987, a trans-Pacific service from Atlanta to Tokyo, via Portland, Oregon.

The Boeing 767

United States manufacturers were surprisingly slow to react to the threat of the European Airbus A300B, which made its first flight on 28 October 1972, and began to penetrate world markets. Douglas looked carefully at a twin-engined version of the DC-10 but put the drawings back on the shelf, as its DC-9 developments kept the production lines busy. Only in the next decade did an American challenger take to the skies. The **Boeing 767-200** made its first flight on 26 September 1981, and went into service with United in September the following year. **Delta Air Lines** (together with American) was the launch customer for a General Electric CF6-80 version that possessed true transcontinental range and introduced its new type on 15 December 1982.

Earlier that year, Delta, had suffered unusual financial losses because of a downturn in traffic but, unlike its similarly-affected competitors, did not react by laying-off staff. In a remarkable demonstration of reciprocal loyalty, Delta's employees raised $30 million through payroll deductions to purchase the airline's first Boeing 767, which was suitably named *The Spirit of Delta*.

The Boeing 757-200 utilized the Boeing 727 fuselage cross-section, jigs, and tools.

The Boeing 757

Coming hard on the heels of the Boeing 767 was what could be described as the ultimate development of an outstandingly successful airliner, the Boeing 727. But the development was so comprehensive that the **757** — as it came to be designated — bore little resemblance to its predecessor. Like the wide-bodied 767, it was a twin-engined variant, with two Rolls-Royce RB.211 wing-mounted engines replacing the rear-mounted JT8Ds of the 727. It had a brand-new, super-critical wing, a redesigned nose and a conventional(versus the T-shaped) tail. Also like the 767, it had a completely new flight deck with an integrated digital system for flight control and navigation combined with digitally-generated cathode-ray tube (CRT) displays (the so-called "glass cockpit")which reduced crew workload and made both types suitable for two-pilot operation. The 757 made its first flight on 19 February 1982.

The 757 exceeded beyond measure the hopes of its maker. Its engines and super-critical wing gave it either a shorter take-off run or longer range than the 727. It was also a quiet airplane, both inside and out, and that pleased everybody, the FAA, the passengers and even the local noise abatement societies. By the end of 1989, over 600 of this remarkable commercial airliner development had been sold.

Delta Air Lines was the launch customer for the more powerful Pratt & Whitney PW2037-powered version on 12 November 1980, with a massive order for 60 aircraft to replace DC-9s and 727s. The 757 entered service with Delta on 28 November 1984, almost exactly two years after the debut of the 767, and by 1990 Delta was operating the largest fleet of 757s in the world.

One of Delta's Boeing 767-332s.

DELTA'S BOEING 757 & 767 FLEET

Regn.	MSN	Regn.	MSN
757-232		N659DL	24421
N601DL	22808	N660DL	24422
N602DL	22809	*Fleet Numbers 601-660; delivered*	
N603DL	22810	*from Feb. 85. Another 13 on order,*	
N604DL	22811	*plus 57 options.*	
N605DL	22812		
N606DL	22813	**767-232**	
N607DL	22814		
N608DA	22815	N101DA	22213
N609DL	22816	N102DA	22214
N610DL	22817	N103DA	22215
N611DL	22818	N104DA	22216
N612DL	22819	N105DA	22217
N613DL	22820	N106DA	22218
N614DL	22821	N107DL	22219
N615DL	22822	N108DL	22220
N616DL	22823	N109DL	22221
N617DL	22907	N110DL	22222
N618DL	22908	N111DN	22223
N619DL	22909	N112DL	22224
N620DL	22910	N113DA	22225
N621DL	22911	N114DL	22226
N622DL	22912	N115DA	22227
N623DL	22913	*Fleet Numbers 101-115; delivered*	
N624DL	22914	*from Mar. 83. N102DA named* The	
N625DL	22915	Spirit of Delta.	
N626DL	22916		
N627DL	22917	**767-332**	
N628DL	22918		
N629DL	22919	N116DL	23275
N630DL	22920	N117DL	23276
N631DL	23612	N118DL	23277
N632DL	23613	N119DL	23278
N633DL	23614	N120DL	23279
N634DL	23615	N121DE	23435
N635DL	23762	N122DL	23436
N636DL	23763	N123DN	23437
N637DL	23760	N124DE	23438
N638DL	23761	N125DL	24075
N639DL	23993	N126DL	24076
N640DL	23994	N127DL	24077
N641DL	23995	N128DL	24078
N642DL	23996	N129DL	24079
N643DL	23997	N130DL	24080
N644DL	23998	*Fleet Numbers 116-130; delivered*	
N645DL	24216	*from Nov. 86. Another 8 on order,*	
N646DL	24217	*plus 4 options.*	
N647DL	24218		
N648DL	24372	**767-332 (ER)**	
N649DL	24389	N171DN	24759
N650DL	24390	N172DN	24775
N651DL	24391	N173DN	24800
N652DL	24392	N174DN	24802
N653DL	24393	N175DN	24803
N654DL	24394		
N655DL	24395	*Fleet Numbers 171-175; delivered*	
N656DL	24396	*from 1990. Another four are on*	
N657DL	24419	*order, plus 16 options.*	
N658DL	24420		

Delta's Trusty Boeings

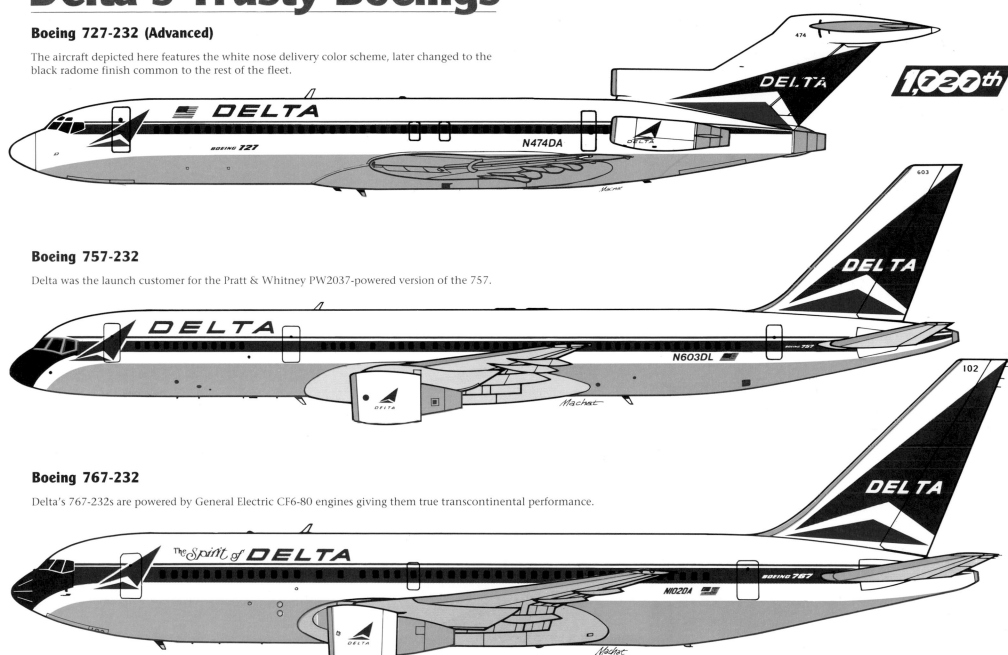

Boeing 727-232 (Advanced)

The aircraft depicted here features the white nose delivery color scheme, later changed to the black radome finish common to the rest of the fleet.

Boeing 757-232

Delta was the launch customer for the Pratt & Whitney PW2037-powered version of the 757.

Boeing 767-232

Delta's 767-232s are powered by General Electric CF6-80 engines giving them true transcontinental performance.

Short-Range Choice

The Super Eighty

The Douglas Aircraft Company had always been masters at the technique of building commercial aircraft that were capable of development into bigger and better variants of the original series. The DC-1 had led to the DC-2 and DC-3; the DC-4, 6, and 7 all came off the same fuselage jigs. The DC-8 and the DC-10 were both developed into aircraft far superior to their prototypes. But no Douglas airliner was developed so much, or so often, or with such good effect, as the DC-9.

Some of this is summarized on pages 78-79, as is Delta's role as the launching customer, inaugurating the first DC-9 service on 8 December 1965, less than a year after the aircraft's first flight on 25 February. Since that time, Delta has never been without a substantial fleet of the ubiquitous Douglas twin-jet, but during the 1980s it was far outnumbered by the Boeing 727. The folks at Long Beach could have been been forgiven for believing that the old relationship between Donald Douglas and C.E. Woolman had disappeared into history, never to return. Even the new version, the **DC-9 Super 80**, or the MD-80 (to recognize the McDonnell Douglas amalgamation) did not appear to impress Delta when it made its first flight on 18 October 1979, and went into service with Pacific Southwest Airlines (PSA) on 17 December 1980.

Delta, one of the few airlines then making money, issued a requirement for a new 150-seat aircraft in spring 1981 and Long Beach offered its D-3300 ('D' for Delta) design. However, this project was canceled late in 1983 and Delta turned to the Boeing 737-200 for its immediate needs. Nevertheless, the **Delta-3** specification (so-called because Delta had been instrumental in the design of two previous transports, the DC-9 and L-1011 TriStar) remained. The re-engined Boeing 737-300 looked as if it would win Delta's substantial order until prop-fan engines (called Unducted Fans or UDF engines) appeared which promised major fuel savings. As the 737 could not be re-fitted with these "jet-propeller" engines, Delta's interest turned to the MD-80 series which was adaptable to the new technology should it prove commercially viable. With the MD-80 also able to cruise efficiently at Boeing 727 speeds, the choice was made and in January 1986 **Delta** ordered 30 142-seat **MD-88s** plus 50 options.

Based on the MD-82 (DC-9-82), the MD-88 featured a number of aerodynamic improvements already introduced for later MD-82s, including a re-designed tail cone, plus an updated "glass cockpit" (see pages 102 and 108). The first eight aircraft were delivered as MD-82s and subsequently converted to MD-88s. Delta introduced the MD-82 on 1 April

W.T. "Tom" Beebe joined Chicago & Southern Air Lines in 1947, succeeded Charlie Dolson in 1970, and was Delta's Chairman from 1971 to 1980.

David Garrett joined Delta Air Lines as a sales agent in 1946 and rose steadily through the ranks to succeed W.T. "Tom" Beebe as president in 1971, and served as chairman from 1980 until 1983.

1987, and the first MD-88 entered service on 21 December the same year.

McDonnell Douglas took the DC-9 one step further in 1989 when, after deciding that prop-fan technology was viable but too expensive to develop until fuel prices increased considerably (thus making jet aircraft less economical), proposed a new family of aircraft based on the MD-80. The **MD90** series featured a new, quieter, and more fuel-efficient engine, the International Aero Engines (IAE) V2500, to replace the Pratt & Whitney JT8D-200 of the MD-80s. In November 1989, **Delta** launched the 150-seat **MD90-30**, 57-inches longer than the MD-88, with an order for 50, with another 110 on option for delivery from 1994.

An artist's impression of the MD90-30 which, together with the Boeing 737-300, will form the backbone of Delta's short-range fleet in the 1990s.

The McDonnell Douglas MD-88 is a development of the original Douglas DC-9, with twice the passenger capacity of the first version, and modernized engines and avionics. (Photo by Frank Hines)

McDonnell Douglas MD-88

142 SEATS ■ 574 mph

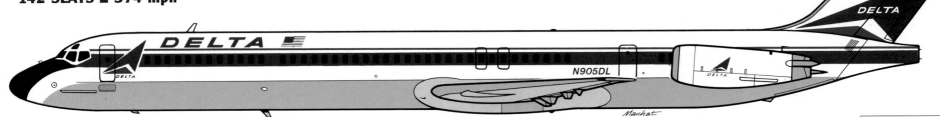

The "Wally Bird" logo depicted above was prepared for the Delta-Western merger day, 1 April 1987, and applied to this particular aircraft delivered during the merger celebration at Los Angeles. It remains part of the aircraft's color scheme today.

LENGTH 148 feet
SPAN 108 feet
HEIGHT 31 feet

Pratt & Whitney JT8D-219 (20,000 lb.) x 2 ■ 149,500 lb. max. gross take-off weight ■ Range 1,800 miles

DELTA'S McDONNELL DOUGLAS MD-88 FLEET

Regn.	MSN	Regn.	MSN	Regn.	MSN	Regn.	MSN
N901DL	49532	N918DL	49583	N935DL	49722	N952DL	49883
N902DL	49533	N919DL	49584	N936DL	49723	N953DL	49884
N903DL	49534	N920DL	49644	N937DL	49810	N954DL	49885
N904DL	49535	N921DL	49645	N938DL	49811	N955DL	49886
N905DL	49536	N922DL	49646	N939DL	49812	N956DL	49976
N906DL	49537	N923DL	49705	N940DL	49813	N957DL	49977
N907DL	49538	N924DL	49711	N941DL	49814	N958DL	49978
N908DL	49539	N925DL	49712	N942DL	49815	N959DL	49979
N909DL	49540	N926DL	49713	N943DL	49816	N960DL	49980
N910DL	49541	N927DL	49714	N944DL	49817	N961DL	49981
N911DL	49542	N928DL	49715	N945DL	49818	N962DL	49982
N912DL	49543	N929DL	49716	N946DL	49819	N963DL	49983
N913DL	49544	N930DL	49717	N947DL	49878	N964DL	49984
N914DL	49545	N931DL	49718	N948DL	49879	N965DL	53115
N915DL	49546	N932DL	49719	N949DL	49880	N966DL	53116
N916DL	49591	N933DL	49720	N950DL	49881	N967DL	53161
N917DL	49573	N934DL	49721	N951DL	49882		

Fleet Numbers 901-967; 901-908 delivered Mar.- May 87 as MD-82s (DC-9-82s) and converted to MD-88 standard 1988, MD-88s delivered from Dec. 87. Another 16 are on firm order (30 Nov. 89) plus options held for a further 67 for a total of 150.

THE McDONNELL DOUGLAS DC-9 FAMILY

Type	Dimensions (ft)			Typical Seating	Engines (2)		MGTOW (lb)	First Service		No. Built
	Length	Span	Height		Type	Thrust (lb)		Date	Airline	
DC-9-10	104	89	27	80	JT8D-1	14,000	90,700	8 Dec. 65	Delta	137
DC-9-20	104	93	27	80	JT8D-9	15,000	87,000	23 Jan. 69	SAS	10
DC-9-30	119	93	27	97	JT8D-7	14,500	108,000	1 Feb. 67	Eastern	662
DC-9-40	125	89	28	107	JT8D-9	14,500	114,000	12 Mar. 68	SAS	71
DC-9-50	133	89	28	114	JT8D-17	16,000	121,000	24 Aug. 75	Swissair	96
DC-9-80 (MD-80)	148	108	30	142	JT8D-209	18,500	140,000	5 Oct. 80	Swissair	654*
DC-9-87	130	108	30	109	JT8D-217	20,000	140,000	14 Nov. 87	Swissair	33*

* At 31 Jan. 90, production continues. All the DC-9/MD-80s have a cruising speed of approximately 560 mph.

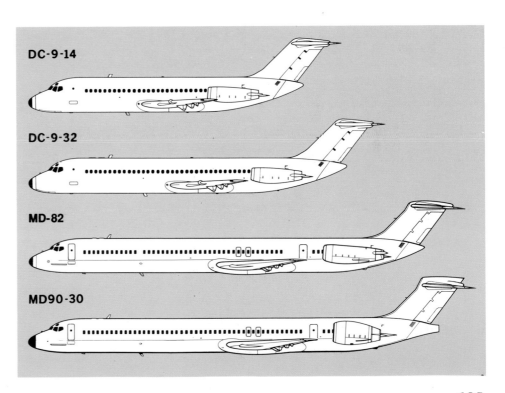

DC-9-14

DC-9-32

MD-82

MD90-30

The Delta Connection

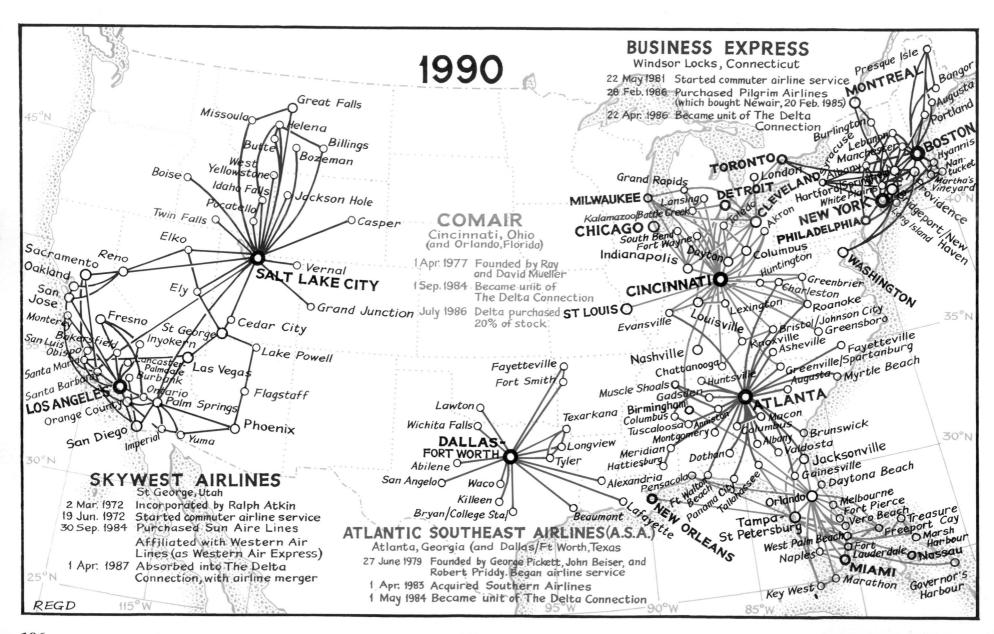

1990

BUSINESS EXPRESS
Windsor Locks, Connecticut
22 May 1981 Started commuter airline service
28 Feb. 1986 Purchased Pilgrim Airlines
(which bought Newair, 20 Feb. 1985)
22 Apr. 1986 Became unit of The Delta
Connection

COMAIR
Cincinnati, Ohio
(and Orlando, Florida)

1 Apr. 1977 Founded by Ray
and David Mueller
1 Sep. 1984 Became unit of
The Delta Connection
July 1986 Delta purchased
20% of stock

SKYWEST AIRLINES
St George, Utah
2 Mar. 1972 Incorporated by Ralph Atkin
19 Jun. 1972 Started commuter airline service
30 Sep. 1984 Purchased Sun Aire Lines
Affiliated with Western Air
Lines (as Western Air Express)
1 Apr. 1987 Absorbed into The Delta
Connection, with airline merger

ATLANTIC SOUTHEAST AIRLINES (A.S.A.)
Atlanta, Georgia (and Dallas/Ft Worth, Texas
27 June 1979 Founded by George Pickett, John Beiser, and
Robert Priddy. Began airline service
1 Apr. 1983 Acquired Southern Airlines
1 May 1984 Became unit of The Delta Connection

REGD

All Part of the Family

When, during the mid-1980s, all the major airlines (formerly trunk carriers) adopted the practice of establishing partnerships with their regional (formerly commuter) brethren, **Delta Air Lines** was well to the forefront of the movement. Eschewing the popular "Express" suffix, the Atlanta airline chose **The Delta Connection** as a group title that more precisely defined the role of the junior members of its adopted family.

On 1 May 1984, **Ransome Airlines** of Philadelphia, and **Atlantic Southeast Airlines (ASA)** of Atlanta, entered into code-sharing agreements with Delta. The two feeder airlines were able to use the two-letter DL reservations code, and were assigned a special series of Delta flight numbers, a mutually beneficial arrangement that stimulated connecting traffic potential through the common airlines. A third commuter airline, **Rio Airways**, from the Dallas/Fort Worth hub, joined The Delta Connection exactly one month later, and **ComAir** of Cincinnati came on board 1 September of the same year, to bring the number of Connectors up to four.

Delta had thus put itself emphatically on the code-sharing map; but the first years were not entirely successful, as two of the four had withdrawn by the end of 1986. On 1 June of that year, J. Dawson Ransome sold his airline to Pan American Airways, which badly needed a feeder system radiating from New York; while on 14 December of the same year, Rio Airways went bankrupt.

By this time, however, an important addition had been made in the northeast, so that the loss of Ransome was not as serious as it appeared. **Business Express**, a commuter airline formed at Hartford, Connecticut, in November 1984 when the Marketing Corporation of America purchased Atlantic Air, was serving New England, which had always been a problem area for airlines as far back as the infant days of Boston-Maine and Central Vermont Airways in the early 1930s (see page 38); and where the distribution of urban population among dozens of medium-sized cities has given headaches to airline planners ever since. Business Express's network, at least the northern half, is uncannily similar to that of Northeast's ancestors half a century ago.

When Business Express joined Delta in July 1986, the latter had only just bought **Pilgrim Airlines**, which in turn had bought **Newair**, operating on many parallel routes, in 1985. Established by one of the true pioneers, Joe Fugere, at Groton, Connecticut, on 1 April 1962, Pilgrim had cemented strong airway links between most of the cities in the Connecticut hinterland and New York's airports on Long Island, to which the surface road connections were circuitous and time-consuming.

The Delta Connection was back to a quartet again when the parent company merged with Western Air Lines on 1 April 1987, and inherited a commuter airline operating as Western Express. Formed in 1972, **Skywest Airlines** had grown vigorously, especially by absorbing **Sun Aire Lines** in 1984. It was serving an area of the western states that would have been envied by some of the trunk airlines before deregulation.

Meanwhile, Delta had plugged up some gaps. ASA established a second hub at Dallas/Fort Worth, as a substitute for the late Rio Airways; and ComAir, already thriving mightily at the booming Cincinnati hub, established a second network throughout Florida, the fastest growing state in the nation.

Today, with a fine fleet of modern airliners, some of which are shown in the photographs on this page, and neatly complementing the main line Delta Air Lines system, The Delta Connection does exactly what its name implies.

A Business Express SAAB SF340A over Manhattan. The Delta Connection regional airline has a fleet of eleven 34-seat SAABs. (Photo by SAAB)

ASA operates a 49-strong fleet of 30-seat Embraer Brasilias. (Photo by George Hamlin)

A ComAir 15-seat Embraer Bandeirante at Orlando. (Photo by Norbert Raith)

Nineteen-seat Fairchild Metros make up the bulk of the fleet of Skywest Airlines. (Photo by Steve Caisse)

Long-Range Choice

Stretching the Ten

During the early 1970s, with a peak of activity in the marketing, market development, and planning departments of McDonnell Douglas at Long Beach in 1973, the idea of a larger DC-10 was the subject of intense discussion. Partly because of the fuel crisis, there had been a lull in sales of wide-bodied aircraft. Boeing particularly, after a dramatic start with the 747, experienced a stagnation period of about 20 months. Airlines were reluctant to commit themselves at a time when the optimistic forecasts of intercontinental air traffic growth were being questioned.

Remembering its successful program of stretching the **Douglas DC-8** (see page 77), many proposals were studied with the objective of doing the same thing with the DC-10; and there were also ideas to make a smaller, short-range **DC-10 Twin** version. Design studies for the latter looked so much like the Airbus A300 that discussions were even held to explore ideas of cooperation. At the time, a family of airliners consisting of the basic DC-10-10 and DC-10-30, teamed up with a lengthened DC-10 with almost as many seats as the 747 and with almost as much range, plus either a DC-10 twin or an A300, would have comprised a formidable marketing combination of incalculable strength.

For a number of reasons, not least the considerable development costs and the need for more engine power than was available at the time, the early ideas for a stretched DC-10 were dropped. But the soundness of the development strategy was not forgotten, and in 1979, the technical analogy with the DC-8 was revived with talks about a series that would have been named the **DC-10-61/62/63**.

During the early 1980s, there was a "Super 10" proposal — an airliner that could have been described loosely as an aircraft very much like the Lockheed L-1011 with winglets, or a McDonnell Douglas equivalent of the Boeing 747SP. This was followed by the MD-EEE — "Economy, Efficiency, and Ecology" — but this nomenclature was quickly dropped as it seemed to invite other interpretations.

By 1983 all the effort, procrastinating and ambivalent though it may have been, began to crystallize and the project studies finally led to a design clarification of an aircraft provisionally designated the **MD-100**, which was basically a DC-10 with its fuselage stretched by 30 feet, allowing up to ten more seat rows, or a total of 270 passengers.

The Avionics Revolution

Trying to decide how to produce a larger DC-10 and to define its exact specification must have been frustrating for Long Beach. Yet these delays may not have been entirely in vain. For the mid-1980s witnessed an acceleration of pace in the development of flight instrumentation and systems, to the extent that the term electronics revolution would not be too much of an exaggeration.

A new collection of words crept into the language of aviation, already suffering from a glut of meretricious phraseology. "Fly-by-wire," "CRTs," and "glass cockpits" epitomized the far-reaching changes that were being made, to the magnitude that even the accepted usage of the term avionics came into question. The fly-by-wire expression referred to a flight-control system with electric signaling, which abolished direct mechanical control, manual or servo-operated, from the flightdeck to the ailerons, elevators, and rudder. The dial indicators that had served the purpose for 80 years gave way to cathode-ray tubes (CRTs) that portrayed speed, altitude, attitude, and other essential parameters in a far less ambiguous, more readable manner.

Advances in Structures and Materials

During the past three or four decades, a process of evolution has occurred that could be called the "sleeping revolution." The development of fiber-glass and reinforced plastics had already resulted in certain applications in aircraft construction as early as the 1950s. Such materials had strength limitations, however, and the metals were still superior, with plastics used mostly for non-load-bearing surfaces.

Then came the new composites. Research revealed that certain non-metallic elements such as carbon and boron could be processed in such a manner as to produce compo-

nents as critically stress-demanding as turbine blades for jet engines. Aluminum alloy itself had already had to give way, in some instances, to the use of titanium, where metallic surfaces and components that were subjected to intense heat were still expected to maintain their inherent strength. The great advantage of both composites and titanium was that they were lighter in weight than other metals that could offer the same properties of strength.

Getting It All Together

All these technical and technological developments, refined after the DC-10 entered service in 1971, eventually combined to permit the Long Beach plant to do in the late 1980s what it had found to be an insuperable task in the early 1970s. The avionics, the composites, and the metals: all these elements had one characteristic that was common to all: they saved weight. Together with engine power increments and the efficiencies conferred by the synthesizing of the bypass principle, the company announced a DC-10 development that was so different from the initial aircraft that it was given a new name, incorporating of course the corporate ownership, the **McDonnell Douglas MD-11**.

Nobody's Perfect

Mr. Murphy, jealously guarding his famous **Law,** must have been irritated beyond measure by **Delta Air Lines'** steady, unspectacular progress, expanding its network inexorably to become one of the leading airlines of the world, ordering vast quantities of aircraft, making sensible acquisitions, and all-in-all acquiring an enviable reputation for reliable, courteous, and human service. True, a regrettable fatal TriStar crash on 2 August 1985, at Dallas, had tarnished a good safety record, but the windshear problem that had proved to have been the cause was highlighted; and the lessons learned from Delta's "Flight 191" accident led to greater precautions.

For Murphy, perhaps the successful entry into service of the MD-82 on 1 April 1987 (see page 104) was the last straw. For during two eventful weeks of the summer of 1987, Delta hit the headlines on four separate occasions. Thankfully, none of the unrelated in-flight incidents that occurred during this hectic period resulted in injury, although many faces in Atlanta were red. But as a result of this spate of human errors, Delta completed a thorough review its training and operational policies which were subsequently modified and upgraded to meet the challenges of new equipment and new horizons scheduled to appear in the 1990s.

McDonnell Douglas MD-11

276 SEATS ■ 580 mph

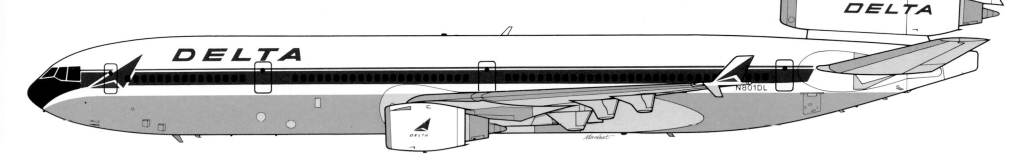

Pratt & Whitney PW4460 (60,000 lb.) x 3 ■ 305 tons max. gross take-off weight ■ Range 8,000 miles

Formally launched on 29 December 1986, the **MD-11** uses the basic fuselage cross-section of the DC-10 but it is nearly 19 feet longer. In addition, a number of aerodynamic refinements are incorporated, including a 10-foot increase in wingspan with the addition of winglets, a new tail cone, streamlined pylon-engine joints, and a smaller horizontal stabilizer containing fuel tanks that can be used to trim the aircraft. Extensive use is made of composite materials and a "glass cockpit" permits two-crew operation (see opposite page).

    Delta Air Lines placed an order for nine MD-11s, with Pratt & Whitney PW4460 engines, in September 1988, with another 31 on option. With 276 seats in mixed class, they are intended to replace the L-1011 TriStars on existing Pacific routes from 1991 until well into the 21st Century. The long-range MD-11 will also enable Delta to expand its network across the Pacific. In May 1990, Delta announced it would lease two MD-11s with delivery in November 1990 in addition to its order, since increased to eleven aircraft.

LENGTH 201 feet
SPAN 170 feet
HEIGHT 58 feet

Ronald W. Allen, President, Chairman, and Chief Executive Officer of Delta, joined the company in 1963.

DELTA'S McDONNELL DOUGLAS MD-11 FLEET

Regn.	MSN
N801DL	48472
N802DL	48473
N803DL	48474
N804DL	48475
N805DL	48476
N806DL	48477
N807DL	48478
N808DL	48479
N809DL	48480
N810DL	48565
N811DL	48566
N	48411
N	48412

First eleven on order for delivery from 1991, plus 31 options. Last two aircraft leased from Aircraft Leasing & Management for delivery Nov. '90.

The first MD-11 just prior to its first flight from Long Beach, California, on 10 January 1990. (Photo by Mike Chew)

Delta's World

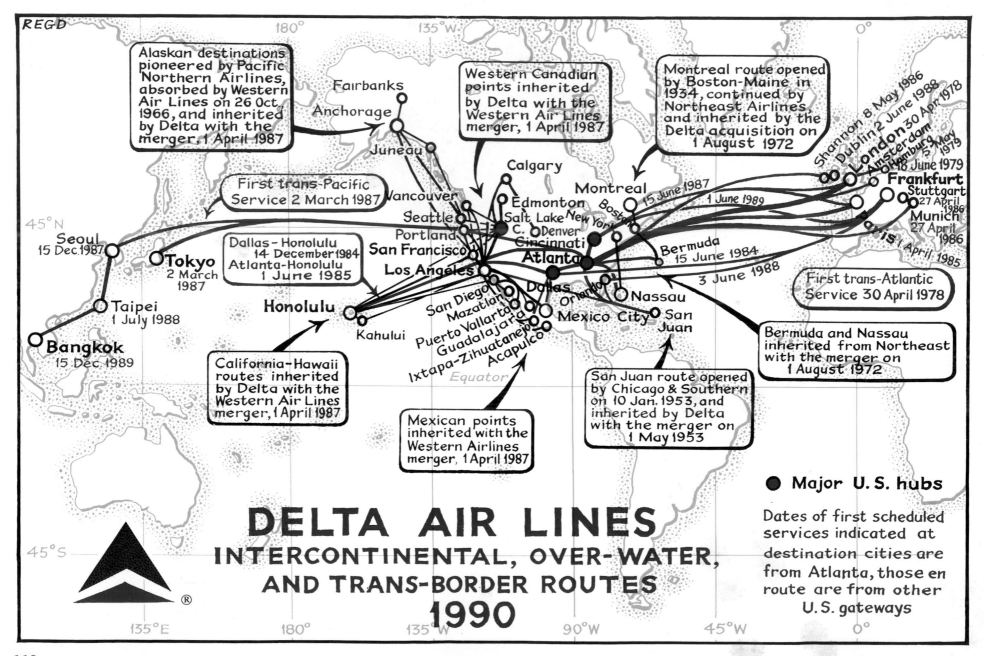

REGD

Alaskan destinations pioneered by Pacific Northern Airlines, absorbed by Western Air Lines on 26 Oct. 1966, and inherited by Delta with the merger, 1 April 1987

Western Canadian points inherited by Delta with the Western Air Lines merger, 1 April 1987

Montreal route opened by Boston-Maine in 1934, continued by Northeast Airlines, and inherited by the Delta acquisition on 1 August 1972

Fairbanks

Anchorage

Juneau

Calgary

Montreal

Shannon 8 May 1986
Dublin 2 June 1988
London 30 Apr 1978
Amsterdam 5 May 1979
Hamburg 18 June 1979

First trans-Pacific Service 2 March 1987

Vancouver

Edmonton

Seattle

Salt Lake C.

New York

Boston

15 June 1987

1 June 1989

Frankfurt

Stuttgart 27 April 1986

Portland

Denver

Cincinnati

San Francisco

Atlanta

Munich 27 April 1986

Seoul 15 Dec. 1987

Dallas – Honolulu 14 December 1984 Atlanta-Honolulu 1 June 1985

Los Angeles

Paris 1 April 1985

Tokyo 2 March 1987

Bermuda 15 June 1984

Taipei 1 July 1988

Honolulu

San Diego

Mazatlan

Dallas

Orlando

Nassau

3 June 1988

First trans-Atlantic Service 30 April 1978

Puerto Vallarta

Guadalajara

Mexico City

San Juan

Bangkok 15 Dec. 1989

Kahului

Ixtapa-Zihuatanejo

Acapulco

Equator

California–Hawaii routes inherited by Delta with the Western Air Lines merger, 1 April 1987

Bermuda and Nassau inherited from Northeast with the merger on 1 August 1972

Mexican points inherited with the Western Airlines merger, 1 April 1987

San Juan route opened by Chicago & Southern on 10 Jan. 1953, and inherited by Delta with the merger on 1 May 1953

● **Major U.S. hubs**

Dates of first scheduled services indicated at destination cities are from Atlanta, those en route are from other U.S. gateways

DELTA AIR LINES
INTERCONTINENTAL, OVER-WATER, AND TRANS-BORDER ROUTES
1990

The Delta Family Tree

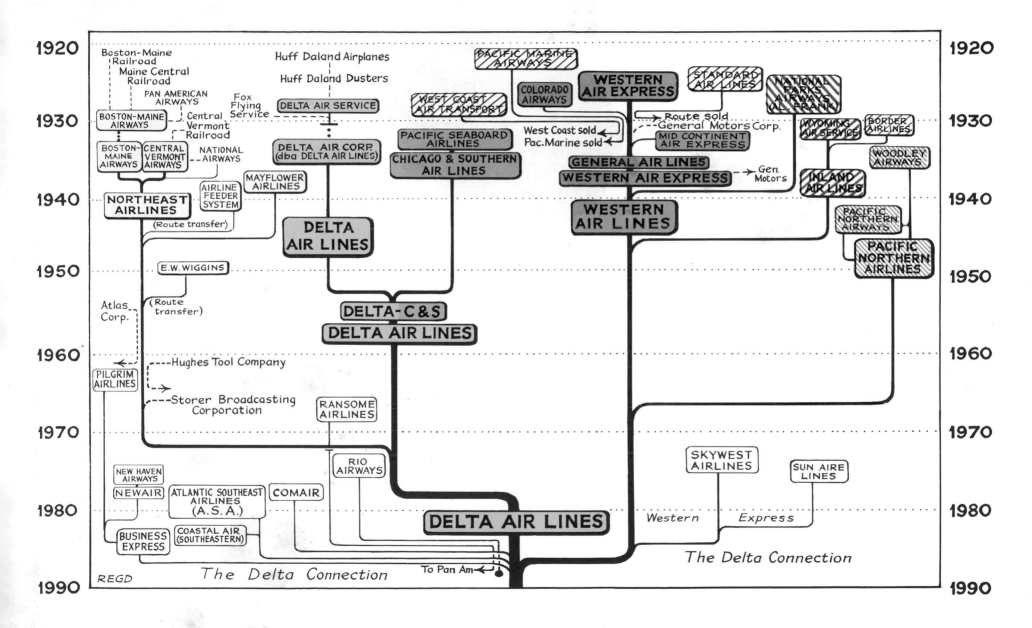

INDEX